# CHICANO PRISONERS

## The Key to San Quentin

# CHICANO PRISONERS
## *The Key to San Quentin*

By

R. THEODORE DAVIDSON

*El Camino College*

**Waveland Press, Inc.**
Prospect Heights, Illinois

For information about this book, write or call:

Waveland Press, Inc.
P.O. Box 400
Prospect Heights, Illinois 60070

SBEND    BEV42955B

# Foreword

## About the Author

Of necessity, being from a large family, R. Theodore Davidson worked his way through college. Before becoming an anthropologist, his job experience had been considerable. This proved to be an extremely valuable personal asset while conducting his research. The jobs ranged widely as the following examples indicate: life insurance salesman, bartender, magazine salesman, roofer, D-8 cat driver, laborer, taxi driver, carpenter's apprentice, surety bond underwriter, journeyman meat cutter, and others. He began his undergraduate studies at Menlo Junior College. Later, after two years in the army and two years of work to repay educational loans, he entered the University of California at Berkeley, receiving a B.A. in English in 1961. After two and a half years in the corporate world, he began his graduate studies in anthropology at San Francisco State College. Later, while at the University of California at Berkeley, he began his doctoral field work at San Quentin Prison. While conducting his research, he transferred to the University of California at Davis, receiving his M.A. in 1969. Since his research was so timely and of such social import, it was agreed that he should take a leave of absence from his doctoral program at Davis to write this and perhaps one other book. He taught anthropology at Cabrillo College before his present position as an associate professor of anthropology at El Camino College. His formal field work was conducted in San Quentin Prison for 20 months (1966–1968). However, his research still continues on an informal basis with Chicanos and convicts he met in prison, yet who are now paroled or discharged. He foresees at least two additional works from his current research: one dealing with the Chicano *barrio* culture as manifest through the life history of an ex-convict, and a second dealing with the particulars of his research experience.

## About the Book

The Chicano prisoner, like the migrant worker or a black child in a ghetto school, is a member of a group that is prejudicially treated by members of the mainstream society. The Chicano prisoner suffers double jeopardy because he is

v

both Chicano and a prisoner of the state. Like the black child or the migrant worker, the Chicano prisoner has special means of coping with the acute deficits of his particular situation. The sanctions of this group, however, are more powerful than those of migrant workers and black children. Chicano prisoners are able to present a strong, unified front to the staff and other prisoner groups through the creation of a "Baby Mafia"—a secret group that has been renamed "Family." Being a member of Family automatically places a convict in a dominant position vis-à-vis others who are not. Complete loyalty exists between Family members; disloyalty is punished by death.

Ted Davidson explains the important differences between being a "convict" and an "inmate." Both convicts and inmates generally believe they are "being punished, not rehabilitated," and most of them will at least superficially "play the game" of becoming rehabilitated for the staff. However, an inmate may individually go much farther to better his own position (such as by snitching to the staff), even though it might be detrimental to another prisoner. In contrast, convicts display a strong unity in opposition to the staff, especially when important, covert prisoner activities are involved. A convict is not a snitch. Chicanos make up three-fourths of the convict group.

The author began this study at the request of the prison administrators at San Quentin, who wanted to see if an anthropologist could determine what subcultural factors were responsible for the excessive violence and reluctance to participate in the rehabilitation activities exhibited by Chicano prisoners. The study is unique in that it presents a prisoner subculture as the prisoners themselves experience and know it. The author, himself, became, insofar as it was physically and socially possible, a participant observer in the prisoner culture. Acceptance of an outside researcher by the prisoners is indeed rare. The focus of the study is on those areas that are most meaningful and important to the prisoners, as they define these areas: their own economy, leadership, social control, and law. Since there were only 375 guards for 4000 prisoners, the men were not under constant surveillance. The majority of areas and buildings were not subject to immediate supervision and many areas were seldom visited by guards. This explains how a complete set of subcultural and illegal activities could exist side by side with officially sanctioned prison activities. Since Family controls the major economic activities, and since almost all Family members are Chicanos, a large portion of the book deals with Family and Chicano convicts.

It is interesting that the major conflict situations are not ethnic in nature. The convict group, for example, includes cooperative representatives of all ethnic groups who observe the "convict code." The real hostilities, both overt and covert, exist between convicts and inmates, between "snitches" and nonsnitches, and between the aggressive homosexual and the weak "punk." Violence and death frequently result when a prisoner fails to live up to an unwritten, yet understood, agreement.

Ted Davidson adeptly takes the reader from the world outside the walls of the prison, comprised of the officials' homes with neatly groomed lawns, to the prisoners' world inside the walls with blocks of 11-by-4½ foot cells of concrete and steel and treeless, grassless, concrete yards. He succeeds in helping the reader to understand why prisoners think and act as they do in their particular ecosphere.

GEORGE AND LOUISE SPINDLER

# Acknowledgments

I wish to express my gratitude to those staff members and administrators at San Quentin who sincerely desired to understand the Chicano prisoners better. Without their concern and cooperation, this study would not have been possible. They opened many doors for me; often the doors were steel ones.

I owe a deep, special debt of gratitude to the many prisoners who shared the depths of their world and their lives with me. For some rather obvious reasons, they will remain nameless. However, to each and every one of them, I give my thanks. To several of my close convict friends who read most of this book in either draft or manuscript form, and who collectively represent over one hundred years of time served in the prisoner culture, little can be said to express the degree of my gratitude; we share a friendship-convict bond that is much deeper than mere words.

I am grateful that for one year, beginning in September 1968, my research was supported by a National Institute of Mental Health Predoctoral Fellowship 1-F1-MH-34, 148-01A2 (CUAN) BT TBT 313. During that year I was spared the burden of working and borrowing to personally finance my own research as I did at other times.

Finally, to Mary Anne, Arlen, and Jalin go my very special thanks for their familial understanding, toleration, and support.

R. THEODORE DAVIDSON

# Contents

# Introduction

My field work among prisoners at San Quentin began in June 1966, when I was a graduate student at the University of California, Berkeley. Prison administrators at San Quentin wanted to see if an anthropologist could determine what subcultural factors were responsible for Mexican-American prisoners being excessively violent and excessively reluctant to participate in rehabilitation activities. With the understanding that it would be necessary to view the prison in a holistic manner, I began my study. I was given total freedom of movement throughout the prison—except for Death Row. As a participant observer, I went to where the prisoners were; my shoes were my office; I purposely took no notes while at the prison. Prison administrators realized the delicate nature of the type of information I would probably encounter if I were to accomplish my task, so it was agreed that I would not have to reveal any confidential information to the staff. The only exception would have been if I had learned that someone was going to be physically harmed or that the prisoners were going to destroy the prison in some manner. My research formally continued for 20 months, until February 1968. At that time, prison administrators abruptly withdrew their permission to allow me to enter San Quentin, because (as an informed citizen and social scientist) I had discussed events that were taking place inside prison with the news media. Since that time, my research has continued on an informal basis, primarily with men that I knew inside prison who have either been paroled or discharged. At times that informal involvement has been extremely intense, as you may come to appreciate by the end of the book. In Chapter 4, after the necessary background for a full understanding has been given, I will make some additional comments about my research methods.

I want to note immediately that I do not normally use the term "Mexican-American" in this book. While I was conducting my research, the term "Chicano" came to be commonly used as a chosen term of address among Mexican-American prisoners. I doubt that there is a single man from the Mexican-American ethnic group in California prisons who does not think of, or refer to, himself as a Chicano. My use of "Chicano" is similar to my use of "black" as the chosen term of address among Negro prisoners.

It should also be noted that I use the term "prisoner" as an adjective, rather than having to continually use "prisoners'" throughout the book. Consequently, using prisoner as an adjective, I refer to a variety of prisoner things such as the prisoner perspective or the prisoner culture. Occasionally I emphasize my use of prison*er* (in contrast to *prison*) by putting part of the term in italics. This is purposely done to draw the readers' attention to the fact that I am very definitely referring to a prison*er* thing. For example, the prison*er* economy is quite unlike any existing description of a prison economy; the latter would deal with economic aspects of the formal prison system and have little if anything to do with the vast, generally covert, prison*er* culture.

The purpose of this ethnography is to present the prisoner culture in a holistic manner, as a complete world, treating the complex, largely covert, yet quite real totality that the prisoners perceive, experience, and know. This is a view of the prisoner culture that has never been presented to outsiders before. It should fill an existing void and prove extremely useful to students, professionals, and the general public. In order to present the prisoner culture from the prisoner perspective, from the ultimate depths of their culture, it is necessary to describe the sizable portion of the prisoner culture that is covert or purposely hidden from outsiders. From the staff's perspective, these activities are viewed as illegal or against the rules and are supposed to be stopped. However, the prisoners realize that secrecy is necessary to assure the success of these activities. Some of these activities (most of which are economic in nature) are so vast and important that they are even hidden from the majority of prisoners by the relatively few prisoners who are knowledgeable of and control the fundamental levels of the prisoner culture. Since those in control are the Chicano convicts who are members of a secret organization called *Family* (formerly called the "Baby Mafia"), and since the entire prisoner culture can be seen and known *only* from their perspective, this ethnography will principally use the perspective of Chicano convicts. In addition, since Family controls the major economic activities in all California prisons, it should be noted that much of what is presented in this study is applicable to other California prisons, too.

As the prisoners would say, this study "tells it like it is." This is *not* an ideal, or partial, or distorted description of prison life. This is *not* an idealized view of the prison—presenting the prison as prison administrators would have outsiders think it is. Instead, it is a presentation of the real prisoner culture—a reality based on the actual patterned behavior of prisoners. In order to present this world in a holistic manner, a detailed analysis of the most significant aspects of the prisoner culture is necessary. This analysis focuses on those things which are most meaningful and important to the prisoners themselves, such as *their own* economy, leadership, social control, law, types of prisoners, ethnic divisions, and levels within their culture. This analysis will *not* include things that may seem important to staff members or outsiders, such as the prison industries, the formal prisoner leadership, and the like—things which are rather extraneous to the real prisoner culture. However, this study will include a consideration of the ways that prisoners perceive and react to certain aspects of the official prison system that significantly intrude into their lives, forming a part of their culture. Ultimately, the reader will be given a full view of the prisoner culture, a view of reality that often is painfully felt by prisoners.

I openly admit that it has been impossible for me to view the prisoner culture with total objectivity. I believe that those who would make such a claim have never been involved enough to be allowed to fathom the ultimate depths of that culture. As a participant observer, I came to know many prisoners well; some of them continue to be my close friends. They have openly and generously shared their thoughts, experiences, and emotions with me. Consequently, I have been able to observe, sense, feel, and know the reality of the prisoner culture—often with considerable emotion. I recognize that the prisoner perspective is subject to biases, and my use of this perspective exposes this study to those biases. However, I have simultaneously attempted to temper my necessary involvement with the detachment of an outsider and anthropologist. Hopefully, I have been able to avoid the excessive ethnocentrism of some prisoners and present the prisoner world in a culturally relativistic manner. It should be stressed that the outsiders' perspective (the one which usually is used by those who write about prisoners) also is subject to biases—a different set of biases. In addition, the outsiders' perspective is relatively far removed from the vast amount of activity that covertly takes place within the prisoner culture. Had I not become involved as I did, I could never have comprehended the real prisoner culture and presented it as a culture that is unique among existing ethnographies. I believe that if we are searching for the reality of a culture, for as true a picture as possible, we must endeavor to see, sense, and feel that culture as its members do. I maintain that it has been necessary and fruitful to do as I have done. The resultant knowledge, emotions, feelings, and biases have been the necessary foundation of this study. Hopefully, my application of a degree of objectivity has enabled me to write an ethnography that comes as close as possible to the true reality of the prisoner culture.

# 1 / The setting

Hopefully you will be able to suspend your ethnocentric judgment long enough so that, by the end of this book, you will have penetrated to the vast, complex, covert depths of the prisoner culture. You will have been taken behind those cold, silent prison walls to see some of the world in which the prisoners live. It is a full, real world, with joys and sorrows, laughter and pain. Through the stark reality that they face, prisoners have their own view of their world behind walls. It may differ from views held by outsiders and staff. However, it is important to realize that the prisoner perception of the prison world is what governs their actions. In this respect, their view of their world is quite real. Granted, their view may be subject to ethnocentric limitations and distortions, but to no greater degree than the view of the prisoner world held by outsiders and staff. Of necessity though, it is first necessary to briefly describe the physical setting in which this prisoner world is found.

San Quentin is the oldest, largest, and most complex prison in the California prison system. The system includes nine prisons and three conservation centers, in which 27,000 convicted adult felons are prisoners. This is the largest prison system in the United States; its prisoner population even exceeds that of the federal prison system by several thousand prisoners. In addition, the California prison system supervises nearly 15,000 convicted adult felons on parole. The prison system was euphemistically renamed California Department of Corrections (CDC) in 1944. This *correctional* or rehabilitative emphasis is reflected in a listing of CDC's nine prisons. Only San Quentin and Folsom are actually called prisons. The other seven prisons are euphemistically called medical facility, institution for men, institution for women, correctional institution, correctional training facility, vocational institution, and men's colony. With its annual budget that now exceeds $100,000,000, CDC has been able to experiment in corrections. It has gained the reputation among some penologists of being one of the most progressive prison systems in the nation. However, not all people agree. Prisoners have frequently endured great personal hardships to protest against what they see as the hypocrisy of the prison system. They are fully aware that all nine of the California "correctional institutions" are prisons, regardless of what seven of them may euphemistically be named. Among the general public in California, there has been an increasing awareness of the shortcomings of the state prison system, resulting in a growing tide of strong criticism against CDC. In addition to penologists and legislators,

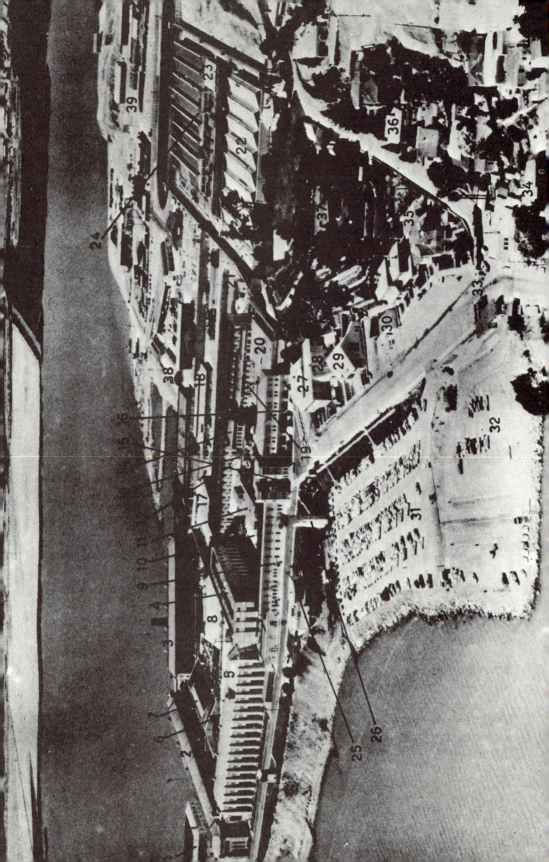

many others have urged and continue to urge that changes be made in this vast, costly system. California legislative studies have shown that CDC is grossly ineffective and wasteful of tax dollars. Prisoners, too, have long been aware that rehabilitative efforts generally are a waste of the taxpayers' money. As prisoners frequently say, "If a man makes it on the streets after prison, it's not *because* of the prison system, it's *in spite* of it."[1]

In 1852, two years after California became a state, San Quentin was established as the first permanent state prison. San Quentin is only a 13-mile drive north of San Francisco, across the Golden Gate Bridge. Except for a few small private homes near the main gate, San Quentin is relatively isolated on an undeveloped peninsula that juts into the San Francisco Bay. The prison facilities are built inside a chain-link fenced area—on about 40 of the 420 acres owned by the state. The real prison, though, is limited to about 14 heavily walled acres. In 1964, administrators indicated that San Quentin was a $67,000,000 prison—to which "must be added a multi-million dollar industrial plant, as well as many other special facilities." This prison has a rated capacity of 2700 prisoners. However, by double-celling prisoners in cells that were originally built for single occupancy, San Quentin receives the overflow of prisoners in the system so that other prisons will not have to exceed their quotas. There have been times when San Quentin has exceeded its own maximum capacity of 5000 prisoners.

It is obvious that things such as walls, sharply restricted personal freedom, confined living quarters, and absence of females make prison life quite different from life on the streets (outside of prison). The physical world of the prisoners is limited to the prison. In a few ways though, the prison setting is somewhat comparable to a small, remote company town. Supplies and materials must be brought

---

[1] The author is fully aware of the repeated use of the terms "prison" and "prisoner" throughout the book. However, from the perspective of the prisoner culture, it is unrealistic to use euphemisms for the "correctional facilities" of the state of California; the men who are locked inside those walls know that those "institutions" are indeed "prisons." Also, as will be explained in Chapter 4, "prisoner" is used in a specific manner which precludes the use of some of the common substitutes that might be used by other writers.

---

*Aerial view of San Quentin Prison: 1. hospital; 2. South Block; 3. West Block; 4. North Block; 5. East Block; 6. upper yard; 7. south mess hall; 8. north mess hall; 9. staff cafeteria, bachelor officers' quarters; 10. library; 11. Adjustment Center; 12. maintenance shops, old gym; 13. education building; 14. education building; 15. count gate (main entry through prison walls); 16. custody staff offices; 17. gym; 18. laundry; 19. prisoner activities offices; 20. chapel buildings; 21. lower yard (north end); 22. furniture factory; 23. industries maintenance shops; 24. cotton textile mill; 25. staff snack bar; 26. armory, gun tower; 27. administration building; 28. fire house; 29. staff recreation building; 30. staff gas station; 31. staff parking lot; 32. visitor parking lot; 33. main gate; 34. private homes (outside prison grounds); 35. state-owned homes for administrators; 36. state-owned homes for administrators; 37. warden's home; 38. warehouse area; 39. ranch area (no longer used as such). (Courtesy of California Department of Corrections)*

*Block worker in North Block, watching television during the day after cleaning up. Tiers and cells on right; gun rails and outer wall on left. (Courtesy of California Department of Corrections)*

in by truck; however, most of the basic consumer services are performed by the residents. In addition, the manufactured products from their specialized industries are trucked out to be distributed and used elsewhere. Continuing the comparison with the small company town, inside the walls you find about two dozen buildings which include the following: four huge cell blocks, two mess halls, a hospital, an "Adjustment Center" (a prison within the prison), maintenance and vocational training shops, an education building, a library, a gymnasium, a religious chapel, the guards' offices, prisoner activities offices, a laundry, a steam plant, a cotton textile mill (recently replaced by a mattress factory), a clothing factory, industrial maintenance shops, an auto body-repair shop, and a furniture factory. For most prisoners, this is where they spend virtually all of their time while at San Quentin.

A small percentage of the prisoners are assigned to prison jobs that take them outside the walls. They work in, or maintain the nonwalled areas of the prison which are seldom, if ever seen or visited by most prisoners. Therefore, in many respects, it can be seen that the portion of the prison which is outside the walls really is beyond the physical setting in which most of the prisoners live and in which the prisoner culture is to be found. This portion of the prison is necessary for its functioning, but it is somewhat extraneous to this study, which is primarily concerned with the prisoner culture. To briefly give the reader an idea of what this outer portion of the prison is like, it should be noted that the buildings outside the walls near the main entrance include the following: the administration building, a staff snack bar, a staff cafeteria, a fire house, a staff recreation building, a staff service station, and about a dozen large, attractively landscaped state-owned homes in which prison administrators live. Also outside the walls, but on the other side of the prison, are warehouse buildings, ranch buildings (no longer used for that purpose), and a settlement of modest state-owned homes that are provided at low rent to staff members, most of whom are guards.

Visually, the prison is a dull, drab world—quite unlike the picture postcards of the outside of the prison that seem to overemphasize the colors of the sky, the bay, and the landscaping around the administrators' homes. The contrast could be seen especially during the Christmas season when a sparsely decorated tree was set on a high platform outside the East Block, supposedly to be enjoyed by the prisoners when they were in the upper yard. Yet inside those walls, even that battle-scarred Christmas tree seemed to be in black and white.

## CELL BLOCKS

Inside the prison, the majority of prisoners are housed in the four huge, gloomy, poorly ventilated cell blocks—each being named according to its correspondence with the four cardinal points of the compass. The West, North, and East Blocks each have 500 single cells. In contrast, the South Block initially was built as a single cell block, with two regular sets of cells placed end to end. However, with its 1000 single cells, it proved to be so large that it has long been separated by steel doors into four separate units: A, B, C, and D Sections. Even though each of these 2500 cells in San Quentin was planned to house a single prisoner, a second steel bunk bed has been added to most cells. In this way, San Quentin is able to house almost twice as many prisoners as its rated capacity. North Block differs from the other blocks in that it has a separate floor that is built above the normal cell block ceiling. Here, in stark isolation from all normal prison activities, is where Death Row is located.

People who view the prison from the outside only often form a mistaken impression of a cell block. Many are likely to imagine that prisoners' cells are immediately behind the long, narrow windows placed high on the sides of the cell block building. Actually, all that can be seen from the outside is the long, tall, rectangular, reinforced concrete shell that completely encloses a much smaller structure inside. The smaller structure inside is formed by 500 cells. Stretched along the middle of the cement floor are two long, separate rows of 50 cells. The cell doors in each row face out toward their side of the long rectangular shell. Behind each row of cells and separating the two rows is a narrow maintenance passageway. Collectively, these two rows of cells form the first 100-cell tier. The tier is about 27 feet wide and 275 feet long. On top of this are four more identical tiers of cells. The reinforced concrete ceiling of one tier also serves as the floor of the next tier. Collectively, the five tiers are about 40 feet tall, but they fall well short of the ceiling of the outer shell. At this point, looking at a single long side of this tiered structure, one might imagine this solid reinforced concrete structure as a gigantic, long waffle that had been set on its edge; each of the waffle indentations is a concrete pigeonhole that has been made into a prison cell. Added to this, the second through fifth tiers each has a rather narrow, railed walkway (about $3\frac{1}{2}$ feet wide) that extends the length of the tier, in front of the row of cells. These walkways are connected to the stairways that are located at both ends of the tiers. The outer shell is about 10 to 12 feet—across open space—from the walkway railings. This prevents prisoners from reaching the long, high windows in the outer shell. Perhaps the tiers and the outer shell (the two basic structures of the cell block) can be better understood if one imagines them as a long, narrow, five-layered, gray, rectangular layer cake which has been iced with a waffle iron, over which a much larger, long rectangular cover has been placed.

## CELLS

The cells are 11-by-$4\frac{1}{2}$-foot reinforced concrete cubicles with 7-foot ceilings. The open end is covered by 13 steel bars which extend from the floor to the ceiling. Seven of these bars are independently framed in heavy gauge steel and are hinged to serve as a door. Inside the cell are found double-deck steel bunk beds, a toilet (without a toilet seat or cover), a wash basin with cold running water, two shelves across the back wall, and a light fixture on the wall opposite the beds. The cell is really little more than a small restroom with two bunk beds in it. Each cell door can be independently locked. However, there is a second locking mechanism that locks 25 cells at a time. When all the cell doors are closed, a huge lever at the end of the tier can be moved to lower a single hinged steel bar about four inches below the top of the doors of half of the cells on that side of the tier. Once the "bar has been dropped," there is no way to open a cell door, even if a cell's lock is unlocked. It can be opened only when "the bar is raised."

A small, yet significant group of prisoners is kept in what is euphemistically called the Adjustment Center. This is a small, somewhat self-contained prison within the prison. Here, men who the staff think are habitual troublemakers within the prison or men who are suspected of committing serious crimes inside the prison are brought for long-term punishment. Also, about 30 percent of the men

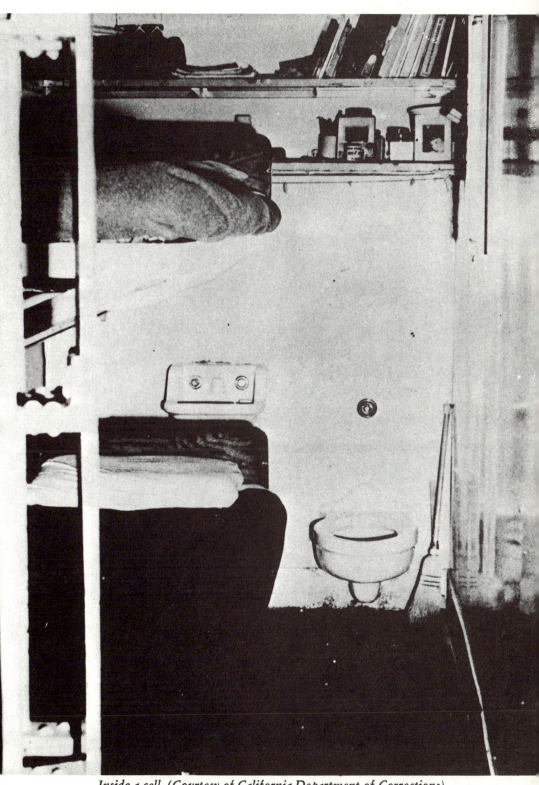

*Inside a cell. (Courtesy of California Department of Corrections)*

in the Adjustment Center (commonly called "AC") are there for long-term protective custody (protection of a prisoner from other prisoners who may have reason to bring physical harm to him). The Adjustment Center is a relatively new building with staff offices and a small mess hall on one end of the building. The prisoners in AC are subjected to a rigorous routine which entails sharply reduced privileges, severely restricted movement inside AC, and isolation from the rest of the prison and prisoners. A much tighter security is imposed over these prisoners by the staff with the aid of newer facilities—such as a mechanism permitting them to independently lock and unlock cells from the staff portion of the building, outside the cell block area. The floor of each tier extends to the reinforced concrete wall of the building. Therefore, AC does not have an outer shell like the other four cell blocks do. There are 34 cells on each tier, but the cell block area is constructed so that each side, with its 17 cells, is isolated from all other parts of AC. Since the last execution in San Quentin's gas chamber, in 1967, the moratorium on executions led to over 100 prisoners being held under sentence of death. To accommodate these prisoners, the top two tiers of AC were converted into an additional Death Row. This has reduced AC to three tiers which hold about 102 prisoners. Consequently, B Section in South Block (commonly referred to as "the hole"—where prisoners are sent for short-term, in-prison punishment) has been expanded into A Section to accommodate the overflow from AC. Additional descriptive details about "the hole" and AC will be given in the next chapter.


## MISCONCEPTIONS

A misconception frequently held by outsiders is that the prisoners are under constant surveillance by the staff. This is not true. There is no way that the 375 guards can be divided into three daily shifts and still have enough men to watch all the nearly 4000 prisoners at all times. Except for some of the open areas and places where prisoner movement is restricted or where tight security must be maintained, the majority of areas and buildings inside the walls are not subject to immediate supervision or surveillance by the staff. During the daytime especially, most prisoners have much more freedom of movement and a great deal less supervision than outsiders normally imagine. Just like in a small town, there are many places and areas in the prison that are seldom visited by a freeman[2]—and even less so by guards. For example, I usually went to where the prisoners normally were, so the majority of my time with prisoners was spent somewhat isolated with one or a few of them. It was normal to spend several hours at a time with them without seeing a guard or a freeman. The impossibility of constant surveillance by staff, coupled with the size, complexity, and relative self-sufficiency of the prison are important factors that enable prisoners to engage in their own extensive activities

---

[2]"Freeman" is a term prisoners use to refer to male nonprisoners. Work supervisors, doctors, teachers, visitors, and people who have no connection with the prison system would be freemen. However, administrators, guards, and counselors are such an integral part of the system that they are not considered freemen. Administrators are referred to by name or title; guards (bulls) and counselors are referred to as such.

*A postcard-type view from behind prison administrators' homes with the San Francisco Bay and Marin County hills in the background. (Courtesy of California Department of Corrections)*

*The main gate, where tourists often view the prison at a distance, through the bars of the gates which normally are closed. (Courtesy of California Department of Corrections)*

—which are primarily illegal and economic in nature. It must be stressed that the world of George Orwell's *1984* is very far removed from San Quentin.

Occasionally outsiders will have a misconception about the guards' use of guns. Actually, the majority of the guards are unarmed, and all guards who actually work among the prisoners are unarmed. Normally, the only guards who have guns are the few who are assigned to the posts on the gun rail. This is a single, elevated, continuous, railed catwalk that runs along the top of the prison walls, around the outside of some of the cell blocks, suspended under the roofed part of the upper yard, and with extensions that lead through steel doors to the gun rails that are elevated on the inside of the shell portion of the cell blocks and on the high walls of the mess halls. In times of emergency, additional armed guards may be assigned to the gun rail. It should be stressed, though, that no armed guards are allowed inside the walled area on the ground level where prisoners may be. This restriction of weapons to the elevated rail prevents prisoners from being able to take guns away from guards.

## RELATIONSHIP WITH THE OUTSIDE WORLD

The prisoner relationship with the outside world is quite one-sided. Most prisoners are able to listen to either of the two local radio stations that are monitored by the prison staff and made available for prisoners—through speakers in some work areas and through headphone outlets in the cells that may be used by prisoners (if they have earned the privilege of having headphones). The monitored stations tend to have a great deal of music and very little news. If a prisoner lives in East Block or North Block (honor and semihonor blocks respectively), he is able to watch television in the evenings and on weekends. Also, prisoners who legally have money may subscribe to newspapers and magazines (subject to certain restrictions) which are delivered through the mail. Often a subscriber will pass his newspapers on so that many prisoners are able to read the paper, because few men inside can legally afford this luxury. In addition, through approved visitors and correspondents (old friends and family members), it may be possible to keep abreast of activities of friends and family. However, the 400-mile trip from the heavily populated Los Angeles area often prevents poor people from visiting their friends or relatives in San Quentin. A significant percentage of the prisoners have few if any visits while in certain prisons. Even though there are numerous limitations and problems in this system, prisoners are generally able to keep fairly well informed of what is happening on the streets.

For people on the streets—the general public and even state legislators—the flow of information from inside prison is limited in many ways. For example, outsiders may subscribe to the biweekly prison newspaper, the *San Quentin News*. The reporting is done by and for the prisoners, but staff restrictions limit the news to activities of formally approved prisoner organizations, recreational activities, and the like. As you continue reading, you will see that these are activities that take place on the superficial, overt level of the prisoner culture, and that they have a minimal impact (at the most) on the lives and activities of the majority of prisoners. In contrast, prisoner activities and interests that take place on the vast covert levels of the prisoner culture (that probably would be deemed newsworthy by outsiders) are omitted. Even when those activities and interests do surface and become overt, they are not reported in the *San Quentin News*, because the prisoner reporters are not allowed to write of violence, defiance of authority, or violation of prison rules. In Chapter 8, you will read of *The Outlaw*, an illegal, truly underground prisoner newspaper which came from the covert depths of the prisoner culture. *The Outlaw* reported things that were very important to the majority of prisoners, important to taxpayers and legislators, and threatening to the status quo of CDC. Actually, the serious articles in *The Outlaw* dealt with the real prisoner culture, not with the ideal one which is treated in the *San Quentin News*.

Public access to knowledge of situations and events inside prison is further limited. For example, San Quentin guards are to censor outgoing prisoner mail for statements about: the "reputation of the institution," "mistreatment of inmates," criticism "of law, rules or policy," and "attitudes toward discontent or racial friction." If a prisoner's criticism should be too strong or persist, disciplinary action may be taken against him. Also, in written rules, staff members are ordered: "Do not discuss institutional affairs off duty, or with outsiders. Refer all inquiries from the public, to the Office of the Warden." If a staff member should publicly criticize the prison or CDC, or even openly approach a state legislator to discuss problems within the prison system or at a particular prison, the staff member is subject to being directly (or indirectly, if necessary) fired and actively blackballed from other similar employment. Even outsiders who volunteer their time to work with prisoners in a variety of ways are beholden to the prison administrators for entry into the prison and would be denied entry if they publicly criticized the prison system. Even a man who has just been paroled from prison is limited to what he may say publicly about prison by restrictions that are stated in the Parole Agent Manual and enforced through conditions number 10 and 12 of the parole agreement, which the man must sign to be released on parole. Also, those approved visitors who do visit a prisoner are reluctant to use any information that is critical of the prison or CDC, which may verbally be transmitted to them. They are aware that if they should attempt to publicize such information, the prisoner who gave them the information could be indirectly, yet severely, punished for such action. Prisoners are fully aware, and some staff members privately admit, that these and other restrictions make it virtually impossible for most outsiders to know what is really going on behind prison walls.

## ABSOLUTE POWER

Prison administrators, who are not subject to the restrictions discussed above, know much of what goes on behind the prison walls. However, in the past, they often have been less than candid. It appears that they are so much a part of the system that some of them have gone to great lengths to hide or distort the reality inside prison from the public. In fact, they have tried to perpetuate an ideal view of the prison system which is remote from the real prisoner culture that the prisoners know and experience behind the walls. Coupled with the restrictions treated above, the actions of administrators generally assure that the prison remains a closed system—one that keeps both the prisoners and the truth tightly locked behind the walls. For example, many members of the news media are fully aware that a news story about prison almost always comes directly from a prison administrator and that it is never given to them *inside* the prison walls. A few exceptions may occur when dealing with officially approved public interest stories, but normally lower-level staff members and prisoners are not allowed to be interviewed by the news media. Also, it is impossible for an outsider to casually visit a prison and talk with the prisoners; he first must go through official channels. The outsider may sign up for a warden's tour, but it is impossible to even begin to see the reality of the prisoner culture on any kind of a guided tour. Regardless of what occurs inside, prison administrators have the almost absolute power to control the flow of information from within the prison; and occasionally it has been tyrannically used to conceal or disguise the reality behind the prison walls.

In order to illustrate how this absolute power has been used in the past, let me note some details from an instance which will be more fully treated in Chapter 8. The example is used here to show the credibility gap that surrounds the administrators' public statements about the prisoners' "Convict Unity Holiday" on February 15, 1968. This was the first day of a peaceful strike that lasted for more than a week. The strike was the result of prisoner grievances over parole procedures, the indeterminate sentence, and other serious matters that had been strongly felt by the prisoners of CDC for several years. The legitimacy of the prisoner demands is reflected in the fact that prison administrators were forced to allow the prisoners to communicate formally with the State Assembly Criminal Procedure Committee and that several legislative bills which were introduced later in 1968 dealt with some of the topics that formed the prisoners' list of ten demands. For our purposes, we are interested in the number of prisoners that went on strike that day. Two months after the strike, on April 22, Warden Nelson spoke to the Berkeley-Albany Bar Association. In reply to a woman's question about the Unity Holiday, he noted that "three men stayed out" on strike. There is a serious credibility gap, however. San Francisco newspapers were on strike and not publishing at that time, but several of the *San Francisco Chronicle* reporters were publishing a small newsstand daily. In their paper, *Friday*, February 16, they reported the following: at 8:30 A.M., Warden Nelson reported that none of the prisoners were on strike; at noon, Associate Warden Park said that 20 above normal were absent from work; and at 3:00, the absentee rate was given as 20 to 40 above normal. Prisoners contend that, on the evening of February 15, on the prison radio, Warden Nelson admitted to 59 prisoners having struck. However, employees (who actually have prisoners assigned to them) collectively tried to pool their information and arrive at a reasonable figure; they contend that 20 percent of the nearly 4000 prisoners were on strike—almost 800. The prisoners themselves tend to confirm the 20 percent figure. Obviously, there is a credibility gap; it appears to be possible because of the closed nature of the prison system.

To conclude this chapter, I would like to note that this restrictive attitude is not unique to San Quentin. It is a condition that is more or less general throughout

CDC and most prison systems in the United States. A few California legislators have been trying to bring about changes in this situation. However, their efforts have not yet succeeded to the degree necessary to guarantee that tragedy will not occur from public ignorance of, and inaction toward, the reality which lies hidden behind the facade of the ideal prison system. Unfortunately, through their use of this type of absolute power, administrators have been able to prevent meaningful communication by the prisoners with the outside world. I personally contend that this type of power and the resultant public ignorance of the real prison system is an important—and perhaps the most important—root cause behind the Attica Prison massacre in 1971. As of the actual date of writing these words, California has been fortunate to avoid similar tragedy. Luckily, (even though the Folsom Prison strike was not reported to the public as such) major strikes protesting abusive actions by the Adult Authority (parole board), at Folsom in 1963 and at San Quentin in 1968, have been peaceful. However, the major abuses within the system have not been corrected yet. I will have more to say about the subject in later chapters. Now, I would like to take you behind the prison walls to show you the *real* prisoner culture, to show you the prison system that the prisoners see and experience.

# 2 / Entry into
# the prison world

After being arrested, jailed, and convicted of committing a felony, a man who is sentenced to CDC for the first time usually begins serving his sentence with a four-to-eight-week stay in one of CDC's two reception-guidance centers. The major function of these centers is the physical, psychological, and social testing of men as they enter CDC. Many prisoners, staff members, counselors in particular, and even Adult Authority (parole board) members question the validity and usefulness of much of this testing—which is never repeated, regardless of how long a man stays in prison. Nevertheless, the results of the testing become the basic foundation of a man's permanent "jacket" (record file) and influence decisions regarding the man—even if the decisions are made ten or twenty years after the testing. Although the reception-guidance centers are inside the prisons at Chino and Vacaville, the real shock of entering prison normally does not hit the prisoners then, because these centers are unlike the regular prisons. There is a very different feeling among prisoners at the centers than is present when they enter a real prison such as San Quentin as a "fish" (new arrival). Since the major function of these centers is testing, prisoners feel that the center staff are more considerate than those at the regular prisons. Prisoners note that even the guards at the center tend to have a more tolerant attitude than guards in most CDC prisons. In addition, all the prisoners are "fish," so none are in a position to take advantage of the situation.

## CULTURE SHOCK

For the "fish" who arrives at San Quentin from the reception-guidance center on the prison bus, the actual beginning of prison life is when he passes through those walls. Others have described this experience as the process by which a prisoner's "self is mortified" (Goffman 1961: 12–74) and "the pains of imprisonment" to which prisoners are subjected (Sykes 1958:63–83). From conversations with prisoners and personal observations, I believe there is a more valid, fruitful way to describe this type of experience. A simple, yet accurate explanation can be developed by using the concept of culture shock.

Drawing on some of the ideas presented by Philip Bock (1970:Foreword), it is acknowledged that culture shock frequently may arise when one is directly exposed to a strange culture. Disturbing emotional feelings may arise from one's inability to make sense out of, or predict, the behavior of others. The resulting disorientation and helplessness is especially disconcerting and unpleasant if one must, of necessity, learn to live in that strange culture. A prisoner who had read widely in the literature on prisons commented on the use of the concept of culture shock as opposed to other descriptions of the experience of entering the prison world. "It's not so much a problem of loss of identity when coming into a joint as a fish as it is a problem of confusion. You're too busy learning the new culture to worry about things like being stripped of your identity, or figuratively castrated, or deprived, or rejected by society. A lot of that's off base anyway. Your biggest problem is that you're unable to make sense of things. You think something means one thing and later find out that it means another. You don't know the routine or what to expect from anybody. When do you shower? When do you change your clothes? How can you avoid trouble with the bulls and other convicts? These are the things that are on your mind."

Put yourself in the shoes of a fish. Imagine, for example, that it is an evening during your first week in your cell, in this new, all too real prison world. One of the almost endless number of things you have been told was something about showering once a week. It has been over a week since your last shower, at the reception-guidance center, and you are more than anxious to have one. You hope that tonight is the night for men on your tier to go down to the showers on the ground level at the end of the cell block. You hear something about showers over the loudspeaker. You even hear the bar slip so that you can open your cell. You are nervous and don't want to make any mistakes and get into trouble with either the guards or with other prisoners. Therefore, you just peek out on an angle through your bars to see if the men in the cells next to you are going. They don't open their cells. Because of the bars, you can't see any further; but you assume that tonight is not shower night for your tier and that the few prisoners walking by are from another tier. Later (too late) you learn that tonight *was* shower night for your tier and that the men in the cells next to you didn't shower because they shower every day at their prison jobs. Later you rather meekly ask a guard about seeing if you could get a shower. In very brusque terms you are told that you are just one of so many hundred men in the block and that you can wait until next week. And, next week, after you have had your long overdue first shower at San Quentin, you will have learned one more of the seemingly limitless number of things you must learn before you overcome the culture shock and cease to be a fish.

Sooner or later all fish learn the prisoner culture well enough to get along in it, to lose their fish identity, and to become a member of the prisoner culture. This period may range from a few hours to a few weeks to several months. At one extreme, the "loner" (who remains aloof except when it is absolutely necessary to talk or interact with other prisoners, and who refuses to ask questions) usually finds that it is a long, difficult process to learn the prisoner culture. In contrast, Chicano prisoners do not have that problem. Many prisoners openly acknowledge

When passing through the count gate into the prison proper, the visitor's first view is of the carefully landscaped Portal Plaza area. This area sharply contrasts with the rest of the prison. (Courtesy of California Department of Corrections)

Another view of the Portal Plaza area, looking from the Adjustment Center toward the chapel buildings. Flowers, fishponds, and fountains are only for passing enjoyment when on official business—no loitering of prisoners allowed! (Courtesy of California Department of Corrections)

that "Chicanos are better off than any other group in prison." One of the reasons for this statement (others will become evident in later chapters) is that Chicano family, friendship, *barrio* (neighborhood), and ethnic loyalties serve to preclude any Chicano fish from being without the close, personal support and guidance of other Chicanos. For example, a Chicano fish who enters prison usually has a relative, a friend, a friend of a relative, or a relative of a friend there. If not, there will be someone there from the same *barrio*, or at least the same part of the state or country. One or several of these individuals will "clue the fish in on the situation." Usually within a few hours of arrival, a Chicano fish is relatively oriented to the situation and set up with any essentials (such as toilet articles or cigarettes) that he may need. He also knows where he can get answers to his questions. Since the staff assign the prisoners to cells, it may be that none of these individuals are celled near the fish. In these cases, another Chicano who is celled near the fish would be brought into the picture, to help the fish. These Chicanos continue to aid, offer suggestions to, and answer questions for the fish. Their support is somewhat like that of a mother as she aids her child through the long process of enculturation. It can be seen that the culture shock experienced by Chicanos is relatively short-lived and mild compared to what other prisoners undergo.

## CHARACTERISTICS OF PRISONERS

It is generally recognized by CDC officials that most California prisoners are from the lower levels of the socioeconomic scale. Rarely is a prisoner from a group other than the poor, the disadvantaged, or the ethnic minorities. CDC officials have admitted that the majority of the prisoners would not be in prison if they had the advantages that most readers of this book have had. Over 75 percent of the men are under 40 years of age, with the median age being 32. About 65 percent of these men have less than a ninth-grade education, with the average being a seventh-grade education. Job skills, training, and experience among these prisoners normally are grossly inadequate or entirely lacking. With an average of about 30 percent black prisoners and 18 percent Chicano prisoners, one can see that the ethnic minorities are overrepresented in the prison population. There does seem to be some basis for the prisoners' feeling that there is a selective administration of justice in the United States. For example, one of their arguments against the death penalty illustrates their feeling: They simply state, "There are no rich men on Death Row."

Prisoners are expected to be able to get along without money in prison because the state supplies all goods and services that are deemed absolutely necessary. All prisoners are supposedly reduced to an economic level that is close to poverty. However, if a prisoner legally has money in his personal account, he may draw up to $45.00 in token money each month for canteen luxury purchases such as candy, cigarettes, toilet articles, and magazines. In reality though, the majority of prisoners do not routinely receive (and many never receive) money from sources such as family outside or from the relatively few prison jobs that pay from 3 to 16 cents an hour. Legally, the majority remain near the poverty level. It can be seen that the economic disparity between those with nothing and those with $45.00 to spend at the canteen each month is considerable. However, as will be shown in Chapter 6, legal economic activities are almost completely overshadowed by the vast scope of the prisoners' illegal economic activities. It will become apparent that even the full, legal $45.00 monthly draw is rather insignificant compared with the extent and volume of illegal consumption and use of consumer goods and services. Many times those who legally have nothing are the very ones who reach the highest economic level possible in the prisoner culture. Later, when treating the prisoner economy, it will again become evident that "Chicanos are better off than any other group in prison." At this point it should merely be noted that a Chicano fish does not have to undergo the required six-week wait until he can make his first legal draw. Regardless of whether or not a Chicano fish will ever receive a legal draw, he is almost immediately set up with desired extra necessities—beyond those provided by the state.

## ROUTINE BASIC ACTIVITIES

A fish soon becomes aware that life in San Quentin is subject to a basic routine from which many variations develop. Four major variations are evident when one considers the routine in each of the cell blocks. Life in the four cell blocks can be seen as a series of graded steps, beginning at the bottom with South Block and progressing to East, North, and finally to West Block. There are graded demands of conformity to prison rules that must be met in order for a prisoner to qualify to be moved to a higher step. Such conformity is judged by things such as a man's work and conduct record and is reflected in his custody classification (degrees of custody range from maximum to minimum). With each move up these steps, there are fewer legal deprivations, more legal privileges, and more toleration of petty rule-breaking.

South Block is the worst block in the prison. It is a catchall that has considerable variation between its four sections. B Section (commonly called "the hole") has a very different routine which will be treated later. In the other three sections, there is a strong emphasis on control and security, with activities other than the standard daily movements being minimized. There is no television, and most prisoners are restricted to their cells in the evening. The largest number of unassigned (to a job or to school) prisoners are celled here. The jobs that are filled by men from South Block are most likely to be nonpaying. If legal income is considered, prisoners in South Block generally are on the lowest legal economic level. Normally a fish is first celled in D Section. Here is where many hospital workers, ambulatory convalescing medical patients, and special diet patients are celled. After being classified by staff for admittance to the general prisoner population and perhaps being assigned to a job or school, the fish often will be transferred to C Section where men await cell openings in East Block. Kitchen workers and some prisoners from the general prisoner population are celled in A Section. However, as will be detailed later, the expansion of "the hole" has intruded into the top three tiers, so A Section effectively is limited to two tiers now.

The majority of prisoners in East Block have some sort of school or work assignment. However, those who do have jobs tend to be assigned to some of the poorest, nonpay jobs in the prison. In East Block, the prisoners' activities usually revolve around the standard legal daily movements for meals, jobs, and school. Formal evening activity generally is restricted to the movement of those who are allowed to go to and from special evening activities such as school, church, and meetings of prisoner organizations. However, for the large number that remain locked in their cells, there is a vast realm of informal rule-breaking and illegal activity in which they may take part. The nature of much of that activity will become obvious when the prisoner economy is treated.

Most of the prisoners in North Block (the semihonor block) have job or school assignments and clear conduct and work records. Those with jobs tend to have better jobs, some being paid for their work. As a reward for conformity to prison rules, the men are allowed more evening freedom. They are not locked in their cells; but are allowed to attend special evening activities outside of the block, as well as to watch television on the ground floor if they wish. Also, their greater mobility makes it much easier for them to engage in their rule-breaking and illegal activity.

In the West Block (the honor block), the prisoners generally have the best work and conduct records and monopolize the highest paying jobs. They have the greatest number of privileges and the most freedom of movement of all prisoners. The bars that lock the cells are dropped only at night. During the day and evening, they may have their cell locked or unlocked by a prisoner tier tender whenever they wish. They have their own large recreation yard that they may use even in the evenings—as well as television and special evening activities outside the block, in other parts of the prison. It should be stressed that the daily routine of prisoners —regardless of what block they live in—involves considerable illegal and rule-breaking activity.

The basic legal routine of a generalized weekday in San Quentin is as follows. Prisoners are awakened by a bell at 6:30 A.M. Cell doors are opened at 7:00 and the men file to the mess halls to eat, finishing by 7:30. After a half hour to mingle on the upper yard, "work call" is sounded at 8:00. Assigned men go to their job or to school (including vocational training). Unassigned men and those with evening or night jobs either stay in the yard (to pass the time there, in the gymnasium, on the lower yard, in the library, or in some out-of-the-way place) until lunch lineup, or voluntarily lock up in their cells for the morning. At 11:30, prisoners line up in the upper yard for lunch. The mess halls are cleared by 12:30, giving the men another half hour on the upper yard until work call is sounded at 1:00 P.M. Again, the men either go to their assignments or pass the time until the work day is over. Beginning at about 3:30, men gradually gather in the upper yard prior to filing into the cell blocks for the regular count. Between 4:00 and 4:30, the guards carefully count every prisoner in the prison—most prisoners are required to stand at the bars of their cell while count is being taken. Dinner is served at 5:00, after which the prisoners return directly to their cells. At 6:20 the prisoners who are scheduled for early evening activities are let out of their cells. Some who are scheduled only for later evening activities are let out at 8:20. Other activities such as scheduled showers and clothes changes take place within each block during the evening. All evening activities are concluded by 10:00, with all prisoners being locked in their cells by "lights out time" at 10:30. Prisoners control the lights in their individual cells, so they may do things such as read or listen to the radio (if they have earphones) as late as they wish.

On weekends, the basic legal routine differs in many ways. Breakfast is served an hour later, and the day's routine ends an hour earlier—at 3:00 P.M. Since few men have weekend assignments, the majority are free to pass their time in their cells or in the yard. Athletic events with outside competition and movies highlight the weekend for many prisoners. Church services and meetings of prisoner organizations are important for some prisoners in a personal sense; but these meetings and services (as well as those held during the week) actually have little impact on the prisoner population as a whole. Often prisoners attend merely to please the Adult Authority (parole board) or to break the routine of prison life. There are few scheduled evening activities on weekends, so the evenings tend to be very long.

If the vast number of rules that govern the prisoners are added to the legal routine described above, an outsider is quite likely to be impressed with the order that the staff is able to impose upon prisoner activities. For example, some of the rules for the upper yard include: no running at any time; no horseplaying, body-punching and the like; no playing of any musical instruments; no domino playing under the "big shed"; and for meals, movies, and lockups, the men are to line up in a single file, in appropriate lines, as soon as the whistle is blown.

However, the outsider's impression of orderliness should be countered by viewing this routine as it really happens. Often, when large groups of prisoners move, uproar and confusion prevail. Generally there are only two or three guards in each block per shift, with only a single guard in the honor and semihonor blocks on the graveyard (after midnight) shift. During the 4:00 P.M. count though, there is a double shift, with a few additional guards moving in to each block to aid in the count. In the East Block for example, about nine guards handle the operation. However, when the roughly 900 men swarm in, even nine guards can do little more than wait until the uproar and confusion die down. At these and other times, when large numbers of prisoners move in or out of their cells, the guards have little real control over the prisoners.

The guards' inability to maintain real control at all times is well understood by the prisoners. Consequently, the prisoners have a vast illegal, rule-breaking routine that is covertly joined with and dependent on the daily legal routine. Most of this covert routine is economic in nature and will be treated in Chapter 6. At this point though, it should be noted that most legal activities and movements can be and are used for illegal, rule-breaking purposes too. For example, the confusion of hundreds of prisoners simultaneously moving to or from their cells enables prisoners to do many things—such as passing by cells on other tiers and picking up or delivering illegal goods. Or, a prisoner's signing up to attend religious meetings on a weeknight may have absolutely nothing to do with his religious or moral convictions; it may just be an excuse to routinely get out of his cell and to enable him to take care of some business. And, in the blocks with limited evening movement, the prisoner "tier tenders" legally carry hot water to the prisoners and pour it through their bars to them; and illegally, the tier tenders pick up and deliver all sorts of things for those who are locked in their cells. For example, a prisoner who is busy illegally making bacon and tomato sandwiches in his cell may rely on the tier tender to deliver the sandwiches to the other prisoners throughout the block who want to buy them. The aroma from the frying bacon advertises the product and usually brings calls of cell numbers from prisoners who want to buy a sandwich. On weekends there is even less control exercised over the prisoners, for the majority are free to pass their time in their cells or in the yard. Therefore, the volume of covert routine activity (which involves things such as gambling, loans, alcohol, and drugs) increases considerably.

## ROUTINE ACTIVITIES IN AC AND "THE HOLE"

A prisoner constantly faces the potential of getting into trouble with the staff or with his fellow prisoners. If this should happen, the prisoner may be subjected to the very different routine of the Adjustment Center (AC) or B Section ("the hole"). As noted in Chapter 1, the Adjustment Center is a prison within the prison. It is here that the staff keep men who are thought to be habitual troublemakers within the prison, men suspected of committing serious crimes inside the prison, and men in need of long-term protection from other prisoners. A prisoner will be kept in AC for at least the major portion of a year, if not several years; for the AC is not used for short-term punishment. Upon entry into AC, a prisoner usually is first put in "isolation." Later he enters grade 3 segregation and potentially may work his way up to grade 1 segregation.

Legally, a man cannot be kept in isolation for more than 29 days. However, there are ways that the staff can technically (on paper) get around this limitation if they have strong, negative feelings against the prisoner. The most extreme type of isolation occurs when a man is put in a "quiet cell." Here the prisoner finds himself in a stripped cell, with just a mattress on a cement block and a metal toilet and sink. He is allowed no personal property other than the clothes on his back. There is a small cement block entryway with a solid steel door outside his regular barred door. He can see and hear nothing that is happening outside his cell. The lights are controlled from the outside (as they are in all isolation and grade 1 and 2 segregation cells); and, if the guards are really down on the prisoner, they will shut the door and keep the lights off—except during meals. If their feelings are extreme, they may not even turn the lights on at meal time, when the food is pushed in to the prisoner through the slot in the bars. The previous maximum of 29 days in a quiet cell has legally been reduced to 10 days, but staff are still able to circumvent the rule by letting the prisoner out for less than an hour and then putting him right back in.

For regular isolation, a prisoner is not put in a quiet cell. However, the prisoner still is locked in 24 hours a day, with no personal property, and with no smoking permitted. Technically, the prison rules allow prisoners in isolation to have pencil and paper for corresponding with an attorney or for preparing a petition to the court. However, in reality this depends on the guard. The prisoner may get a pencil and no paper, or vice versa, with some excuse being given about not being able to find the other. Or, the word may come down from the captain that the prisoner is not to have any. Even if he is given both pencil and paper, there is no way for him to check that the guards mail his correspondence.

After a prisoner serves his isolation time, he is put into grade 3 segregation. Occasionally a prisoner who is being held for investigation (not for punishment) will go directly into grade 3. At grade 3 segregation, the prisoner is kept in his cell 23½ hours a day. He is allowed outside, in the corridor in front of his cell, for exercise for a half hour every day; but he is not allowed to go to the AC exercise yard. He eats in his cell. Most of his personal property is kept from him; but he is allowed to use the state-issued tobacco (which prisoners claim is a very poor roll-your-own variety). He is not allowed to listen to either of the two prison-monitored commercial radio stations.

When the staff decide the prisoner is ready, he is graduated into grade 2 segregation. Now the prisoner's lot improves. He is allowed to have his wallet, comb, toothbrush, and toothpaste. He may exercise in the AC yard for an hour a day. Also, he goes to eat in the small AC mess hall. He is allowed to have earphones and access to the library cart that brings books through the AC. In addition, he can order canteen items (if he legally has the money in his prisoner account)—within a $12 monthly limit.

At grade 1 segregation, a prisoner is out of his cell for longer periods. He is allowed to go to the AC yard for one hour in the morning and one and a half hours in the afternoon. He is given the freedom of having an AC job—such as pushing carts, cleaning up, and such. He is allowed to order almost a full draw each month from the canteen. He may have all of his personal property, except for those items in glass containers. When the staff decide it is time, the prisoner's next graduation will be from AC to the "mainline" population where he will probably be celled in C Section of South Block for a while.

The AC is directly inaccessible to the mainline. It is harder for mainline prisoners to get illegal goods in to prisoners in AC than it is to those in B Section, for there is less movement of prisoners in and out. However, there are ways—such as a guard bringing a carton of cigarettes in each time he comes inside. The mainline prisoners who make the arrangements will give the guard 20 or 40 dollars every so often for his effort.

In the southwest quarter of South Block, B Section stands in grim contrast to the new and relatively clean Adjustment Center. Commonly called "the hole" by prisoners, B Section is used for short-term punishment of prisoners, for holding a man for short-term investigation, or for holding a man under protective custody. Many prisoners claim that this is the worst place to be locked up in all of CDC. Chain link fencing is welded outside the rails of the walkways that run along the second through fifth tiers, making an additional cage that is used to control prisoners and prevent them from throwing guards or other prisoners over the railing when they are moving to or from their cells. In certain places, concertina wire (coiled barbed wire) is a grotesque reminder that prisoners are not to try to get to certain places. When a prisoner is taken to B Section, other prisoners generally refer to his being "thrown into the hole." Technically a prisoner is either in isolation or in one of the 3 grades of segregation. When pressed for further distinctions, prisoners acknowledge that only the quiet cells are actually the hole.

The six quiet cells on the ground tier in B Section are strip cells similar to those in AC. However, these have no cement block—the mattress is just put on the floor. In the mid 1960s, there was only a hole in the floor where the toilet had been and no wash basin; the prisoner was given a bucket of clean water for drinking and washing, and an empty bucket in which to perform bodily functions. The buckets were changed daily. Now there are metal toilets and sinks in most of them. However, they are not much better than the bucket routine; for the guards flush the toilets from the outside only once a day; and they "stink to high heaven" and are almost impossible to clean (the prisoner has nothing with which to clean them)—especially in the dark. Occasionally, when guards have very strong feelings against a prisoner, they actually go beyond the limits of punishment prescribed for isolation. In these instances a prisoner may find himself stark naked, in a totally stripped cell, where even the metal toilet and sink are removed—"for his protection." Utter darkness, profound silence, foul odors, bare skin, and cold concrete prevail.

The rest of the cells in B Section are strip cells, with the remainder of the cells on the bottom tier being regular isolation cells. The routine in regular isolation is the same as in AC. In B Section though, a man may just serve isolation time, without even being graduated to grade 3 segregation, for the lengths of punishment are shorter than in AC, and perhaps there is no time left for working up through the 3 grades of segregation.

The routine of segregation in B Section corresponds with the three grades described for AC. As in AC, a prisoner under investigation (who is not being punished) will immediately be put into grade 3 segregation, without going before disciplinary court and without serving isolation time. In B Section, all three grades are shuttled to meals in small groups—usually a tier and a half at a time, with only half of each group eating together, because they use two of the four sections of the south mess hall. Grades 2 and 1 have access to a small exercise yard next to the hospital. Once in segregation, if a prisoner has no bad reports, disciplinary court will graduate him to the next grade after 30 days, except for the move from grade 1 to the mainline population.

A special group of prisoners are those who are held in B Section under protective custody. These men are not being punished for breaking rules or laws. They are being held for their own protection, to keep them from getting hurt by other prisoners who may have reason to do so. For example, if a man has overextended his credit and cannot pay his debts, he may go to the guards and request that they lock him up so that those to whom he owes money cannot get to him. The guards oblige if they think the case merits such action; however, they do not want the situation to be too pleasurable. If it were, they might be deluged with such requests. Therefore, these prisoners are put into segregation; and they have to work their way up to grade 1, as do those who are being punished. The only difference is that these men usually are double celled, and the bunk beds are not stripped from the cells. During the last 30 days in grade 1, the guards consider the man's

*A view of "the hole." Prisoner in the third isolation cell from the right, by holding a mirror through the bars, is able to view the activity down the tier. (Photograph from the* San Francisco Chronicle*)*

*One section of the south mess hall ready for inspection. The mural depicting California's history was painted by a Chicano prisoner. (Courtesy of California Department of Corrections)*

situation as it relates to the yard. If it is relatively safe (such as those to whom he owed money having been transferred to another prison), he is released to the yard (the mainline population). If not, staff may transfer him to another prison, hoping that he will make it better there.

B Section is more readily accessible to the mainline than AC is, and therefore illegal goods can be brought in to those prisoners who are being kept there. In this way, prisoners are often able to mitigate some of the punishment that is imposed on them. However, there is no question that the daily routine of B Section is punishment. And, prisoners have very strong feelings about the negative "extras" that may be imposed by a guard who feels in a punitive mood. Prisoners see much of this "extra" punishment as being more humanly degrading than the actual physical punishment.

## PRISON GUARDS

Of the roughly 650 staff members at San Quentin, about 375 are custody personnel. The warden and three associate wardens are the top administrators. In descending order below the associate warden custody are the following: one captain, four program administrators (in charge of the four cell blocks), about 21 lieutenants, about 55 sergeants, and over 275 "correctional officers." The latter term is merely a euphemism for what is more commonly known to outsiders as prison guards and to prisoners as "bulls." The roughly 275 positions below the associate warden, administration and the associate warden, care and treatment would include the following: a business manager, secretaries, accountants, clerks, counselors, doctors, dentists, nurses, school teachers, vocational instructors, a librarian, chaplains, a food manager, cooks, and maintenance foremen. Most of the employees in this latter group are hired for a specific job that usually requires educational background, professional skill, or previously acquired job training. Many of these employees have little if any direct contact with prisoners, and those who do tend to do so in a professional capacity only. For our purposes, the custody personnel—and in particular the guards—are most important in that they deal directly with the prisoners and have a direct impact on their lives. The bulls are the ones who are responsible for keeping the legal daily routine going, and they also attempt to thwart the prisoners' vast illegal, rule-breaking routine.

A guard's job is rather onerous at times; it is far from being the most stimulative or desirable of jobs. In order to attract men to the position, the pay must be high or the requirements must be low. In this case, the pay leaves something to be desired. A guard starts at $650 per month; and after many years of service, he may be able to work up to the maximum of $790 per month. However, for someone who lacks qualifications to rise above the lower levels of the job market, it is not too undesirable to land a job that begins at $650 per month by merely showing his high school diploma and passing a relatively simple civil service examination. In fact, some staff members privately admit that some guards have obtained their jobs by using bogus high school diplomas. For a man on the low end of the totem pole of job status and opportunity, the job as a guard is relatively soft and well paid compared with other employment opportunities. In addition to the pay, there are other compensations such as free shoe shines and haircuts, reduced rates at the prison laundry, very low rent (with free garbage service and garden care) if one lives in one of the state-owned "company houses" near the ranch area, and a heightened sense of personal status and worth in comparison with the prisoners—convicted criminals who tend to come from even lower levels of the socioeconomic scale than the guards do.

Being fully aware of the potential shortcomings of, and exceptions to, any generalizations about a large group of individuals, I still think that it will be fruitful to note some distinctive characteristics obvious to many observers that enable them to discuss the types of people who tend to become guards. It should be stressed that not all guards fit into one of the five distinct types that are observable. However, the majority do, and some fit into more than one of the types. The observers are prisoners; prison guards themselves, observing their fellow guards; a wide variety of staff members, including some of the administrators; and myself. One type is comprised of retired military personnel. These men—about 20 to 25 percent of the guards—seem to fit into the authoritarian prison routine quite well. Many of these men were master sergeants in the military service, so their position of power over the prisoners is not unlike their position of command in the military. A second type is made up of humanitarians, who sincerely feel that they will be able to help "rehabilitate" the "inmate" in California's "correctional" system. Unfortunately, most of these men soon learn about the *real* prison system—that is quite different from the *ideal* "correctional" system they had heard about. Many of these men quit their job in disgust and frustration. Some of them try to bring about changes and find themselves forced out of the system. A few of them undergo a basic change, which is brought about by the system; they lose their humanitarianism and become hardened toward the prisoners. A third type includes individuals who have generally failed at the jobs they have tried in the past. Usually in their forties or early fifties, these men have such poor work records that few employers will even consider hiring them. Many of this type appear to be somewhat less than quick-witted. A fourth type is comprised of men who may be characterized as poor white Southerners. They tend to hold racist attitudes and appear to be of less than the highest level of intelligence. Some of these men have also experienced employment difficulties and fit into the third type too. A fifth type contains out-and-out sadists. Fortunately very few of these individuals are guards, but they do have a definite impact on the prisoners at times. The administrators are aware of this tendency in most of these men and have taken measures to discourage those inclinations. Under normal circumstances, the measures are effective; but in acute situations, the repressed sadism may reappear.

To illustrate the kind of considerations which lead observers to draw conclusions about guards and which give rise to the five types noted above, a few examples of the intellectual and educational shortcomings of some of the guards will be given. One instance involved a rather sharp, humane lieutenant who had responsibility for the continued training of guards. In a private conversation, he discussed the many problems of dealing with a staff comprised of members "with quite different levels of intelligence." He detailed some of his problems, noting that "the guards are not the sharpest mentally."

A second example was related by a prisoner who rather bitterly told of the problems that arise for prisoners from the guards—"who are from the bottom of the barrel." He went on to illustrate how the "limited intellectual capacity of the bulls is a problem at times." He and a friend had been leaning on a tier railing in the East Block, discussing semantics. Referring to something they had read in a textbook, he was saying, "It isn't reasonable to expect a dog to understand certain things that you might say, so you don't blame him if he does something wrong." While this was being said, a guard walked by. Since they were not talking about something that should be concealed from the guards, they had not changed the topic of conversation and continued as the guard walked by. Suddenly the guard stopped and rushed back. He gave them a very bad time, accusing them of being insolent and threatening to write them up for disciplinary infraction. Finally, the prisoners were able to talk him out of it. The guard, who had never heard of semantics, came by the prisoner's cell later to discuss it; but the guard never did believe that the two prisoners would be talking about something like semantics. He refused to believe that these prisoners could be above him in any way.

A final example involves a younger guard who became a counselor while I was at San Quentin. As a counselor, he was no longer relegated to the back tables of the employee snack bar as the guards seem to be. When discussing this, he expressed his sense of relief from the tedium of the nonintellectual conversations that are typical of the guards. As a counselor, he could sit at the window booths, among the noncustody staff, and partake in conversations that he felt were varied, stimulating, and intellectual in comparison with those of the guards.

To conclude this consideration of guards, I would like to temper the negative implications that may come from the discussion above. In attempting to give a realistic view of the prisoners and their culture, it has been necessary to treat the guards in a realistic manner, even though it may be somewhat unflattering. Some prisoners would claim that all guards are evil brutes; however, the majority of prisoners realize that most of the guards are far from that. Generally, the guards seem to be working-class men who have somewhat limited opportunities for jobs and status. The guards are frequently reminded that *custody* always is of utmost importance. Yet they work in a "correctional" system that publicly stresses its *treatment* programs—that it is not punishing the prisoners, but rehabilitating them. The difficulty (if not practical impossibility) of enforcing custody and carrying out treatment at the same time comes to be understood by most guards. This predicament is one of the root causes of the long-standing covert antagonism between custody and treatment staff.

From discussions with guards it became apparent that many of them learned to accommodate certain of the negative aspects of their job with their personal life by maintaining a strict separation between their role as a guard and the numerous other roles that they assume when away from the prison. In a variety of ways, guards discussed their partial involvement with their job and the often striking discrepancy between their behavior and attitude as a guard and as a husband and/or father. For example, a guard who was recognized for his sadistic tendencies by both staff and prisoners was discussed by two guards who knew him socially away from prison. They had the highest praise for him as a friend, husband, and father; but strongly condemned, and could not understand, his occasional acts of brutality against prisoners. Another example of this partial involvement is manifest in the paranoia among fellow staff members. Many times, in reply to my initial questioning, guards expressed a "formal" view about some aspect of prison life or some incident. However, with time, some of them overcame their paranoia, realized that I was not a threat to their job, and gave me a much different "private" or "personal" view (one that frequently paralleled the view of prisoners). Once this pattern of behavior became obvious, it gave me additional reason to be dubious of official staff views.

Unlike the guards' partial involvement with the prisoner culture, the prisoners' involvement is total. Therefore, it is understandable that the prisoners' view of their culture would be different from the view held by the guards—who actually are outsiders in many ways. With time, all prisoners learn the basic legal routine discussed in this chapter and some of the covert, illegal routine which will be treated in later chapters. However, it will become evident that not all prisoners have the same degree of understanding of their culture. All prisoners learn it well enough to function in it. However, some learn its covert, inner workings so well that they are able to exercise a control and influence over it. Others—regardless of how long they stay in prison—will never really know the prison culture. By the end of this book, you will have been given a view of the ultimate depths of the prisoner culture—a view that even is unknown to the majority of prisoners.

# 3 / The reality behind
## the formal prison life cycle

When first entering prison, a prisoner not only faces the vast, complex, partially covert prisoner culture, he also enters into what can be seen as a formal prison life cycle. This series of stages through which each prisoner usually passes during his life in prison includes stage 1, serving time prior to being eligible for parole; stage 2, serving time while being eligible for parole; stage 3, serving time after being given a parole date (failure at this stage results in being returned to stage 2 for at least one year); stage 4, parole (failure at this stage results in parole revocation, refixing of sentence to the maximum and return to stage 2—usually for several years); and stage 5, discharge from CDC.

This formal prison life cycle is the result of and is controlled by the imprisonment and parole system in California. A combination of features—the indeterminant sentence law, the Adult Authority (parole board, or "the board"), the parole system, and the methods by which parolees have their parole revoked and their sentences refixed to the maximum—determine when, how rapidly, and how far prisoners move through the formal prison life cycle. Each prisoner gradually learns the reality of this formal cycle, a reality that often bitterly contrasts with the publicly acknowledged goals and ideals of the imprisonment and parole system in California. Each prisoner passes through this life cycle as an individual. Collectively however, California prisoners have long felt the injustice of the real system and seen the hypocrisy of the ideal system. Let us point out what some of the key features of this system should ideally be and examine the reality behind those features, as the prisoners perceive it.

## THE INDETERMINATE SENTENCE:  A BASIC DEFECT

When the Department of *Corrections* was established to replace the Department of *Penology* in 1944, a new emphasis was placed on the "correction" and "rehabilitation" of prisoners—instead of punishment. A new parole board, the Adult Authority, also was established. Under California's indeterminate sentence law, the judge who sentences a convicted adult felon to prison does not fix the term or duration of imprisonment. Except for certain felonies that carry a mandatory life sentence, a minimum and maximum term of imprisonment is fixed by statute for each felony. Ideally, within legal limits, the Adult Authority supposedly administers certain parts of the indeterminate sentence in a more scientific manner than the earlier parole board did. Within those limits, the Adult Authority has the power to determine the total time a prisoner is to serve in prison and on parole (conditional release from prison under the supervision of CDC)—presumably based on when the prisoner becomes rehabilitated. As an ideal example, a first termer usually becomes eligible for parole after serving one third of his sentence in prison. If he is rehabilitated, he may be paroled from prison when eligible; but he must serve the remainder of his minimum sentence on parole. If successful on parole, he is discharged from CDC's authority when he completes his minimum sentence. But, if he does not become rehabilitated, he can be kept in prison until he has served his maximum sentence—to protect society and to punish him as a non-rehabilitated prisoner. When the maximum is reached though, he must be discharged. However, if he should become rehabilitated at some point between the minimum and maximum, he is to be paroled at that time and discharged after successfully serving about two years on parole.

Two examples will make clearer the way the indeterminate sentence system ideally functions. For burglary, the sentence is 1 to 15 years. As with all one year minimum sentences, the prisoner must serve the minimum in prison; but if he becomes rehabilitated, he may be paroled or discharged after serving that one year. If he fails to become rehabilitated, he is kept in prison for the entire 15 years or until he does become rehabilitated. Even though he may never become rehabilitated, he must be discharged from CDC after serving 15 years. In contrast, many sentences have a "life top." For example, armed robbery carries a sentence of 5 years to life. After 20 months, the prisoner may be paroled if he has become rehabilitated. However, he would have to serve the rest of the 5 years on parole; then he could be discharged. If he is not rehabilitated by 20 months, any time thereafter, when he becomes rehabilitated, he can be paroled and/or discharged —as long as the total time served in prison and on parole totals 5 years. If the prisoner has a poor disciplinary record in prison and fails to become rehabilitated, he potentially can be kept in prison for the rest of his life—for the protection of society and as punishment for his crime and for failing to become rehabilitated.

It can be seen that movement from stage 1 (serving time prior to being eligible for parole) to stage 2 (serving time while being eligible for parole) is automatic, as fixed by law. Also, if a prisoner has not been discharged earlier, his movement into stage 5 (discharge for CDC) is automatic too, unless his sentence carries a life top. With a life top, movement into stage 5 is determined either by the Adult Authority or by the prisoner's death.

The ideals that underlie California's indeterminate sentencing system are commendable. Ideally, the system is intended to protect society, while being humane and fair to prisoners. Within the maximum and minimum limits set by law, the Adult Authority is supposed to tailor the amount of correction and/or punishment each prisoner receives according to the individual needs deemed necessary for each prisoner. Unfortunately, these underlying ideals will never be achieved under the existing system, because there is a basic defect in the way that the indeterminate sentence is administered. This basic defect has never been realistically acknowledged or faced by CDC and the Adult Authority. In the above examples

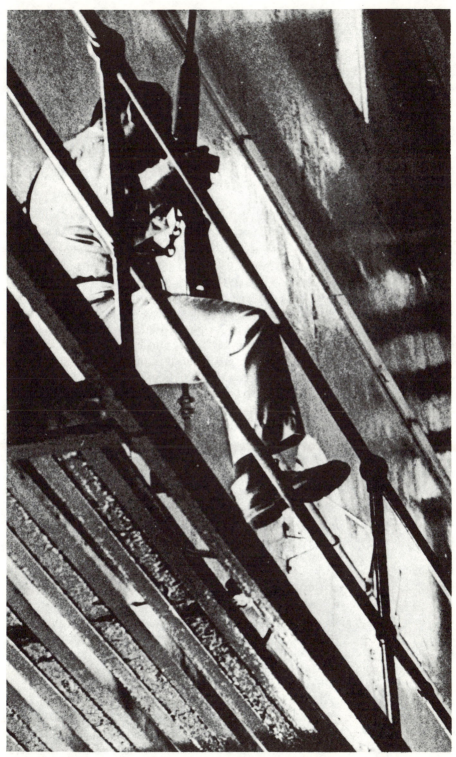

*Armed guard on gun rail in B Section. (Photograph from the* San Francisco Chronicle*)*

of the ideally functioning system, it is evident that the key factor is the point in time *when the prisoner becomes rehabilitated.* Unfortunately, the system in practice stands in bitter contrast to the theoretical system. The basic defect is that *there is absolutely no way to judge if a prisoner has become rehabilitated or not.* Prisoners have long been aware of this. However, with the cooperation of CDC, the Adult Authority has been able to effectively sidestep this issue. In lieu of admitting the impossibility of determining when and if a prisoner is rehabilitated, the Adult Authority has used its quasi-judicial and administrative power to set up a system that ignores many of the ideals that supposedly underlie California's indeterminate sentencing system.

Legislative reports have indicated that the Adult Authority "operates without a clear and rationally justified policy" (California Legislature 1968:40 for example). The parole board ignores the basic defect noted above, acting as if it is possible to determine when and if a prisoner has become rehabilitated. In addition, a deeper, more basic defect prevails throughout CDC. The board seems to go along with the false assumption that it is possible to rehabilitate men in a prison setting, especially a large prison. In reality, rehabilitation does *not* occur in California prisons. For example, after a visit to San Quentin in 1967, former United Nations criminologist, Professor Manuel Lopez-Rey, corresponded with me about this subject. He wrote, "I never believed in programmes carried out in prisons as big and depersonalized as San Quentin. Whatever is done will affect very little the future of the inmates." Most prisoners are fully aware of the failure of rehabilitation efforts in prison. However, they also realize that they must "program" (play the rehabilitation game) if they are to be paroled or discharged before reaching stage 5 (when a prisoner *must* legally be discharged by CDC).

The Adult Authority has taken a cautious approach to granting paroles. By making most prisoners spend from just under, to well over, the majority of their minimum sentence in prison, it appears that the board has generally been able to avoid being criticized by the general public for being too lenient. Some observers feel that this is why the board has generally increased the median times served by prisoners in California throughout the years.

Most prisoners, staff members, and many outsiders are inclined to believe that the Adult Authority has its own implicit understanding of how long the minimum time in prison for each offense generally should be—*regardless of a prisoner's record in prison;* and the board's minimums are well above those prescribed by law. For example, prisoners repeatedly stress their observation that ordinarily, regardless of what a prisoner does inside, it is very unlikely that a prisoner will get out much before the minimum time *established by the board.* Prisoners claim, and give examples to illustrate, that a man can have an exceptionally poor record for his first years in prison, but that if he "cleans up his jacket" (stays out of trouble) and programs the last 1½ or 2 years before he reaches the average time that the board is requiring for that particular offense, he will get out just as early as the prisoner who has had a spotless record and who has programmed all the time he has been in prison. When the board's minimum time is reached, the board is likely to judge both of these prisoners to be rehabilitated and release them on parole. If, before he has served the board's minimum, the prisoner who programs from the beginning protests that he has become rehabilitated and should be paroled, he is likely to be told that he is merely trying to manipulate staff members and the board into thinking that he is rehabilitated. In contrast, the prisoner who cleans up and programs for the last 1½ or 2 years may be noted as an example of how the programs work—that he finally became rehabilitated. However, if a prisoner continues to get into trouble and refuses to program, the board is likely to keep him in prison until he plays the rehabilitation game, or until he must legally be discharged.

## THE PAROLE BOARD:   IDEAL VERSUS REAL

California Penal Code, Section 5075, authorizes the governor to appoint nine members to the Adult Authority. "Insofar as practicable members shall be selected who have a varied and sympathetic interest in corrections work including persons widely experienced in the fields of corrections, sociology, law, law enforcement, and education." The Adult Authority's primary functions are to fix and refix sentences, grant paroles, set conditions of parole, and revoke paroles. The board employs about eleven representatives who help the board members conduct the parole interviews held at the prisons throughout the state and make recommendations to panels of board members—the recommendations are almost always followed. Owing to the nature of their duties, it is reasonable to assume that these case-hearing representatives would have qualifications similar to those of the Adult Authority members.

Turning from the guidelines in the California Penal Code which reflect some of the ideals that underlie California's indeterminate sentencing system, let us consider the actual composition of the present (late 1973) eight-member board. Unfortunately, it is heavily weighed toward law enforcement. Governor Ronald Reagan has appointed men with the following backgrounds: one retired FBI agent, one retired police chief, two former deputy district attorneys, one assistant commander of the Los Angeles police department's detective bureau, and three former CDC employees. A major criticism of the board is that it is not balanced, that it has no members from the fields of law, sociology, and education. Also, there are those who criticize the absence of meaningful minority representation. In reply, the board proudly notes that one of the former CDC employees is a Negro and another is a Mexican-American. However, black prisoners quickly point out that the Negro member certainly is not a black—there being a difference between a Negro and a black. Instead, they contend that he is an "Uncle Tom." Similarly, Chicano prisoners maintain that the Mexican-American member is not a Chicano, but that he is a *Tio Taco* (the Chicano equivalent of an Uncle Tom) and a *"Vendido"* (sellout). In addition, it should be noted that all of the case-hearing representatives are former CDC employees.

## PAROLE HEARINGS:   A GRIM REALITY

A major task of the Adult Authority (members and representatives) is to conduct hearings for prisoners who are legally eligible for parole. Usually several teams of two men each hold hearings for several days at one prison and then move on to another prison. During these hearings, the board determines which of those prisoners that are heard will be given a parole date and which will be made to wait another year to be reconsidered for parole. Due to the number of individual hearings that must be held each year, time is limited. Therefore, the hearings average about 10 to 15 minutes each. During the hearing, while one member of the team is questioning one prisoner, the other member of the team is busy skimming the "jacket" (record file) of the next prisoner to be interviewed and simultaneously half listening to the current interview. When the prisoner leaves, the members discuss the case briefly and come to their conclusion. Usually within 3 to 5 minutes, they are ready for the next prisoner. When the next prisoner is brought in, the member who has skimmed his jacket during the preceding hearing conducts this interview, while the other member half listens as he is skimming the jacket of the prisoner who will follow this one. Members repeat this routine for the entire day—for weeks, months, and years. If such interviews become perfunctory, it is understandable.

Critics contend that the time spent on each individual case is so short that it is impossible for the board to come to any meaningful decision as to whether or not the prisoner has been rehabilitated. The board counters this criticism by noting the 2 or 3 page "preboard report" that is prepared on each prisoner by his counselor at the prison. This report supposedly is an updated compilation of the man's entire jacket—all in 2 or 3 pages. Prisoners and some critics who know the prison system well enough to see beyond the board's argument are fully aware of the true nature of preboard reports. Each report is the end product of a counselor's 15 to 20 minute interview with the prisoner—with the counselor often perfunctorily rushing through the several pages of standard questions and later summarizing the answers and/or his feelings. Counselors have admitted that anything over 25 minutes is too much time to spend on one of these interviews. A few admit that, in a tight situation, they are able to conduct the interview in 5 minutes and "fake the rest." Normally, most prisoners only see their counselor this one time each year, because the counselors are too busy to do little more than prepare the preboard reports and take care of those few prisoners who seem to continually complain. Even if the counselors did have considerable free time, most prisoners would not go to a counselor with a personal problem anyway; most prisoners do not think of counselors as such. If a prisoner has a personal problem, he is more likely to turn to a fellow prisoner for help than he is to go to a counselor. Some prisoners contend that counselors are little more than preboard report clerks. Regardless of the prisoners' feelings, the total annual time spent judging whether or not a prisoner has become rehabilitated usually is between 25 and 35 minutes. Prisoners and critics argue that this is not enough time to be able to make such an important decision.

The parole hearing, regardless of the prisoner's outward appearance, is a grim, emotional encounter for him. Perhaps you can understand this better if you imagine that *you* are a prisoner and view it as a prisoner might.

You have thought about and planned for this hearing for a long time—at least a year. It's your chance for freedom. Since you are legally eligible for parole, you may get a parole date if everything goes well. If you "blow it" though, it will be another year before you get a chance. You have planned and know what you will and will not say. It's your turn. A guard ushers you into the hearing room. With a quick glance, you see the two board members, dressed in business suits, sitting in stuffed leather chairs behind a long, massive wooden table. Off to the side, beyond the end of the table, you see another man in a suit and recognize him as one of the counselors from the prison. He's there to take a few notes and act as a clerk for the board members. You are told to take a seat in a solitary straight chair that is across the table from the two members. The chair seems to be isolated in what appears to be a vast expanse of empty floor. Seated, you try to act relaxed. Inside though, you are tense; you recognize the tremendous power these men have over you. You may have many negative personal opinions about them, but you keep them to yourself now. If they say something, you try to agree; the last thing you want to do is argue with them. You may have even memorized a little talk about your plans for life on the streets—hopefully to impress them. However, as with so many prisoners in the past, your emotions blank out your memory; so you're forced to play it by ear. They ask you about what you've been doing in prison to rehabilitate yourself and what you plan to do on the streets. You present answers that you think will impress them with how prison has rehabilitated you. Suddenly it seems that the 10 to 15 minute hearing has ended before it really began. As you leave, you hear the oft-repeated phrase, "We'll let you know."

Perhaps the best way to convey some of the harsh truth faced by prisoners in these hearings is to give two examples from the board hearings that I attended as an observer. The first example involves a Chicano prisoner who was questioned by the board representative who had skimmed his jacket during the previous hearing. After several rather perfunctory questions, the prisoner was asked about the crime for which he had been convicted. This led to some rather pointed questions about the activities of his alleged crime partner who had not been convicted. The prisoner made considerable effort to hedge the questions, but they were asked again. Finally the prisoner was in such a tight spot that he had to answer. This was an extremely emotional moment for the prisoner since the board represented the potential of freedom. The final question had been worded in such a way that he would have to either snitch on his alleged crime partner or tell an evident lie. With much anguish, the prisoner finally told them an obvious, yet qualified lie. He prefaced his answer with the phrase, "since you make me answer." After the prisoner left the room, the two representatives actually laughed about it and noted, to me, that it was an example of how "the Mexican-Americans will never rat on anyone." The representatives had no valid reason to question the prisoner the way they did. The crime had already been processed through legal channels, the prisoner had refused to inform on his crime partner before, and he was serving a sentence that took all of this into consideration. It appeared to me that they did this merely as a humorous example. They seemed to have no compassion for the prisoner and no understanding of the conflict situation in which they placed him as a fellow human being—forcing him to tell them an obvious lie when they held his life in their hands. These were men who had been hired for their supposed ability to understand the conditions and situations faced by other human beings.

The second example is from the hearing of a prisoner who was returned to prison for violating his first parole by writing a bad check four months after his release. The board representative was verbally reviewing what had taken place two years earlier. Routinely the prisoner would nod or murmur the expected agreement. The representative's rather callous comments (punctuated by affirmative nods or murmurs from the prisoner) went somewhat as follows: "I see that we let you out on parole to a job, but that you were fired from the job in about two weeks. Then, after about three more weeks, you were able to find another job; but that one only lasted a couple of weeks too. You were pretty good at getting jobs though; you got another one in three weeks; but you were fired again within a couple of weeks. Then, after about three or four weeks, you wrote a bad check. Now don't you know how stupid that was? What you should have done was line yourself up with one of the many small loan companies out there—for a small loan to tide you over until you got yourself lined up with a steady job." Without betraying his true feelings of astonishment, the prisoner muttered agreement. The representative, apparently satisfied with having proved his point, concluded the hearing. Fortunately, for the prisoner, his performance was worthwhile and successful. Since the prisoner had served two years for the violation and now saw his error, the representative concluded that the prisoner was again ready for parole. The representative demonstrated apparent ignorance of the larger world in which the prisoner must live when he is released on parole. I doubt that there is a loan company in existence that would have knowingly lent the parolee money under those circumstances. Even if there were, I doubt that there is a parole agent working for CDC that would have given the parolee approval to sign such a loan contract.

It has not been my intent to add to the existing reams of criticism directed toward the Adult Authority and the way it abusively administers California's indeterminate sentence system. However, if you, the reader, are to begin to understand some of the truth behind the formal prison life cycle, the circumstances that give rise to this criticism of the board must be presented. Hopefully, you will see the hypocrisy of the Adult Authority and of California's indeterminate sentence system that becomes obvious to most prisoners as they pass through the formal prison life cycle and learn what actually happens behind the ideal facade that is presented to outsiders. There are many ways that the board and CDC staff sidestep the ideals of rehabilitation, but they are too numerous to be presented here, and some of those abuses are not directly relevant at this point. In Chapter 8, several other ways that the ideal system is averted will become evident.

From my own observations, I would like to briefly go a step beyond those critics who argue that the board members should be better qualified and that the board should be enlarged to allow more time to be spent for each parole hearing. I contend that these critics' have mistakenly assumed that with more time and better qualified members, the board would be able to succeed. I do not think so, because the basic defect noted earlier will always remain. There still will be no way to get behind the "in-prison" or "before-the-board" roles played by prisoners and to know what they actually will do when released on parole. Hopefully, by the conclusion of this book, you will be able to better understand why I strongly feel that a prisoner's actions in prison are *not necessarily* a reflection of what his behavior will be on the streets. It must be stressed that these men are not atypical human beings; it is the prison situation that is atypical. It is in this atypical world that prisoners have developed and maintain their culture. And, as members of that culture, prisoners learn to live in it and assume one or several of the various roles found there. If prisoners act in what appears to be a negative way, outsiders must try to realize that the prisoners' actions are those of typical human beings who are reacting to an atypical situation. Even in a complex culture such as ours in the United States, most individuals become quite adept at playing a variety of roles that frequently may have conflicting demands. Yet people normally are not condemned for this, because those who are successful at playing roles are usually able to keep the conflicting roles separated. Why shouldn't prisoners be able to do the same? Why should prisoners be condemned for playing in-prison roles before they are given a chance to show if they are able to keep those roles separated from the roles they will be expected to play on the streets?

## THE PAROLE SYSTEM:   CONFLICTING FUNCTIONS

The parole system is directly related to a prisoner's movement through the formal prison life cycle. If he succeeds on parole, he may be able to move to stage 5 (discharge from CDC) before he has served his maximum legal sentence. However, if his parole is revoked, he will be returned to stage 2 of the cycle, usually for two or more years, before he will be allowed to move through the remainder of the cycle again.

Before being released on parole, a prisoner must first sign the Adult Authority's parole agreement, whereby he agrees to the rules, terms, and 14 standard conditions of parole—as well as any special conditions the board may impose. The standard conditions of parole deal with requirements and/or restrictions in areas such as residence, work, monthly reports to the parole division, use of alcoholic beverages, association with former prisoners, use of motor vehicles, cooperation with parole division and parole agent, personal conduct, and civil rights. The parole division of CDC enforces these rules, terms, and conditions of parole. It is the parole agent's duty to supervise the parolee—through surveillance, counseling, job placement, and restoration of civil rights.

Primarily, the parole agent is expected to perform a support function *and* a police function in his relations with the parolee. However, in contrast to the ideal expectations, the parole agent generally fails to successfully carry out either of these two primary functions. Parolees generally contend that supportive programs and efforts frequently look better on paper than they do in practice. Also, they know that parole agents seldom apprehend a parolee in a criminal act. If a parolee is arrested, it usually is by the police. Regardless of whether or not he recognizes it, a parole agent's two primary prescribed functions generally are seen as mutually exclusive by parolees. Actually, the parole agent cannot be a truly supportive influence and a policeman at the same time, because most parolees will not accept him as such. Therefore, the police function usually defeats the support function. In the majority of cases, when a parolee finds himself in a tight situation, he will turn to others of his own subculture before he will ask his parole agent for help. Parolees do approach their parole agents for help and interact with them, but this usually is done on a superficial level where little if any real communication takes place. In fact, this situation breeds much dishonesty, with most parolees learning to play the parole game with their parole agent. Normally, most parolees are able to successfully present a front to their agent that is in accord with the agent's expectations, regardless of what may actually be occurring when the agent is not present.

## PAROLE REVOCATION:   REASON FOR PROTEST

Prisoners generally regard parole efforts as ineffective and wasteful of tax dollars, and the part of the parole system that is most intensely criticized by prisoners is the method by which a man's parole is revoked. The Adult Authority has the statutory power to suspend or revoke parole for good cause; and since suspension always precedes further investigation or the revocation hearing, suspension may be based on a mere belief that good cause exists. Prisoners, attorneys, and other critics contend that the Adult Authority frequently abuses its power in this area. For example, parole may be suspended if a parolee is in jail, pending prosecution on a new criminal charge; and usually the suspension order is prepared so that it cites additional noncriminal violations of parole such as driving a motor vehicle without *written* permission, failing to cooperate with the parole agent, or association with individuals of bad reputation. Normally such noncriminal violations are not used as grounds for violation, because the board realizes that all parolees usually break some of the conditions of parole from time to time. However, by including noncriminal violations in its charges against the parolee, the board is able to revoke parole anyway, even if the parolee is not convicted of the criminal charge. When the parolee is acquitted, the board still has the power to determine whether or not his conduct in connection with the criminal charge was such to be grounds for revocation. In fact, there have been instances when a parolee has been found guilty of a crime by the board, even though he had already been acquitted of the same crime in a court of law. Also, the board has judged parolees guilty of crimes for which they were never prosecuted. Since a parolee may have his parole revoked for noncriminal violations of parole, and since almost all parolees (successful or not) commit parole violations, a mere documentation of some of those violations can be used by the board to support its decision to revoke a parole in a case that is based on grounds that might be of questionable validity in a court of law.

If, after suspending a man's parole, the Adult Authority intends to revoke his parole, the parolee is returned to prison to await his revocation hearing. Prisoners realize that once a man has been returned to prison, it is almost a foregone conclusion that he will have his parole revoked, have his sentence refixed to the maximum, and be returned to stage 2 (serving time while being eligible for parole) for at least two years. Prisoners do concede that the board has just reason to revoke the parole of many parolees. However, they bitterly contend that this is not true in many instances. For more than 25 years now, California prisoners have been protesting the fact that the traditional rights of due process of law have been denied them at parole revocation hearings. At this hearing, the prisoner is allowed to admit or deny his guilt; but he is *not* allowed the normal safeguards such as to have legal counsel, to confront and directly challenge his accusers, and to call witnesses in his own defense. Prisoners argue that the parole revocation hearing resembles a kangaroo court hearing. They feel that they have valid reason to protest.

Prisoners realize that the board's decision to revoke parole, coupled with the automatic refixing of their sentences to the legal maximum when parole is revoked, means that they may end up serving almost as much time in prison for a parole violation as they originally did for the initial crime. In fact, some men (especially if they openly react against the injustice they perceive) serve more time for the violation than for the original conviction. For example, let me note some of the details of a Chicano prisoner's parole hearing before the board in 1967, two years after his parole had been revoked. He was in stage 2 for the second time, trying to get into stage 3 again. At the time of the hearing, this man was 33 years old. He was born in California, but most of his family lived in Mexico. He had worked hard most of his life as a migrant farm laborer. About 5½ years earlier he had been convicted of committing a burglary—during the long winter months when agricultural employment generally is unavailable. He had served 3 years of his 1 to 15 year sentence when he was granted a 3 year parole by the board. If he had successfully completed the 3 year parole, he would have been discharged after a total time in prison and on parole of 6 years. However, after a few weeks on parole, he was missing. His parole agent assumed he had absconded (was running from parole), so a routine all points bulletin was issued for his arrest. Apparently he had not really understood the conditions of parole (which had been written in English) and had merely followed the crops to stay employed. Later, in another part of the state, he was picked up for parole violation—failing to report to his English-speaking parole agent. His sentence was refixed to the maximum, so he still faced the potential of serving the remaining nearly 12 years of the original 15 years. After serving 2 years in prison for the noncriminal violation, his parole hearing which I observed went about as poorly as his experience on the streets. The board representative who was reviewing his case verbally noted that the lack of Spanish-speaking counselors and parole agents had been a problem for the prisoner. And, it was obvious from his single-word replies to several questions asked by the board representative that he did not really know what the questions had been. It appeared to me that he had understood a couple of words and assumed the rest —this assumption turned out to be wrong. Because of his poor performance before the board, the prisoner was denied parole for another year. After that third year in prison during his repeat of stage 2, he would have served a third year—as much time as he did for burglary. I do not know the outcome of his hearing in 1968; but if he was not granted parole at that time, he served more time for the noncriminal violation than for the crime that originally sent him to prison.

(The United States Supreme Court's *Morrissey* decision in June 1972, dealing with the rights of an Iowa parolee facing return to prison, granted the man a preliminary court hearing—where some due process of law exists—before being returned to prison. Some of these *Morrissey* rights are being implemented in California and have resulted in changes in the manner in which California parolees have their parole suspended and revoked. However, prisoners contend that the procedural changes have had a minimal effect in actuality. Apparently, the full impact of this decision in California is yet to be determined in the courts. In the meantime, prisoners recognize that the decision did not go far enough. Therefore, in November 1972, a group of California prisoners filed a class action suit in the U. S. District Court in San Francisco. The suit charges that disciplinary, parole, and parole revocation hearings are completely lacking in both procedural and substantive due process.)

Although much more could be written about the reality behind the formal prison life cycle, at this point you should have some understanding of why, for more than 25 years, California prisoners have been trying to make the public, the state legislature, and the courts aware of that truth, too. In Chapter 8, on social control, some of the prisoners' efforts to bring about that awareness will be discussed. With this basic understanding of the discrepancy between the real and the formal prison life cycle, let us turn to a consideration of the types of prisoners who enter into that life cycle.

# 4/Types of prisoners

The attention in previous chapters has been focused on the general prison population. Some readers may have become conscious of my apparently stubborn refusal to use the two common synonyms for prisoner—convict and inmate. However, there have been valid reasons for my persistent use of the term prisoner, as should become more apparent as you continue reading. In California prisons, all prisoners are called inmates, because staff intentionally began using that term many years ago. Now, even the prisoners themselves refer to other prisoners or to the general prison population as inmates. In contrast, the terms prisoner and convict seldom are used by either staff or prisoners. Application of these terms has been discouraged by the staff of California Department of *Corrections*. It must be remembered that there has been a shift of emphasis. California no longer has a *prison* system. Instead, convicted felons are locked up in the *correctional* institutions (only two of the nine CDC institutions are actually called prisons). Yet, prisoners will readily admit that those "correctional" institutions are really prisons, regardless of what they are called. The term convict has almost become taboo in normal staff conversations. Convicts have suggested that the staff had hoped that convicts would disappear if no one used the term. If so, staff hopes have not been fulfilled. Convicts still exist.

## CONVICTS AND INMATES

Many prisoners make a definite distinction between two types of prisoners—convicts and inmates. However, the majority of inmates (who also are the majority of prisoners) merely have a general awareness of the differences. They are not aware of—nor do they have reason or opportunity to become aware of—many of the important details of the differences. Those who routinely use the terms convicts and inmates to distinguish the two types of prisoners are not confused by the fact that the term inmates also refers to all prisoners. The meaning of inmate is obvious to prisoners from the context of their conversation. However, having two possible meanings for the term inmates is confusing to outsiders. Therefore, as an aid to the reader, I have taken the liberty of replacing one of the uses of inmates by the term prisoners. Henceforth, prisoners—*not* inmates—will be used when referring to all prisoners. This will eliminate the necessity of having to qualify the term for the reader when its meaning is not clear. In addition, I refuse to insult convicts by calling them inmates, or by calling inmates convicts. Occasionally there are common prison expressions that include the term "inmate" as it refers to prisoners in general—such as a prisoner's "inmate" account. When it must be used as such, "inmate" will be set off by quotation marks so that the reader will be aware of its meaning.

Background of Convicts

In order to distinguish between these two types of prisoners, it is best to begin with the background of convicts. It is important to realize that convicts have been around for a long time. Years ago, before the present emphasis on rehabilitation had begun, prisoners knew exactly why they were in prison. They were being punished, and the guards were instrumental in the administration of that punishment. Then, as now, much of the prisoners' most meaningful activity was either against the law or against the prison rules. This illegal or rule-breaking activity also was important to staff, for it was their duty to stop it. Because of these activities, the prisoners were in an almost continual state of warfare against the staff. This fierce opposition between the prisoners and staff promoted an intense unity among the prisoners—a unity against a common enemy. This opposition also was a key element that contributed to the existence of convicts. In this situation, convicts would interact with the staff—but only to receive orders or to answer direct questions. A convict did not want to be caught interacting with the enemy on a friendly or excessive basis. To do so would invite the suspicion of other convicts if staff should learn and act upon secret details of the convicts' activities. Few rewards were available from staff, and convicts thought none of them worth betraying their fellow convicts for. Consequently, these convicts would never do anything for their own personal good that would be detrimental to the group. Convicts would never snitch on other prisoners. And, it was expected that no prisoners would snitch. Therefore, informers were not tolerated. Granted, some prisoners surreptitiously snitched and got away without being suspected. And, a few snitches were so obvious that they were never privy to important communications; and since they did not really pose a threat to the rest of the prisoners, they were avoided and tolerated. However, the prisoner who was caught giving or selling important secret information to the enemy was eliminated. He was executed by the convicts who had judged him and found him guilty under the convict code—the convicts' unwritten law which generally forbids a convict from snitching or doing anything for his own personal benefit that would be damaging to the group or another member of the group.

An important change came about when emphasis on rehabilitation began many years ago. When implemented, the rehabilitative nature of the new programs became apparent to prisoners. They were now told by staff that they were in prison to be rehabilitated, not punished; that guards were "correctional officers" there not to administer punishment, but merely to keep the prisoners confined; that confinement was necessary to protect society while the prisoners were being rehabilitated. Prisoners began to wonder why they were in prison. Supposedly, the staff was no longer an enemy; it was a partner, who was helping the prisoners. The fierce opposition between prisoners and staff seemed to disappear, thus effectively destroying that intense unity among prisoners. Without an obvious opposition or enemy, most prisoners saw no reason for unity. Simultaneously, convicts (as a type of prisoner) seemed to fade into insignificance while a new type of prisoner appeared—the inmate.

An integral part of the new rehabilitation programs was the effective interaction between prisoners and staff. A prisoner's release became contingent on his "programming." To program, a prisoner had to actively participate in several of the offered rehabilitation programs—the ones that staff suggested. Prisoners now were serving sentences under the indeterminate sentence laws; and if a prisoner was to be released before his maximum sentence, he first had to be rehabilitated. Under this system, prisoners did almost anything to prove to the staff that they were rehabilitated, regardless of how it would affect other prisoners. Since unity no longer existed among most prisoners, each inmate was a single individual, trying to get out as soon as possible. Inmates thought they could further impress staff into believing they had become rehabilitated by telling staff about the illegal and rule-breaking activities of other prisoners—activities in which prisoners have always engaged. This "law-abiding" snitching became wholesale and made it difficult for the relatively few remaining convicts to continue many of their activities; they were forced into even more covertness than before. For convicts, the staff was not the only enemy now. Inmates were a new enemy who could not be privy to convict activities, because they did not adhere to the convict code.

With the passage of time, more and more prisoners began to question the validity of the rehabilitation programs and the sincerity of those who administered them. They came to recognize the general inability of programs inside a prison to effect rehabilitation and the hypocrisy of the indeterminate sentence system. In their new role, the "correctional officers" did more than merely confine the prisoners; they continued to harass, repress, and punish the prisoners as they had before. A general disillusionment began to grow among most prisoners. More and more prisoners recognized that their own illegal and rule-breaking activities were more important to them than the staff's rehabilitation activities. Although even convicts superficially played the game and programmed, the basic opposition between staff and prisoners became apparent to more prisoners. With growing numbers of convicts, the opposition became fierce, and an intense unity once more prevailed against the staff as enemy. The convicts who had earlier faded into insignificance reappeared and multiplied. It has taken them years to rebuild the California convict population, and most convicts are a bit older. Today, even though they are only 8 to 10 percent of the prisoner population, convicts are a significant, powerful type of prisoner. They have been able to mitigate the harshness of the present system through their illegal and rule-breaking activities. Most of those activities are economic in nature and will be treated in Chapter 6.

Prisoners Today

Having personally seen that the prison system generally fails to rehabilitate, most prisoners today also recognize that they must program if they are to become eligible for parole when they have served the "average" time for their particular crime.

But most prisoners are also kept off guard by personal statements made to them by staff members and by the Adult Authority. Those personal statements imply that there always is that possibility that his actual participation in rehabilitation activities—not the amount of the time he has served—just might really be the key, important factor involved in his release. These prisoners begin to doubt the truth of what they, and almost all other prisoners, have observed. Most of these prisoners are so uncertain that they are willing to go beyond the required programming and become inmates. Therefore, the majority of prisoners are inmates.

Now, as in the past, inmates are willing to do just about anything to convince the staff that they have become rehabilitated. Concerned only for himself, the inmate has no sense of duty toward, unity with, or real concern for other prisoners. Inmates frequently report on the illegal and rule-breaking activities of convicts, so it is understandable that convicts think of inmates in terms such as rats, snitches, and punks. Some inmates are dependable, however, in areas that involve their own interests—such as not telling even a friend that he has found a source and is shooting drugs. Still, inmates are unpredictable when they are busted by staff. Normally they will inform on any and every possible person to try to get out of a pinch. But even then, an inmate who is using drugs might not snitch; he might want to protect his source—the source being more important to him than his having to endure some in-prison punishment.

Basically, convicts have not changed. They know that they are being punished, not rehabilitated. They have united in opposition to those who thwart their punishment-mitigative activities. Now they successfully wage warfare against two enemies: inmates as well as staff. This makes for a strange situation where convicts frequently must peacefully interact with their enemies. Convicts successfully accomplish this by perfunctorily programming and superficially talking with staff and inmates—and even known snitches at times if necessary. However, their "talk" is shallow; no real communication takes place. Convicts are concerned about their fellow convicts though. They live by the convict code: never snitching and never doing anything for one's personal benefit that would be detrimental to the group or another member of the group. Convicts almost never snitch; but if one should snitch and be caught, he often would be executed in accordance with the convict code. Inmate snitches do not come under the authority of the convict code. They would not be executed, but ostracized. Inmates are the enemy, and convicts must take care to hide their important illegal and rule-breaking activities from them.

Having presented the general background and salient characteristics of inmates and convicts, it should be noted that inmates or convicts are involved in all aspects of the prisoner culture. Therefore, much additional description and detail concerning these two types of prisoners will be presented in the forthcoming pages. At this time however, a few selected details will give you a better understanding of convicts. For example, inmates generally respect convicts, but it seems to be a respect that arises from the inmates' fear of convicts and their power. Many times inmates will go to great efforts to help a convict because they know that it is wise to stay on the good side of convicts. This way not only will they avoid trouble, but they might be in line for some sort of favor from the convict in the future. From this fearful respect, the misconception occasionally arises that convicts do not always pay their debts. This could happen when an inmate, not wanting to push or bother a convict, fails to remind a convict about a minor debt. The convict, who usually is busy with much more important activities, might forget about the minor debt and never pay the inmate. However, if reminded of a legitimate debt, a convict will honor and pay it. Another illustration of this fearful respect is in the area of key prisoner jobs which allow convicts to control many prisoner activities. Convicts do not work in all of these jobs, but they are able to exercise a powerful control over those inmates who hold those key jobs. There are always the stories about those very unwise, deceased inmates who refused to cooperate with convicts.

Some important details concerning convict unity should be noted. Some prisoners refer to themselves as convicts (they will be treated in detail later), but real convicts would not consider them convicts. Convicts are fully aware of who the real convicts are. They know each other and talk freely in front of each other. This occurs even among convicts who may not really like each other as individuals; but, regardless of their personal feelings, the trust is there. Their unity is in their trust. They know that a fellow convict will not snitch to save himself from punishment when he is busted. An accused convict who is not guilty, but knows who the guilty convict is, will deny guilt. If necessary, he will honorably take the unjust punishment; but he will never reveal who the guilty convict is. Convicts are proud to be convicts. They take great pride in their honor, trust, and unity.

During my research at San Quentin, I came to personally understand and experience that pride. As a participant observer, I was privy to illegal and rule-breaking activities of convicts, and I developed a deep, convictlike relationship with many convicts. However, I did not know who all the convicts were. Apparently most convicts knew who I was though. For example, one day I was returning to South Block from the hospital. There is a very heavy steel door that is either locked or under the immediate control of a bull at all times. It serves as a sort of count gate, because movement in and out of the hospital is very restricted. It takes the guard, at the very least, several seconds to check a prisoner's ID card and papers. Therefore, with considerable effort, the heavy door is closed by each prisoner after he passes through. Freemen are obvious to the guard though and are allowed to pass through immediately. As a freeman, I passed by several prisoners who were waiting to be checked through the door. A prisoner was going through the door, so I hurried to get through before he closed it. Out of the corner of his eye, he caught a glimpse of my freeman's suit. While stopping the closing movement of the door, the prisoner said "Excuse me, I didn't mean to close the door on a freeman." By then he had looked directly at me to excuse himself. He immediately corrected himself and said, "whoops, I mean a convict!" Later, from my description, a close convict friend pointed out that the prisoner was a convict. My friend said that I had been paid a very great compliment—"one which is not given lightly, and it should not be taken lightly."

To temporarily conclude our present treatment of convicts let us discuss the way they interact with staff and participate in programs. Usually convicts can turn most situations to their advantage. For example, a black counselor was quite proud of the fact that he had been able to put together "a multiracial group of very heavy inmates" for a weekly group counseling session. The session was held in one of the classrooms in the West Block yard. The counselor was impressed with how these "heavies really cut it up." In fact, the counselor brought many other staff members to visit. I sat in one time, but I was not too impressed. True, the prisoners (many of whom were convicts) did get emotional and actually yell at each other some of the time. However, the actual topics under discussion were superficial ones. Convicts later discussed this programming. They admitted that they were using the counselor, that they were doing it for ulterior motives. After the hour-long session was over, the counselor would have to rush off to other duties, or he would walk out with his guests. However, the convicts would stay behind and get some of their important business (illegal activities) done in the West Block area—an area that normally is restricted from most prisoners.

A second example will show how very complex this interaction can become. I had been curious about a particular convict who was drunk at least half of the times I saw him. I wondered how he could actually stagger around the yard and never get busted by the bulls. The explanation came from other convicts. Apparently he had what appeared to be a very close working relationship going with one of the lieutenants. The lieutenant thought he was getting quite a bit of important information from the prisoner, so his word was out to the sergeants—and consequently to the bulls—to leave this prisoner alone. Occasionally some bull might bust him anyway; and the lieutenant would come by in a couple of days and get him out of the hole. Why did the other convicts tolerate this convict as a fellow convict, or tolerate his continuing in a situation that would lead most observers to believe that the convict was snitching? The answer was that—even though the convict would actually feed important information to the lieutenant from time to time—the information was always delivered just a little after the information was no longer vital to the situation or individuals involved. Therefore, he never really gave the lieutenant anything of value; although the lieutenant often thought so, especially if he was able to act on the information before the individual who received the information first acted. In addition, the lieutenant was always hoping that, in the future, he would get something that was really hot. If some staff member should question the lieutenant about the prisoner, he would say "Hands off; he's my boy." The staff member would infer that he received information from the prisoner. In reality, if the lieutenant were pressed to tell *what* really useful information was given to him *when*, he would probably have to admit that he had received nothing of value to staff. It was a tricky feat for the convict to give information at just the right time to have it appear hot, while knowing the information had already leaked out some other way. If the information was obviously cold, the lieutenant would catch on. One can see that this was a delicate situation to be in. The risk was worth it for this convict and his· fellow convicts though, for the convict's job gave him almost unlimited freedom of movement throughout most of the prison and enabled him to take care of a lot of business for convicts.


## ETHNIC GROUPS

Temporarily turning from the classification of the prisoners as convicts or inmates, let us now consider the other significant way they are divided. The three major ethnic groups among prisoners are distinguished by CDC staff and adminis-

*North mess hall—where the warden's tour never goes. Weekend movies are shown here. (Courtesy of California Department of Corrections)*

*Another section of the south mess hall in use. (Courtesy of California Department of Corrections)*

trators. A fourth catchall group has been added. These four groups are referred to as Anglo, Mexican-American, Negro, and Other. There may be variations in some of these terms. For example, Anglo is normally used in conversations among staff, but reports and statistical tables may use white or Caucasian to refer to the same group. In a similar manner, the Mexican-American group may be called either Mexican or white, Mexican descent. The Other classification includes American Indians, Japanese, Chinese, Filipinos, and any additional ethnic groups that might be represented in the prisoner population. I have personally modified CDC's terminology to reflect significant social changes that are well known to prisoners. Henceforth, in reference to the same four ethnic groups, I will refer to them as Anglo, Chicano, Black, or Other.

Simplifying computations by leveling out the yearly fluctuations that occurred during the period that I was going into San Quentin, it can be roughly stated that, of the nearly 4,000 prisoners, 50 percent were Anglo, 18 percent were Chicano, 30 percent were Black, and 2 percent were Other. It must be admitted that the American Indians, as part of the Other group, have had a successful program going for several years. However, the impact of the Other group on the entire prisoner population has been relatively insignificant. Therefore, with no intention to slight the Other group, our concern will be primarily with the three major ethnic types.

## TWO LEVELS OF THE PRISONER CULTURE

The three major ethnic types of prisoners significantly fit into two distinct levels of the prisoner culture that correspond with the inmate and convict types of prisoners. The first level—the inmate level—is obvious and superficial. The second level—the convict level—is deeper and relatively covert. It should be noted that the present discussion of these two levels of the prisoner culture will not be complete. Many further differences between these levels will become apparent in the following chapters, especially in Chapter 6, the very long, important chapter that deals with the prisoner economy.

The definite distinctions that prisoners make between inmates and convicts are based on their own observations and experiences. For example, convicts who oppose inmates and staff in many of their activities are fully aware that if they are to successfully continue in their illegal and rule-breaking activities, these must be hidden from staff and inmate view. This necessity has resulted in the development of various levels of prisoner activity—levels that are obvious to an insider. Convicts know the behavior patterns and activities characteristic of each type of prisoner. Those distinguishing features have led to the prisoners' very real typology, and they are also used to determine the first and second levels of the prisoner culture. In other words, those things that an inmate typically does, also are things that are typically done on, or characteristic of, the inmate level. The same is true of the convict level. Accordingly, much of the earlier treatment of inmate and convict types is directly applicable to the first and second levels of the prisoner culture.

It must be admitted that this classification of prisoners into inmate and convict types is based on ideal types. Not all prisoners fit neatly into these two types. Nevertheless, most prisoners either fit into or have a propensity to one of the two types. The majority of prisoners are either inmates or inmatelike. A relatively small number of prisoners are either convicts or incline toward that type. Some prisoners, a very small percentage, are distinct exceptions; they do not fit into either of the two types. Those exceptions will be treated later. Now, an attempt will be made to give a better indication of what is meant by "majority" and "relatively small number."

Convicts admit that any estimate of the number of convicts inside would only be an estimate. A precise number or percentage could never be ascertained. There are convicts who are not active in any business that would allow others to definitely classify them as such. These "inactive" convicts only show their true colors if some situation should require their participation. Therefore, it is very difficult to even estimate their number. However they would certainly be included among those prisoners who are inclined toward the convict type.

Some convicts did attempt to estimate the number of active convicts. It was interesting to note the consistency of their estimate. They insisted that these were only rough estimates; but when their estimate, that between 8 and 10 percent of the entire population are convicts, is compared with their estimates of the percentage of convicts in each ethnic group, the results are surprisingly close. Table 1, using the convicts' estimates of the percentage of convicts in each of the ethnic groups, is based on a total prisoner population of 4,000. The low estimate of 334 convicts represents 8.3 percent of the total prisoner population, and the high estimate of 536 convicts represents 10.9 percent. It should be recognized that, using the low estimate, Chicanos comprise over three-fourths of the convict population; and using the high estimate, they still are over two-thirds of the total. In either case, Anglos make up most of the remainder, with blacks comprising a rather insignificant portion.

Since all prisoners do not fit into the ideal types of convict or inmate, is there some way to get a better picture of the composition of the entire prisoner population? With a full awareness that the following is just a "guesstimate," it is possible

TABLE 1     CONVICTS' ESTIMATES OF PERCENTAGE OF CONVICTS IN EACH ETHNIC GROUP

| | | | Low estimate | | | High estimate | | |
|---|---|---|---|---|---|---|---|---|
| Ethnic Group | Percent of total | Actual number | Percent that are convicts | Actual number | Percent of 334 total convicts | Percent that are convicts | Actual number | Percent of 536 total convicts |
| Anglo | 50 | 2,000 | 3 | 60 | 18 | 7 | 140 | 26.1 |
| Chicano | 18 | 720 | 35 | 262 | 78.4 | 50 | 360 | 67.2 |
| Black | 30 | 1,200 | 1 | 12 | 3.6 | 3 | 36 | 6.7 |
| | | | Total: | 334 | | Total: | 536 | |

to combine those prisoners who are convicts with those who incline toward that ideal type. The actual percentage of those who are convictlike might *very* roughly be estimated to be about the same as those who are active convicts. Therefore, it is quite likely that those prisoners who are convicts or convictlike would not comprise much more than 20 percent of the entire prisoner population. Similarly, if a few percentage points are allowed for those prisoners who are exceptions, a *very* rough estimate would be that about 75 percent of the prisoners are either inmates or inmatelike. These percentages seem to be supported by the way that Chicano and black prisoners fit into the convict and inmate types.

On the streets, as ethnic groups, both the Chicanos and the blacks have long, well-documented histories of experiencing governmental hypocrisy, abuse, and misunderstanding. Generally, each ethnic group has reacted to that negative experience in a different manner. The Chicano prisoners, for example, admit that on the streets there have always been strong individual and *barrio* (neighborhood) loyalties that always are a potential source of conflict within the ethnic group. However, the Chicanos have normally set aside those differences and exhibited an intense unity in their opposition to threat from governmental officials—such as police—who really are not part of their subculture. The principal manifestation of that unity is a refusal to answer any potentially harmful questions about another Chicano. Even if one Chicano knows that a Chicano he personally dislikes is guilty of something, the Chicano will not snitch. The concern for the group—in opposition to the outsiders—is more important than any individual differences or conflicts. This type of unity is directly parallel to the convicts' unity. Therefore, even though half or more of the Chicano prisoners are not active convicts, they certainly do not even begin to lean in the direction of inmates. Some of these Chicano prisoners might be what was pointed out above as "inactive" convicts, and the remainder would probably be convictlike if forced into such a situation. Therefore, almost all Chicano prisoners can be depended on *never* to snitch. Other prisoners are aware of this and usually act accordingly. Chicanos admit that extremely rare exceptions may occur (as they do among the convicts) when a weaker Chicano will snitch; but this would occur only when the situation involved extremely high stakes and an excellent chance of getting away with it.

My discussions with black prisoners, a couple of whom were convicts, reveals a striking contrast among the blacks. Recognizing that exceptions do exist, these prisoners contend that blacks on the streets have never had the same kind of unity that the Chicanos do. Granted, the blacks have been able to attain an open, political type of unity that has not yet succeeded among the Chicanos. However, these black prisoners also feel that many blacks, as individuals, have found it to their advantage to exploit officials as much as possible. Therefore, the reality behind the scenes frequently contradicts the public display of unity, with many blacks covertly exhibiting behavior that shows little real concern for a united front against government officials. To these blacks, anything that will enable them, as individuals, to better their own position, is acceptable behavior; and if they can get out of a tight spot by telling on a guilty black, they are inclined to do it. They are concerned for themselves, not for any group. The black prisoners who discussed this with me are fully aware that this pattern is repeated inside prison. Consequequently, many of those blacks who might be inclined toward a real unity just give up and join the others. They realize that they will be at a personal disadvantage if they do not do the same, because the professed unity is not really there. A black convict agreed with an idea frequently expressed by Chicano and Anglo convicts— that most blacks have an inclination toward snitching that "just won't stop." Accordingly, most nonblack prisoners have come to treat all black prisoners as potential snitches. This inmatelike pattern of the majority of blacks makes it very difficult for the few black convicts to overcome the natural suspicion of other prisoners and to be accepted as convicts.

It was noted earlier that a very small percentage of prisoners are distinct exceptions, that they do not fit into either the convict or the inmate types. These prisoners naturally form two small, but significant factions. Both kinds of prisoners highly esteem convicts, desire to emulate convicts, and are convictlike in some ways; but neither kind is truly convict in nature. Gunsels (also called low riders) are one of the two factions; they are the younger, immature hoodlum element among the prisoners. Gunsels are the rip-off artists who take unfair advantage of other prisoners. They will burn or cheat others whenever possible. Even when caught doing illegal things by bulls, the negative consequences leave them unabashed. In fact, the punishment is something to brag about among fellow gunsels. They are highly individualistic, with no real regard for any kind of larger group. However, they do take pride in their dealings with convicts. They are *not* snitches; so they can be trusted by convicts—even though they really cannot be controlled. In later chapters we will see how gunsels serve a very important economic role—as both a link and a buffer between convicts and inmates.

The other kind of prisoners who are not truly convicts are those who might be called false convicts. These are older prisoners who act like convicts in many, but not all, ways. They personally claim to be convicts—even among real convicts—in an attempt to gain the respect normally accorded convicts. These false convicts definitely are not inmates; and, understandably, they do not want to be called inmates. Neither are they real convicts. Real convicts detest them for making such a claim; but do not contest this claim to their face, because convicts are able to use them effectively to their own advantage. Convicts realize that these false convicts act much like overgrown gunsels would act. In fact, most of them probably would have been gunsels, but they were busted too late in life. They are active hustlers, but they are not as reliable as gunsels. Because real convicts understand this, they have no actual problem dealing with them. Convicts treat them as individuals and limit their conversations and transactions with them.

## CHICANOS—THE KEY TO THE THIRD LEVEL

At this point, a very significant change will be made. The treatment of prisoners and the prisoner culture will turn from the obvious and the relatively covert levels and begin to delve into hitherto unmentioned depths. At an extremely covert level is hidden this third level of the prisoner culture—the *Family* level. If one does not comprehend the Family level, one will never fully understand the real prisoner culture. And, since almost all of the prisoners on the third level are Chicanos, such insight can be achieved only by fully comprehending Chicano prisoners. Consequently, as indicated by the title of this book, Chicano prisoners are the "key" to San Quentin. They are the *only* key to a full, in-depth understanding of the prisoner culture. In addition, it is very important to note the following:. Since Family and the Family level exist in all major California prisons, *the understanding of Chicano prisoners and the third level also is the key to understanding the prisoner culture throughout California.*

Since the next chapter is devoted entirely to Family and since the third level will become manifest there, an actual description of the third level will temporarily be delayed. Also, as with the first and second levels, it should be noted that many additional aspects of the third level will become evident when the prisoner economy is discussed in Chapter 6. At this time, however, turning our attention to Chicano prisoners will accomplish several things. An increased understanding of the Chicanos will enable the reader to see how and why the Chicanos are able to effectively function and control activities at the third level. Further distinctions between convicts and inmates will become apparent. Additional, important differences between the major ethnic groups will be revealed. And, the Chicanos will serve as an example of the potential diversity and complexity that may exist in any of the major ethnic groups of prisoners.

How does an outsider acquire additional information about the very nature of the Chicano prisoners—and not just some of the obvious behavioral manifestations of that nature? Unfortunately CDC staff members were of little help in this regard. They openly admitted that they have no real understanding of Chicano prisoners. That is one of the reasons they requested my study of Chicano prisoners. Even John P. Conrad, who at that time was the Chief of the Research Division for CDC in Sacramento, acknowledged that the Research Division knew of little information that would be helpful in this respect. In addition, there is a dearth of intelligence about Chicanos in the existing scholarly works on California prisons.

Apparently there is only one source that does have the information necessary to help us acquire a deeper comprehension of the Chicano prisoners—which is requisite for a full understanding of the prisoner culture. The chief problem for the outsider is getting the information from the source—the Chicano prisoners themselves. Outsiders, such as staff and researchers, have traditionally experienced difficulty in trying to understand the Chicano prisoners. This is understandable, because Chicano prisoners normally interact with outsiders in a superficial, taciturn manner. The Chicanos' experiences with officials on the streets generally have had negative results. The Chicano prisoners frequently stress the language problem—their inability to properly express in English what they really want to say. Many of them have learned, through painful experience, that they are likely to fail in their verbal dealings with officials and, consequently, be humiliated. Consequently, they have learned that their best defense is taciturnity or silence. If this is coupled with the convictlike qualities of Chicanos, who find themselves united in opposition to the prison staff and all who might be connected with staff, the wariness observed by outsiders is understandable. Many staff members and inmates contend that the Chicanos are the tightest group inside prison—that it is almost impossible to get to know them. Yet that is exactly what must be done to get any information from this source.

Methods Used to Fathom Depths

The methods that I used to conduct my research were one of the key factors that led to my success—in being able to broach the reluctance of Chicano prisoners to communicate and in being able to perceive this hidden level of the prisoner culture. Although these methods were described in the introduction, some additional observations are appropriate at this time.

Social and behavioral scientists have frequently studied prisoners; and many of the prisoners that I talked with had also studied the scientists. A few prisoners had been directly involved in some of the research of those scientists. They were well aware that those scientists usually avail themselves of the prison facilities—such as an office and the use of the ducat system (a system whereby a freeman submits a list to custody staff indicating the time the prisoners he names should report to his office; each prisoner receives a "ducat," or "inmate" pass, and is required to report as indicated)—that are normally proffered by the administrators. In contrast, prisoners were impressed by the relatively unstructured nature of my participant observation. I did not use an office or the ducat system. None of them had ever seen a freeman who used his shoes as an office, who did not take some sort of notes, and who went to where the prisoners normally were. It struck them as strange when they saw me in the following situations: sitting in a cell, lost in conversation with a couple of convicts; standing near a far wall of the lower yard for several hours in a winter drizzle, talking with two gunsels who were reluctant to talk elsewhere; walking to lunch with a couple of prisoners from the industrial area, up the narrow alley among a throng of prisoners; and sitting in an isolated work area, enjoying some home brew with some prisoners. Consequently, it was quite natural that the subject of research methods would arise in the course of our candid exchanges.

Many prisoners, fully aware of the difficulty that any outsider encounters when he tries to delve behind the strong unity of Chicanos and convicts, developed definite ideas about my research methods. Since I had started my study among Chicanos, many of whom were also convicts, most prisoners had initially doubted that I would ever really get below the surface with either Chicanos or convicts. Gradually my use of the participant observation method began to dispel their doubts. In our open-ended discussions, they often learned as much about me as I did about them. I became less and less of an outsider and more and more of a friend. Some of the prisoners were in a position to realize that unless one actually is inside and part of the *real* prisoner power structure, or at least so close that a full knowledge of it is possible, one's view of the prisoner culture would be distorted or incomplete from want of information. In other words, they understood that I was trying to achieve a holistic view of the prisoner culture; and they knew that I would have to understand Family and its power if I was to attain that goal. I gratefully cherish the Chicano prisoners' generosity and friendship—their sharing of their own insiders' view with me.

When discussing the necessity of understanding and viewing the prisoner culture from the Family level, the prisoners readily admit that each group of prisoners has a different view of the prisoner culture, and that each is subject to limitations. However, they stress that all other views are either partial or distorted compared to the Family insiders' view. What this emphasis really amounts to is that Chicanos and Family are the key to the most realistic view possible. These prisoners are fully aware that some prisoners, staff members, and penologists will criticize this emphasis on Chicanos and Family as being unreal or wrong. However, they also realize that these critics will be basing their criticism on their own understanding of the prison, founded on a partial or distorted view.

These prisoners themselves are qualified to act as expert critics. They claim that any "generalized inmate" descriptions are not valid, that they fall far short of the real complexities involved. Some earlier studies, dealing with the prisoner social organization as a social system principally composed of argot roles, have become classic works on prisoners. However, these (prisoner) expert critics strongly argue that those studies are not at all applicable to California prisons. More recently some of these critics—who now are on the streets—have discussed John Irwin's (1970) revised approach which specifically treats the California prison system. Irwin sets forth eight ideal types of preprison "criminal identities" (major behavior systems)—such as the thief, the hustler, the dope fiend, the head, and the square john. Later he shows how these types fit into three "prison-adaptive modes" (alternate styles of living in prison)—doing time, jailing, and gleaning. Unfortunately, these critics contend that Irwin's analysis is not what the prisoners would see naturally, that it is forced and rather unreal to them. In fact, Irwin's use and misuse of the term "convict" frequently conflicts with their own natural categories which are based on observable behavior patterns—their distinctions between prisoners, inmates, and convicts as discussed earlier in this chapter. In 1971, I talked with a friend who had been one of the prisoners who had been on Irwin's "panel of experts." I asked if the type of investigation that Irwin and other penologists have used in their writing is really reflective of the way that prisoners see the situation inside. In reply, he began noting that there was a wide range of prisoners, that many were well-read and so forth. Then I qualified my question, asking if the prisoners would see it that way if they had not read about it. After pondering, he finally replied that prisoners would not see things that way. He also added that much of the penological analysis does make sense to the prisoners who read the penological literature, but that prisoners would never see things that way on their own, because there are better ways to analyze an aggregate of prisoners.

As noted earlier, during our open-ended discussions the prisoners often learned as much about me as I did about them. After all, I was an outsider, and they were curious about me. A few had never even heard of anthropology, so it was necessary to discuss the nature of anthropology with them. Some knew a considerable amount about anthropology, quite enough to realize that anthropologists had never studied prisons. Penologists, psychologists, and sociologists study prisons, but not anthropologists. Accordingly, urban anthropology was the topic of conversation many times. The prisoners learned that recently there has been an increased interest among anthropologists in the study of complex contemporary urban phenomena, with some of the most recent studies dealing with ethnic minorities and urban problems of the American scene. As they came to understand urban anthropology, they made several discoveries. This was the first time that an anthropologist had ever conducted a study of prisoners. In addition, as briefly discussed above, they soon saw that my methods were different from those used by other researchers; and recently they have realized that those methods were a key factor in my success. They also understood that some of the earlier studies in urban settings must have been relatively easy in comparison with the problems that I faced in getting below the superficial, obvious levels of prisoner culture. In recent discussions, some have expressed their feeling that it would be hard, if not almost impossible, to find a more difficult group to study.

This study is an example of the type of contributions anthropologists can make to the study of complex urban phenomena—contributions that are different from those made by other behavioral and social scientists. Several basic anthropological tools—such as the use of the participant observation technique, coupled with a concern for a holistic point of view and the realization that a reasonable period of time must be involved to give proper depth—have led to a true insiders' viewpoint, a view of prisoners that is quite different from the views given by other researchers. For example, there has been little treatment of the differences between Chicano and black prisoners. In fact, the two groups have even been lumped together for statistical purposes, as nonwhites, to be compared with whites; and that is somewhat like trying to compare the two ends of something with the middle. Very important differences between Chicano and black prisoners are made obvious in this book; and, if the importance of these differences in this prisoner culture are considered by those who are interested in the study of the "culture of poverty" in the United States, they should certainly suspect that Chicano poverty and black poverty will be quite different.

It should be stressed that many factors contributed to the success of this study. Many times the study was merely the subject of chance or luck. For example, if I had started my study among black prisoners, I would never have been able to penetrate the lowest levels of the prisoner culture; and my initial association with blacks would have led to a great degree of suspicion among the Chicanos. The Chicanos would have treated me the same way that they treat almost every black —as a potential snitch, and they would have never changed their impression of me. This would have precluded my ever establishing an effective rapport with the Chicanos—who are the key to those levels. And, since the blacks have no in-depth understanding of Chicanos, and certainly not of Family, I would not have been able to understand the depths of the prisoner culture through them.

The preceding consideration of sources of additional, in-depth information about Chicano prisoners has led to a discussion of research methods that proved to be highly successful in a prison setting. Even though it may not directly pertain to types of prisoners, an explanation was deemed necessary at this point in order to allow for a better understanding of forthcoming material. Consequently, it was purposely omitted from the treatment of research methods in the introduction. And, regretfully, the great amount of interesting, relevant, and often exciting material that deals directly with how I conducted my research is beyond the scope of this book. (I intend to present that material in a future book.) At this time, let us return to the Chicano prisoners, as one of the three major ethnic types, and consider them in detail.

## Staff Stereotype of Chicanos

Although most staff members openly admitted that they knew very little about Chicano prisoners, many of them would follow their admission with some discussion of Chicanos. I soon learned that their knowedge of Chicano prisoners seldom extends beyond rather superficial ideas and a few stereotyped traits—most of which are either distorted or false.

A major trait in the staff stereotype of Chicano prisoners is that they are excessively violent in comparison with the general prisoner population. As noted in the introduction, this is one of the reasons prison administrators requested my study —to find out what factors in the Chicano subcultural background make them excessively violent. However, a breakdown of incidents of violence submitted to the Director of Corrections for the calendar years 1962 through 1966 indicates that the Chicanos proportionately were not overrepresented (Campbell 1967:8). Also, a few staff members questioned the validity of the view held by their colleagues. They contend that if one were to go through *all* incident reports, there would be no higher percentage among the Chicanos. They think what actually happens is that when an incident does occur, it is liable to be more serious in final outcome if Chicanos are involved. Upon further questioning, several higher-ranking staff members admitted that this may be true. Since I, too, am subject to the limitations of statistics prepared by staff at San Quentin, I must confess my uncertainty. When all factors are considered however, I believe that the Chicanos are not excessively violent.

It was frequently noted by staff members that one of the major problems in dealing with the Chicanos was the way they gang (or group) together. They are concerned about the antagonism between the El Paso (Texas) group and the Los Angeles group—which often leads to violence. The staff feel that they would be rid of one of their chief obstacles if they could just break up those groups which are such powerful, yet antagonistic, forces among the Chicanos. In 1962, these ideas about Chicano gangs would have been somewhat valid; but by 1966 these gangs, as such, were almost nonexistent. True, the El Paso group is still a very tightly knit group, but only in the sense of *barrio* (neighborhood) loyalty—which will be treated later. (It should be noted that this *barrio* loyalty may be extended to include an entire town or region, such as with the El Paso group which includes the region around El Paso.)

Many staff members felt that the very strict "code" by which the Chicano prisoners live exerts a tremendous influence over them. It is so powerful that events which occur on the streets can later cause violence or even deaths inside, as acts of revenge. They strongly believed that if they could "break that code" and understand it, they would have the key to solve the problems that exist among the Chicano prisoners. Normally, the Chicano prisoners would not think of the basic subcultural values that strongly influence their behavior inside prison as a "code." Regardless of what they are called, these values have resulted in a strong unity— in opposition to staff. Consequently, there is some validity to the staff (from their ethnocentric perspective) characterization of the Chicano prisoners as noncommunicative and tightly knit. However, I seriously question either the wisdom or sincerity of those who initially promoted the idea that there really was some sort of *secret* "code" which—once deciphered—could become a panacea. At this time, before the detailed treatment of these values, let me point out that the mere knowledge that Chicano prisoners are strongly united against staff—or even a detailed understanding of how they are united against staff—will not lead to simple solutions of very complex problems.

A final stereotyped trait that was frequently expressed by staff is that the Chicanos are liars. For example, the associate warden, custody, said that "the Mexican-Americans are not to be trusted. They'll always lie to you. You never know when they are telling the truth. They can be standing right next to someone who is stabbed and later say that they didn't see it and that they know nothing about it" (Wham 1966). He attributes this to their "lack of moral character." However, he fails to realize that he is the ultimate authority among custody staff. He fails to realize that the Chicano, both as a good Chicano and a good convict, will not jeopardize another prisoner by giving information to staff. He fails to realize that the Chicano is exhibiting strong moral character in upholding Chicano-convict loyalty and unity. He fails to see the cultural conflict. A few staff members —freemen instructors or work supervisors—do not agree with the associate warden's characterization. They have worked with and understand the Chicanos. They comprehend the things that the associate warden fails to realize. And, since they are not part of custody (strongly opposed by the Chicano-convicts), their personal experiences have shown them that the Chicano's word is good.

The perpetuation of these and other false traits by a few of the top custody administrators has a negative feedback to staff treatment of Chicanos. If the staff think something is true, they act as if it is true; and by so acting, they may be selectively treating Chicanos differently. In turn, this may actually skew staff thinking and possibly statistical material too. For example, in a typical statement, a Chicano said "my people are usually given a bad time by the bulls when any trouble occurs. Often many Chicanos are locked up even though they aren't in the events—just because the staff see us as being violent and prone to use a knife." A sergeant confirmed this pattern of treatment when he noted that "we usually look for a Mexican-American when there is a stabbing." He apparently found it easier to maltreat Chicanos because "they have low moral values." He continued with his shocking characterization, "They range from an almost subhuman species (not too unlike a hunched-over chimpanzee) to quite upright, good-looking individuals. Perhaps the hunched-over aspect is a hereditary thing of some sort, coming from the type of work that many of them do in the fields." This personal elaboration on the basic stereotype took place even among the professional staff. For example, a doctor at San Quentin, an ear, nose, and throat specialist, added his own ideas to the staff stereotype. He told me that "the Mexican-Americans are a very low caliber type of person. Most of them are that way. Some Anglos and Negroes are of that caliber too, but they are relatively few in number." Obviously, if staff hold these false convictions about Chicanos, they will treat them accordingly.

Initially I was told that the Chicano prisoners were excessively reluctant to participate in rehabilitation activities. As noted in the introduction, this was the second reason prison administrators requested my study. A few administrators and a few staff members who had limited contact with Chicanos supported that initial claim. However, I soon learned that this was not a universally held view among staff members; it certainly was not part of the stereotype discussed above. The classification and assignment lieutenant indicated that, as far as rehabilitation efforts were concerned, he saw "no real difference between the Mexican-Americans and the prison population in general." The group counseling supervisor said that he had "never had problems with Mexican-Americans not participating in group counseling." This was supported by the weekly night unlock sheets for group counseling; for example, on July 1, 1966, Chicanos represented 21 percent of the total prisoners listed. A student from the University of California, Berkeley, prepared a statistical summary of Mexican-American educational participation at San Quentin which indicated that the administration's assumption about nonparticipation of Chicano prisoners in education was wrong (Lowry 1966).

### Diversity of Chicano Prisoners

By this time, the reader might agree with an instructor at the San Quentin high school who exclaimed that I had made a *gross* understatement when I said that most of the staff really know very little about Chicanos; in fact, he pointed out that most staff actually have mistaken ideas about Chicanos. By now, it also should be obvious that the staff stereotype of the Chicano prisoners generally is distorted and false. Those who understand the diversity of Chicanos (or Mexican-Americans, or Spanish-Americans) on the streets in the Southwest realize that they cannot be stereotyped. As an ethnic group, the Chicanos do have some common traits, customs, and values which lead to a consciousness of group identity. However, the diversity in their social, economic, and political composition and experience has effectively clouded the common characteristics and has made valid generalizations quite difficult to make. Most generalizations have effectively been criticized by those who have pointed out exceptions to each. Nevertheless, it should be possible to make observations about the Chicano prisoners that will add not only to our understanding of them as an ethnic group of prisoners, but also to our understanding of that very diversity that exists among Chicanos of the Southwest.

Obviously, "something" (which might be called Mexicanism) must exist to make Chicano prisoners repeatedly express their fear of losing it—even if they do have difficulty defining this "something." A similar awareness has been a key factor in the social-political activities of *La Raza*, for *La Causa* (the active and sometimes militant Chicano movement on the streets). This "something" also has led to the establishment of Chicano study programs at colleges and universities throughout the Southwest. Much of the diversity which clouds this "something" has been brought together in the California prisoner subculture. Therefore it is possible and profitable to view the Chicano prisoners as a subculture within that prisoner subculture.

A better understanding of the nonuniformity of Chicano prisoners can be gained through a study of some of the general characteristics, as well as the potential scope of characteristics, found among them. The El Paso, Texas, Chicanos are representative of a small percentage who are at one end of that range. Most of the roughly 30 men in the El Paso group tend to be the least acculturated of all Chicano prisoners in San Quentin. Most of them have gained little that they can hold in common with the larger United States culture—either from their parents (most of whom were born in Mexico) or from their personal experiences in El Paso. An El Paso Chicano tried to characterize his town by comparing it to one of the worst *barrios* (neighborhoods) in the Los Angeles area—Maravilla in East Los Angeles. The two areas had much in common in the early 1960s. Maravilla was one of the roughest parts of Los Angeles crimewise. In both areas, people lived in shacks, and the streets were unpaved. These people were at the bottom of the economic and social structure, and the El Paso Chicanos were even more uneducated than those from Maravilla. Because of their ignorance of the United States culture and their inability to effectively express themselves, both groups were unable to handle themselves well in a tight situation. Consequently, in the early 1960s, Chicanos from each of these areas formed separate groups, while the rest of the Chicano prisoners seemed to generally mix together. The situation has changed in Maravilla, resulting in a deterioration of that group; but the El Paso group continues to be a tightly knit group—as it has been at San Quentin for about 30 years. An El Paso Chicano admitted that some in his group may *"appear to be too stupid to be sensible,"* but he pointed out that this was a result of their gross lack of education and their vast ignorance of the larger United States culture. He said that "these men are like fish out of water—men without a culture."

The other end of the spectrum of Chicano characteristics potentially found among prisoners is represented by a very few, highly acculturated Chicanos who are so knowledgeable of the larger United States culture, who speak English so well, and who are so close culturally to being Anglo, that they actually may be held in fairly low regard by other Chicano prisoners. Usually these men are from a family that has been in the United States for many generations. Also, they probably have lived in one of the middle class urban centers in the Los Angeles or San Francisco areas. Often, except for name and perhaps physical appearance, it might be difficult to tell that they are not Anglo. They get along so well in the larger culture that they appear to be part of it; and this is why other Chicano prisoners may have negative feelings toward them—because, culturally, "they really are not true Chicanos."

Now that we have accounted for the small percentage at either end of the wide range of potential characteristics found among Chicano prisoners, what group would be representative of that majority in between the ends? Early in my study a sergeant warned against generalizing from my findings about Chicano prisoners to the larger Chicano community outside. He stressed the "fact" that "Mexican-American inmates are almost entirely lower class and would not be a representative sample." In January 1968, Dr. Ralph Guzman (who at that time was Assistant Director of the Mexican-American Study Project at the University of California, Los Angeles) brought three of his Chicano graduate students with him to visit a Sunday meeting of Chicano prisoners. Five hours of discussion in my home and a three-hour meeting at San Quentin left Dr. Guzman and his students astonished. Dr. Guzman admitted that he had no real idea of the grass roots element of the Chicano population from which most of the Chicano prisoners come. He said that even though this part of the Chicano population might show up in much statistical material of the project, there virtually was no contact with them by the researchers. Such comments would lead one to believe that Chicano prisoners are from an atypical part of the Chicano community. However, that is not true.

Chicano prisoners understood Dr. Guzman's comments and discussed some of the possible reasons for his and his fellow researchers' ignorance. Although discussion of prison and admission of having served time is quite open among those who have had the experience, many Chicanos never come into contact with or become aware of this part of the Chicano ethnic experience. For example, parents might cover the extended absence of a son to a neighbor by saying that he has a job in another area or that he is serving in one of the armed services. For the sake of his parents, the son might support the story on his return. Also, on the higher levels of the Chicano socioeconomic scale, even though it might be less likely to occur, the fact that a relative is in prison is more likely to be hidden. The prisoners felt that the Chicano researchers were probably from the higher socioeconomic levels; otherwise they would not have been able to engage in the luxury of a college education. In addition, since those who have been in prison realize that there is no common ground for discussing prison with someone who has never served time, the subject is never even brought up. For these reasons, Chicano prisoners understood why Chicano researchers might think that Chicano prisoners came from some atypical group at the very bottom of the socioeconomic scale.

The Chicano prisoners claim that the majority of them come from the urban-suburban areas in and around Los Angeles, where the majority of California Chicanos live. The following remarks are based on their general characterization of the Chicanos in this area. A relatively high percentage of the Chicanos in this area suffer from unemployment and poverty. Although they might be relatively poor and often underemployed, the majority would not consider themselves as lower class. Perhaps this is a reflection of the difficulties encountered when trying to define middle class. The vast range encompassed by the term middle class allowed a Chicano who considered himself lower middle class to refer to the counselors as "upper class," yet the counselors earn an amount somewhat comparable to a school teacher. Actually, only a few would reach up into the upper side of the middle class. Chicano prisoners claim that all levels of the Chicano socioeconomic scale are represented in California prisons. Owing to peer group activities—especially drug use—even a few on the highest levels are brought into illegal activities and occasionally end up in prison. Yet, they recognize that the lower levels of the Chicano socioeconomic scale are most heavily represented in prison. Also, except for a few Chicanos from El Paso and a few others who speak little or no English, most Chicanos are bilingual and speak English fairly well. Consequently, they disagree with the sergeant's comments. They feel that, even though it may be lopsided, they do represent a cross section of the Chicanos on the streets.

I am aware of the large number of characteristic traits that potentially could be applied to Chicano prisoners. Yet, I purposely have not gone beyond the above characterization which, admittedly, is little more than a generalized framework on which Chicano prisoners fit. Because of the diversity of the Chicano prisoners, it is obvious that no single set of traits would be *the* set applicable to all Chicanos in California prisons. Those who would characterize the Chicanos on the streets have faced a similar problem. Most of these attributed traits ultimately have become one of the many stereotypes validly criticized by Chicanos. I do not want to add another stereotype to that list. Nevertheless, I have observed that Chicano prisoners feel that they really are not part of the larger culture; they perceive themselves as being different. Frequently, an implicit manifestation of this view can be heard when the Chicanos refer to "their" (meaning the Anglos') laws, "their" culture, "their" system, or "their" society. Those differences cannot be dismissed by stating that identification of the underlying traits would merely lead to another useless stereotype. There are valid reasons for the Chicano prisoners' view—of feeling different. The reasons are found in the real world of the Chicano prisoners, in the significant, observable, and distinctive behavior characteristic of all but a few individuals who must be viewed as exceptions. This distinctive behavior is, directly or indirectly, related to a single dominant, characteristic trait, which can eliminate the problem posed by the existing diversity among Chicano prisoners. Hopefully, the following analysis of the behavioral manifestations of this single dominant trait will add to an understanding of Chicano prisoners.

## Machismo

The dominant characteristic trait to which the distinctive behavior of Chicano prisoners is either directly or indirectly related is *machismo*, that fundamental concept on which basic ideas concerning acceptable masculine behavior rest. The complex behavioral manifestations of *machismo* potentially may involve the qualities of masculinity, virility, honor, bravery, pride, and dignity. It should be noted that the concept of *machismo* is not unique to Chicanos, Latin Americans, or Spaniards. Although it may be called something else, the concept is found throughout the world in a variety of cultural-behavioral manifestations. Even the United States Marines have their own kind of *machismo*. The attempted definitions of *machismo* have usually proven to be unsatisfactory. Perhaps the ideas of a Chicano prisoner will help us see why:

> *Machismo* is one of those cultural ideas that are impossible to adequately communicate. You really have to see it and experience it to get a good understanding. With time, you can talk about it and see it in action so that you do know something about it; but a short definition is almost impossible. It's like trying to answer a person—with some degree of fullness—when he asks what kind of person you are. You almost have to either tell him to sit down for several days and we'll talk about it, or tell him to come and live with you for awhile so that he can see for himself.

Therefore, a "short definition" will not be attempted. Instead, we will talk about it and show how it is manifest in *real* behavior—so that you can see it in action. You will come to know something about how *machismo* is manifest in the behavior of Chicano prisoners.

I have encountered a few Chicanos on the streets who seriously question if the concept of *machismo* can still be validly applied to Chicanos. They claim that it is a vestige of the past, that it is no longer real, and that its continued use is deceptive in that it actually misrepresents the Chicanos of today. Most—if not all—Chicano prisoners would disagree with these critics for reasons that soon will become evident. For example, while discussing *machismo*, a Chicano prisoner commented on the masculine orientation of the Chicano:

> He must always be a man. The price to pay is never too high. This idea has been indelibly impressed in his mind all of his life. This cultural attitude is so strong in him that he is inscrutable to those who stereotype him simply because it is easier to do so than to attempt to understand him.

It must be emphasized that, regardless of how real *machismo* is, the Chicano prisoners do perceive it and act according to their perception. Therefore, in this respect, *machismo* is real.

### Machismo *on the Streets*

Drawing on their experiences on the streets, Chicano prisoners frequently discussed two often complexly related problems that are striking manifestations of how the Chicano subculture and the larger United States culture are in conflict. *Machismo* is associated with both of these problems: the use of drugs and the lack of qualifications to earn a decent living. A consideration of these problems will not only add to our understanding of *machismo*, but also will provide some important background on Chicano attitudes toward the law and on why some Chicanos are in prison.

Preadult drug use among Chicanos is common. Marijuana is culturally accepted by the majority of Chicanos—much like the teen-age and later use of cigarettes are in the Anglo culture. Initial use is usually to gain peer group acceptance—to be one of the boys. In contrast, heroin is not generally approved by the Chicano community. If one begins using heroin, it is much like the heavy use of alcohol would be with the Anglo middle class—as a peer group activity. Those involved would be looked down upon by the community. However, use of heavy drugs is considered as acceptable behavior by many in the Chicano subculture; and, as within most groups that use heavy drugs, the activity is not considered as really being criminal. In fact, the peer group use of drugs is a very *macho* activity. Unfortunately, many young Chicanos go directly to prison for their involvement with drugs.

Many Chicanos are left in a disadvantaged condition by their subcultural experiences. In the very important field of earning a living as an adult male, many of them are unqualified to hold a decent job, and the legitimate opportunities provided for them by their subculture are dismal. This imposes a burden of poverty that makes it difficult for them to legally live up to the ideals of *machismo* which are so real to them.

The stark reality of this predicament has placed many Chicanos in a trap of poverty. Numerous conversations revealed that "illegal" acts are often brought about by circumstances. However, if one happens to be the active party in these circumstances, the acts are not considered "illegal." Instead, they are regarded as acts of self-preservation, basic to human survival. For example, in the middle of a long conversation, a young Chicano told me, "When I was out last time, I was making it on $25.00 a week." Judging by his age and the amount of money involved, I assumed he was single; so, reflecting to the days when I was single, I seriously wondered how he had been able to make it on such a small amount.

Continuing, he explained his undoing, "I finally had to write some bad checks, because I just couldn't make it when our third child was born."

This same predicament often proves unbearable. Consequently, some Chicanos turn to the use of drugs, no longer as a preadult peer group activity, but as an escape—to mask out the bitter reality. For example, in poignant detail, a Chicano told how he fruitlessly searched for a "decent" job—one which would pay him more than just enough to survive on, one which would allow him to live with "some degree of pride and dignity." He was seeking something that would somehow allow him to find a meaningful, lawful place in life—to be *macho* without returning to the escape of drug use that brought him to prison in the first place. He did have a job; but the continuing depression of "barely survival" wages led to his going back to drug use, his parole violation, and his return to prison. This time, administrators branded him as a "habitual criminal." He protested, "the only *real* crime that I ever committed was when I stole a shirt out of a store window over twelve years ago."

Another Chicano prisoner related the following hypothetical example. Regrettably, others confirmed that it contains the elements of the truth faced by some Chicanos. The reality which brings about a loss of *machismo* may be so fierce, so emotion-provoking, that some men are ashamed to ever mention it to anyone—some do not even admit it to themselves.

> Assume that you are a married man (either a farm worker or a laborer) who has been unable to find work during the winter. You have tried all the legal means you know to make it through these rough months. Gradually you become desperate. Your wife offers to see if she can find a job as a waitress or something. This, in itself, is a blow to your *machismo*, because you should be able to adequately support your wife. But being panic-stricken, you allow her to do it. Your wife looks for work but fails to find a regular job. However, she may be propositioned. She may bring back this ill-gotten money and lie to you, telling you she did find a job. She may continue to lie, or she may tell the truth in a few days. All this leads to your virtual emasculation as a man. You really hit the bottom and feel helplessly ashamed—no longer *macho*. You spend her money and may turn to drugs or alcohol as an escape. You may even go out together to night spots, drinking and living it up, but this merely is an escape. With time you may become hooked on drugs and later get caught. After serving time in prison, you certainly will know illegal ways to make money, even if you previously had avoided these prospects while on the streets. Again, you may try to make it legally. But, if you exhaust legal means this time, out of fear of preservation of yourself and your family, and out of fear of repeating the painful process of emasculation, it becomes easier for you to turn to illegal means. Sometimes this illegal activity is used merely as a stopgap until you can get out of the hole and line up legal means of economic support. However, for the present, you are able to support your family like a man; and, regardless of your illegal activities, you remain *macho* and escape both drug use and poverty.

Other Chicanos, through their preadult use of drugs, know a great deal about drugs. After experiencing the reality of unemployment or of near survival wages, some turn to selling drugs. Typically, one Chicano commented, "The money was really fantastic, so why not sell dope? It sure beats picking lemons." Another noted, "Dope was readily available anyway, so why not make large amounts of money? It makes much more sense than knocking yourself out in the fields for virtually nothing." From the Chicano's point of view, this type of reasoning is quite pragmatic. They, too, are escaping, but theirs is a different kind of escape. They escape *poverty—the real cause of misery and drug use among many Chicanos.* By selling drugs, they are able to make a "decent" living and maintain a degree of personal dignity; they can be *macho.* And, if they should be caught, doing time in prison as a real convict, although an unpleasant experience, is a very *macho* thing.

By now the very bitter poverty-drug syndrome that faces many Chicanos should be evident. Many Chicanos (such as farm workers, or unskilled or poorly skilled laborers) have learned to endure this poverty. However, the official records would not reveal the number of Chicanos who are in prison as a result of this syndrome. For example, a prisoner would have to be "insane" to admit that the reason he committed a burglary was to support a drug habit, because he would receive a rougher sentence for drug use than for burglary. Also, he would be admitting two offenses instead of one. In addition, he could never use, as a defense in court, the fact that because of the poverty-drug syndrome he had turned to using drugs as an escape. The official records indicate that over several years the average percentage of prisoners serving time for narcotics offenses has been about 15 to 16 percent. Administrators claimed that Chicano prisoners did not significantly deviate from that percentage. However, Chicano prisoners frequently speculated that perhaps 40 to 50 percent of them were in for drugs or drug-related crimes; a few ventured the figures went as high as 75 to 80 percent. This speculation cannot be proven, but the reality of the poverty-drug syndrome does seem to lend support to the Chicanos' conjectures.

At least among those on the lower end of the Chicano socioeconomic scale, there is a realization that circumstances of this poverty-drug syndrome frequently force people into committing illegal acts. In a subcultural relativistic sense, Chicanos feel that the acts may be "illegal," but those who commit them are seldom judged as "criminals." All this comes down to just one question, which can be phrased two ways. Normally criminologists would ask, "Why do some Chicanos break the law?" Some Chicanos might ask, "Why should we obey 'their' law when 'their' culture, in conflict with ours, has failed to provide us legal opportunities and has put us in the predicament of not being able to earn a 'decent' living as adult males?" Regardless of which way *you* phrase the question, now you may be better able to answer it.

## Machismo *in Prison*

Many Chicano men who are caught in the poverty-drug syndrome on the streets find it very difficult to live up to their perceived ideals of *machismo.* They are unable to find adequate, legal outlets through which to demonstrate their own *machismo.* However, on entry into prison, they find many outlets available. In the prisoner culture they can be *macho* without having their actions decried by others in that culture. Now the concept of *machismo* will be treated as it is manifest in the observable, distinctive behavior of Chicano prisoners.

An honorable, *macho* Chicano would never cooperate with law enforcement authorities and admit he is guilty. If possible, he would make the authorities work to prove him guilty; he would never help them. If the authorities do prove that he is guilty, he will accept the punishment, in a *macho* manner, without sniveling and complaining. Admittedly, Chicanos do have very strong feelings about the lack of morality behind some aspects of the kind of punishment they receive, but this is not the same as protesting the fact that they are being punished for a crime. The Reverend Byron Eshelman, one of the two protestant chaplains at San Quentin, questioned my observations. From his experience (which is almost entirely with non-Chicano prisoners), he had encountered a "fair percentage of inmates who have maintained that they are in on a bad rap." This was not so among the Chicanos.

Chicano prisoners agree that, on the streets, the size, complexity, and diffusion of the Chicano communities allow a degree of anonymity and laxness in the behavior of individuals. This may be why the verbal emphasis of some of the characteristics of *machismo* often may be more ideal than real on the streets. Inside, however, the relatively small size of their group and the intensity of their situation in relation to staff and other prisoner groups has changed the frequent verbal emphasis of the ideal into behavioral reality. For example, a *macho* Chicano prisoner is quite concerned about what he does and does not say and do. The validity of his personal word is above question; his "word is gold." Consequently, Chicano prisoners know that certain things that are said and done among Chicanos will never be revealed to outsiders by a Chicano. This is why they can correctly assume that a fellow Chicano prisoner will not snitch. On the streets, the often-claimed family loyalty is quite real. There are similar claims of *barrio* (neighborhood) loyalty and Chicano loyalty too; but, except for a few manifestations such as *barrio* youth gangs and Chicano political activities, these loyalties tend to be more ideal than real. Inside prison, however, those claims move closer to the claimed ideal and are manifest in many ways. Also, there is an additional loyalty among convicts, in opposition to inmates and staff, which involves many Chicanos. Moreover, it will become apparent in the next chapter that there has developed yet another loyalty among Chicano prisoners (*Family*) which is exceedingly intense and intrudes on all the other loyalties. By being true to their verbal claims of loyalty, the Chicano prisoners are being *macho*.

*Violence*  The violence committed by Chicano prisoners is closely related to *machismo* in many ways. Three out of five significant causes of violence by Chicano prisoners pertain only to the Chicanos and are related to the ideals of *machismo*. One cause of this violence stems from the subcultural experience of many Chicanos: They either are, or feel that they are, unable to defend themselves or attack others verbally. The problems of being bilingual, of having English as a second language, while passing through the educational system create strong feelings among many Chicanos as evidenced by this statement:

> Most students like myself would prefer to stay quiet and not participate in class activities. We had learned that if we did, we would probably be humiliated by the teacher or Anglo students because we couldn't speak correctly. The feelings of inferiority and resentment from those childhood days play an important role in our adult lives. Since we can't do it well in English, we seldom even try to

really communicate with them. I think we keep our resentment and hostility concealed so that the Anglo won't have the satisfaction of knowing how much we're really hurting deep down inside.

Actually it is a blow to a Chicano's pride, his *machismo*, to be put down in a discussion or to lose an argument.

In serious verbal confrontation with Anglos or blacks, a Chicano will often remain quiet until pushed to the point of explosion. In an extreme situation of this type, the Chicano is prone to use physical violence rather than try to argue something verbally and lose. This way, as one noted, "We can prove to ourselves that we are as good as he is—and even better if we fall him." The Chicanos regard this as an act of bravery. The nerve and/or strength involved in violence is *macho*. The Chicanos feel that, "Outright physical violence is the Chicano's method of expressing stifled hostility and resentment."

A second cause of violence by Chicano prisoners is when someone unjustly, yet earnestly, insults a group's image or an individual's *machismo*. A striking example that combines this and the first cause of violence involves a Chicano who was convicted of killing his freeman work supervisor in the prison clothing factory in 1965. The Chicano prisoners do not necessarily condone this individual's act, but they poignantly understand the reasons behind his actions. Discussion with several Chicanos who personally know him revealed the following pertinent facts. This individual had lived the majority of his life somewhat separated from the Anglo culture. Primarily, he spoke only Spanish, and had never learned to express himself or really communicate in English. His education ended prior to junior high school. He was very quiet, with an extreme poker face. The California State Supreme Court's review of his case confirmed that, on the day of the killing, this man's supervisor intended to write him up on a sex beef. The prisoner denied complicity in any sex offense; but he failed in arguing his case with his supervisor who insisted that it was his "duty" to report the matter. Later, having been unjustly accused of a sex beef, and having failed to win his argument, this prisoner's long-simmering frustration, resentment, and hostility erupted in the killing of his supervisor—the immediate symbol of authority. Before being taken to the captain's office, where a confession was obtained, he was taken to the Adjustment Center for 30 minutes where he was beaten by about six guards. The Chicanos claim that each time the guards hit him, he cursed them, but did not ask for mercy; he would rather have died first. From this example, it can be seen that this prisoner's seething hostility and inability to express himself, coupled with an unjustified threat to his *machismo*, led him to erupt in a *macho* act and to maintain his *machismo* even when he was being beaten by guards.

Prior events between Chicanos, either on the streets or inside prison, are a third potential cause of violence by Chicanos. If an insult, injury, or death has occurred, it may be avenged at a later, opportune moment. If an individual was insulted or injured, he is the one who must avenge the wrong to maintain his *machismo*. If an individual was unjustly killed, a relative or someone very close and loyal to him might avenge the wrong, to maintain the *macho* image of his family or those close associates. If the wrong was directed toward an individual, as a member of a group, any member of the wronged group might avenge the wrong. An unavenged wrong reflects upon all members of the group as non-*macho*. It can readily be seen that this would lead to groups or series of related incidents of violence among Chicanos.

Things have changed somewhat in these respects though. Older Chicano prisoners observed changes taking place in the late 1950s and early 1960s. The manifestation of Chicano violence gradually changed from fisticuffs to the use of knives. In the past, when only fisticuffs were involved, entire groups were willing to enter into a fight as a gang. With the realization of the potential use of knives, violence tended to be between individuals or small cliquelike groups, not between large gangs. Also, this was a period of time when the power and influence of some of the traditional groups among Chicanos were breaking up. By 1967, there was virtually none of the gang pressure that had existed a few years earlier. It became apparent to many prisoners that the Chicanos had been stabilized, that there was a feeling of relative peace among them. In fact, the entire prisoner population had become relatively tranquil compared to earlier times. The power and influence of Family (to be discussed in following chapters) was responsible for this. At this point, it should suffice to note that there is no other prisoner group that even begins to have the power that Family does in San Quentin, or CDC.

Gang violence among Chicanos has ceased. But, as will be shown in detail later, many deaths result from Family's activities. However, these deaths are ordered executions that are in accord with the convict code. Chicanos judge those who violate the convict code as non-*macho*. Since Family never misses, the individual would not be alive to avenge his own death; and no individual or group would even consider avenging the death either—to do so would be suicide. Consequently, deaths resulting from Family's activities do not lead to series or groups of incidents. Since violence now tends to be on an individual or small-group basis, the series or groups of incidents are fewer in number. They are even further reduced by the change from fisticuffs to knives. A young Chicano commented, "If you have a hassle with someone, you had better get him good. If you don't, you might not live very long. In other words, go for broke for your own ultimate protection." Today, an opponent is not usually given a chance to avenge the wrong and maintain his *machismo*. Therefore, violence by Chicano prisoners now is less likely to result from this third cause (revenge) then it did several years ago.

A fourth cause of violence involves prisoners from all ethnic groups. Before entering prison for the first time, a man will have mistaken ideas about prison life, and he will be uncertain of potential events. Obviously, this leads to a real fear. The Chicanos realize that this behavior is unmanly, so they counter it by turning to violence, which is considered *macho*. For example, many prisoners noted that gunsels (who normally are younger prisoners) really operate on fear— "They are dangerous behind fear." An older Chicano who had firmly established his reputation several years ago told of his own experiences:

> When I first went to jail, I went in fighting. I let everybody know what I could do so they'd stay off my back. I was so keyed up that it was potentially dangerous to even say hello to me. I did it because of what I had heard. The same thing happens at San Quentin with guys who come in.

Being older and having an established reputation, he did not have the same fear when he entered San Quentin. However, he further commented, "If they had sent me here at about 20 or 22, I would have been scared to death. This leads to a natural grouping of the younger ones who really do it out of fear." Their fear of physical violence from others, as well as their fear of not being accepted, leads many of them to somewhat unrealistically overemphasize their *machismo*. Obviously, this results in needless violence. The older Chicano continued, "I was involved in so much fighting that I actually enjoyed it. I became sadistic. It became a way of life for me."

The final cause of violence to be considered applies to all ethnic groups. However, owing to the concept of *machismo*, it seems to be most intensely felt by the Chicanos. It is based on a certain part of the stark reality that prisoners face. Older prisoners discussed this repeatedly, using a variety of terms and examples, all of which referred to the same general situation. They realize that the prison itself—the total environment in which they find themselves 24 hours a day—is responsible for many of the problems that lead to violence. Regardless of their little joys and humor, and the supposedly positive staff rehabilitation efforts, the total environment is negative. It is not conducive to rehabilitation, but it is a setting that generates violence. The prisoners have developed ways to handle many of the problems created by their prison environment. However, there is one problem, which often leads to violence, for which they have not been able to develop a solution. It involves the frustrations of having to tolerate the hypocrisy they observe between the behavior of staff members, especially their unreasonable or racist actions or comments, and the principles of the model prison system.

Usually the prisoners are able to stifle their frustration and anger, realizing that an attack on a staff member will immediately create many serious problems. However, the Chicanos indicated particularly intense difficulty in repressing their feelings in this type of situation because of the importance they attach to a man's words and deeds. Hypocrisy is seen as non-*macho* and untolerable. Even though the Chicanos distinguish between "going along with" and "accepting" certain things in prison, they feel that there is a degree of tacit hypocrisy in even "going along with" certain things. Yet, they must stifle their urge to react directly in a *macho* manner to unreasonable or racist actions or comments which would be a personal challenge in other settings. Prisoners are unable to prevent this repressed frustration and anger from exploding at times. Usually it is some small, normally acceptable act by another prisoner that triggers the explosion. It is unfortunate that all the pent up hostility, frustration, and anger is misdirected to fellow prisoners; because, due to changes in their style of violence, when a Chicano is involved, the violence is likely to be serious.

Some Anglo and black prisoners may not be familiar with the term *machismo*, but they certainly would not question a Chicano's manliness. The Chicanos have a firmly established reputation for their willingness and ability to engage in violence. This reputation serves as an effective buffer between the Chicanos and the other ethnic groups. From a wide variety of comments made by non-Chicano prisoners, it was obvious that not a single individual or group would even consider pushing a Chicano around. Chicano prisoners are proud of this reputation; it is *macho*.

*Rejection of Hypocrisy*   Influenced by *machismo*, Chicanos have reacted to the observed hypocrisy in other ways besides violence. Noting their greater emphasis on a man's word, the Chicanos discussed the difficulty they encounter in playing

conflicting social roles. Those who do play conflicting roles are seen as hypocrites
—not to be admired or respected, because they do not live up to the ideals of
*machismo*. The Chicano prisoners see manifestations of hypocrisy on all levels
among the staff and among inmates who accept the pretense and become part of
it. They refuse to "*really* communicate" with those who are hypocritical. Therefore, it is understandable that almost all staff members and most inmates find it
difficult to understand or get to know the Chicanos.

However, Chicano prisoners admit that they have to expediently "go along
with" the hypocritical rehabilitation programs. As noted earlier in this chapter,
their participation would lead an outsider to believe that their participation in
these programs is normal; but among themselves, the Chicanos openly acknowledge their adamant refusal to submit to the hypocrisy and fawningly "accept" most
of CDC's programs. A Chicano, or one who knows Chicanos well, would be able
to discern from the taciturn or superficial behavior of Chicanos in these programs
that they are, in fact, merely "going along with" them.

Recognizing the actual ineffectiveness of most rehabilitation programs, Chicano
prisoners have pressed very hard for their own programs in the important areas of
education and employment. Their successful Basic Education for Mexican-American Class (BEMA Class) will be used as an example of a nonhypocritical program
in which their behavior sharply contrasts with their conduct when "going along
with" a hypocritical program. The Chicano prisoners who conceived the class
recognized that many Chicanos need to increase their reading, writing, and speak-
ing skills in both Spanish and English. Even though the high school at San Quentin
(operated by the Marin County School System, not CDC) generally was an exception to the CDC's hypocritical rehabilitation programs, they also recognized that
it was ineffective with many Chicanos who had dropped out of, or been pushed out
of, similar educational systems on the streets. These men needed educational
assistance more than others, but they were expected to enter the special class for
illiterates. Understandably, as adult males, they did not want to be "part of the
dummy class." And, when forced into a normal classroom situation, they tend to
be passive participants, because they do not want to speak out and become the
object of ridicule or laughter; they maintain their pride by remaining silent.

The unique aspects of the BEMA Class took subcultural factors into consideration so that most of the problems faced in getting these men into the normal prison
education classes would be eliminated. The class succeeded because of elements
such as the following: most of the actual planning of the class was done by
prisoners, giving the Chicanos a feeling that the class was really theirs; charismatic qualities of the class leaders initially drew and continues to draw Chicanos;
four different educational levels (advanced and beginning English and Spanish)
are represented, to avoid the "dummy" class label; Chicano prisoners, as teaching assistants, do the majority of the teaching, while an "official" instructor
watches from the sidelines; primarily Chicanos attend, so few non-Chicanos are
present to laugh and ridicule; and a continual emphasis is put on correcting their
mutual problems of communication.

It took repeated efforts of Chicano prisoners before the BEMA Class finally was
established as a supplement to the normal high school educational program in

1965. Through my personal involvement on behalf of the Chicanos, I am aware of the often absurd staff opposition the class encountered during the following year. The Chicano leaders of the class who fought the staff opposition did so at the potential risk of being labeled troublemakers and serving additional time through the abuse of the indeterminate sentence system. Apparently the staff finally realized that something meaningful must be taking place when the class of about 35 Chicanos would break up into four groups (according to language level), go to the corners of a single classroom, and begin studying. Each group seemed oblivious to the intent activity of the other three groups. Fortunately, the staff has ceased harassing the class. The BEMA Class continues to be effective, with many young Chicanos entering, gaining confidence, and later actively entering the regular educational program. It remains a positive program which the Chicanos admit is not going to solve all of their problems; but it is a significant step in the right direction, a step that has been taken with pride and dignity. Compared to the hypocritical staff programs, participation in the BEMA Class is *macho*.

As with all generalization, there are exceptions to the above analysis of Chicano prisoner behavior. And one Chicano prisoner was a notable exception. However, the judgement of him by other Chicano prisoners serves to reinforce the general treatment and show how atypical he was. Other Chicanos contended that this individual was trying so hard to change his sentence from "*life without* . . ." to "life *with* possibility of parole" that his thinking and behavior had been distorted. He did more than accept many of the programs that other Chicanos judged hypocritical. He became so much a part of the hypocrisy that he even tried to persuade some of his fellow Chicanos that the programs were not hypocritical. Even though no one actually accused him of having snitched, his name was almost always named when I asked if there might be some Chicano who was a potential snitch. Obviously, this individual's non-*macho* behavior had contributed to his reputation.

Although details will not be given in this chapter, an important point should be interjected here. The behavior of Family members probably comes closer to the ideals of *machismo* than the behavior of any other group of Chicanos—in prison or on the streets. Some Chicano prisoners who know little about Family might disagree; but there are many very *macho* Chicanos who—even though unable to do so—would like to become even more *macho* by joining Family. Therefore, it is possible to view most of the chapter about Family and major portions of the chapter on the prisoner economy as an example of *machismo*—as the ultimate result of *macho* behavior in prison.

## HOMOSEXUAL ACTIVITY

A discussion of homosexual activity among prisoners is relevant to *machismo*. Also, it will show additional differences between the ethnic groups and between convicts and inmates. However, the following material has to be carefully qualified. It was felt that questionnaires about personal involvement in homosexual activity probably would not give the desired results, because the topic is not conducive to the greatest degree of truthfulness or objectivity. A Chicano prisoner conducted a study of homosexual activities in the West Block for a course he was taking at San Quentin. His report was "buttered up" for presentation to the instructor, so he personally discussed the necessary revisions with me. Using some of his resultant ideas as a starting point, the topic was discussed with several convicts who had served a great deal of time and had an excellent understanding of the prisoner culture. The outcome of these discussions came to be called "a very rough guesstimate consensus." Ultimately, many prisoners "generally" agreed with the guesstimate, so it is used here in lieu of the apparently nonexistent relevant data.

It was roughly estimated that about 80 percent of the prisoners have engaged in homosexual activity in prison. But, that figure is deceiving and must be qualified immediately. It is helpful and realistic to distinguish two types of homosexuals: active and situational-inactive. Approximately 40 to 50 percent of the prisoners are situational-inactive homosexuals; and the frequency of their activities is, or has been, quite different from what people might imagine when they hear the term homosexual. The following would be classed as situation-inactive homosexuals: one who had, at one time, been pressured into one or several homosexual acts; one who had briefly experimented homosexually in the past; and one who, on very rare occasions, engages in a homosexual act as a sexual release, perhaps to break the monotony of masturbation. Only about 30 to 40 percent of the prisoners are active homosexuals. Their activity is relatively frequent and routine, even though some may continue to do it only out of fear of physical harm. There are two types of active homosexuals: the aggressive ones who assume the male role and the passive ones who assume the female role. For variety there is reversal of role playing by some prisoners; but if this is discovered or generally known by other prisoners, those who engage in role reversal are classed as passive. In other words, to be passive part of the time is to be classed as such. However, roughly 90 percent of the Chicanos and convicts and an estimated 60 percent of the inmates do *not* reverse roles. Among Chicanos, this is to maintain a *macho* image; among other prisoners, it is to stress their manliness.

Many terms could be used to describe the different types of active homosexuals inside. "Queen" and "joker" denote female and male roles; however, these are staff terms that normally are not used by the prisoners. Several other terms such as "fagot," "gay," "brownie queen," and "commissary punk" are used by some prisoners. However, "broad" is the general prisoner term that is used to refer to a man who has assumed the female role; it is used in a neutral sense. And, it can have very positive connotations when compared with "punk"—the term for the female role which carries negative connotations. "Old man" is the general prisoner term used to refer to one who has assumed the male role; as with broad, it is used in a neutral sense. The negative, derogatory male term is "daddy." Further indications of usage will become evident in the following material.

First, let us put a popular misconception to rest. An illusion from the past is that two men who are celled together are quite likely to have a sexual relationship going between them. This so-called marriage system has been outdated for years. Prisoners may joke about being celled with so and so, or that the bulls sure were nice to perform the ceremony for you; however, it is a false conception. Relatively few affairs occur in cells. Even if two prisoners celled together are having an affair, they almost always take their sex elsewhere. Of course, there are some exceptions; but such in-cell activity is not nearly as extensive as has been thought. The majority of sexual activity takes place in work areas, where there are relatively few bulls and many prisoners to "stand point" (watch out for intruders). In places like the darkroom or the laundry, there are few bulls; and in the chapel, there are virtually no bulls. In contrast in a cell (except in the honor blocks where there is a greater freedom of movement during the evening), there is no one to stand point, and bulls often silently and suddenly appear. In such cases one could easily be caught in a compromising position. In addition, it is often true that an old man has a low regard for the punk he takes pleasure with at work; he might want the peace and quiet of a cell without the punk.

If a prisoner (regardless of whether he is homosexual or not) should be bothered by the sexual overtures of his cell partner, he may be able to get out of the situation legally. If he goes to the captain's porch and admits to being a homosexual and to having trouble with his cell partners, he may be given a cell change, involving a new cell partner or even a single cell. A nonhomosexual may be able to use this method for his ends too, even though he is not being bothered by the sexual overtures of other prisoners. For example, if a man has desired the peace and quiet of a single cell for years, or, if he has tried unsuccessfully to get a job change, he might be able to get his wish. He has to hint to the staff that he is having trouble with his cell partner, or with men at work, that they are making strong sexual overtures to him. He will be asked if he is a homosexual. If he stammers a bit and then adamantly denies it, he may succeed in obtaining the change. However, it is recorded in his jacket that he is a homosexual; yet, the most that will happen in the future is that a counselor might ask him about it once every year, at which time he has to play the denial game. Overall this procedure is much less bothersome than an unwanted cell partner or job; and since the "admission" is to the staff (the enemy), it does not count among other prisoners.

Looking at homosexual activity from the perspective of the different levels of the prisoner culture gives additional understanding. Inmate broads are considered punks. An inmate punk might be allowed or pressured to commit fellatio with a convict old man; however, no one would marry the punk (become involved in a somewhat permanent relationship), and few prisoners have any respect for him. Convict broads usually have sexual relationships only with convicts; convict broads are respected as convicts. Other prisoners deal with them, and usually other convicts will marry them. Granted, another prisoner may not like a particular convict broad, but he will respect the broad as a convict. Seldom would a convict broad become sexually involved with an inmate old man or daddy; if so, he would be considered a punk by other convicts. As for gunsel broads, some are punks; and some would be considered "a punk, but a good dude." It varies with the individual gunsel.

From an ethnic perspective, it appears that the percentages of those involved in all types of homosexual activities do not significantly vary from one group to another. However, there may be fewer Chicanos among the situational-inactive group. Because of their strong group identity and unity, and their reputation for being *macho*, a Chicano would never be pressured into a homosexual act by a non-Chicano. Although a Chicano would never be caught in the following situation, it is indicative of the type of pressure non-Chicanos may encounter. A young, clean-cut Anglo had just come to prison. He had some college background and felt that he really did not fit, so he chose to be a loner and have no friends. Apparently a few blacks thought him very attractive sexually. The first open encounter was a shouting match, but the Anglo adamantly refused to capitulate to the blacks' desires. About a month later, in a second encounter, he was socked in the jaw; but he did not give in. The third and final open manifestation occurred about a month later. He still refused to submit, so the blacks literally beat him to a pulp. The bulls bundled up his bruised, bloody, yet still-living body and sent him off to another prison. A non-Chicano might be able to avoid such attacks by joining a group or clique of prisoners, by carrying a shank (knife), or by being bigger than almost everyone else "in the joint."

Although there also appears to be no significant difference in the ethnic percentages of active homosexuals, the manifestation of Chicano activity is strikingly different. Almost all Chicanos assume the aggressive, male role. This is directly tied in with their feelings about virility and *machismo*. The Chicanos take their pleasure with Anglo broads, but *never* with blacks.

Very few Chicanos assume a passive role because of the non-*macho* implications involved. Of the few Chicano broads, almost all are active only with Chicanos. Some Chicanos claim that there are no bad feelings toward the Chicano broads, as long as they act like convicts and are not false in their dealings. Yet there are conflicting claims which lead one to believe that they may be looked down upon a bit because of their non-*macho* sexual role. If, in rare cases, a Chicano broad should take pleasure with an Anglo, that broad definitely would be held in low regard. Perhaps this reflects a concern for the *macho* group image of the entire Chicano prisoner population. If so, it is even more strongly shown with the outright revulsion felt for a couple of Chicano broads who, in the past, became involved with black daddys. In those cases, not only was the act an insult to the group image, it also was a gross insult to Chicano *machismo* to assume the non-*macho* female role with a black, because Chicanos generally regard the blacks as representing the antithesis of the ideals of *machismo*.

There are differences between Anglo and black broads too. Many black broads have Anglo daddys; but no black broad would ever have a Chicano daddy. Anglo broads normally have relationships with fellow Anglos or Chicanos. Occasionally they may have a relationship with a black; but, if so, they also will have an Anglo daddy as a front. This latter relationship is increasing, but it still represents a very small percentage of the Anglos.

## CHICANO-BLACK CONTINUUM

To conclude this chapter, I would like to set forth what I call the Chicano-black continuum. Obviously, not all prisoners act alike. In many of the prisoners' activities, the differences manifest in the patterned behavior of the different types enable us to make the same distinctions that the prisoners make—between convicts and inmates, and between the three ethnic groups. Our recognition of convicts and inmates allows us to reach depths well below the superficiality of the treatment of all prisoners in the generalized "inmate" sense. The Chicano-black continuum will point out, and keep us from engaging in, the outright distortion of trying to lump the Chicanos and blacks together as "minorities" or "nonwhites" to be compared with the Anglos or "whites"; such comparisons are much like attempts to compare the ends of something with the middle. The Chicano-black continuum orders many of the behavioral differences between the ethnic groups and accounts for the range of behavior that is manifest in many of their activities. The characteristic behavior of the Chicano prisoners represents one extreme of that range. The other behavioral extreme is characteristic of black prisoners. The behavior of the Anglo prisoners tends to be a mixture of behavior from each of the two extremes. It generally lies somewhere toward the middle of the range; but, in certain activities, it may be closer to one or the other of the extremes. Granted, in any of the three ethnic groups, there are exceptions—individuals who display behavior that is different from the behavior of the rest of the group. However, the Chicano-black continuum can help us attain a deeper understanding of the existing differences between the ethnic groups in prison.

Some examples will make the Chicano-black continuum clearer. The following behavioral differences were either directly or indirectly noted and discussed by many Chicanos, some prisoners from all ethnic groups, some convicts—including two black convicts—and some staff members. Earlier, when treating the differences between convicts and inmates, it was shown that almost all Chicanos are either convicts or convictlike. In contrast, most blacks are either inmates or inmatelike. Although the Anglos incline more toward the inmate side, they do represent a mixture of the two extremes. Many of the distinguishing behavioral characteristics between convicts and inmates also apply to Chicanos and blacks. For example, Chicanos and convicts may say little about it, but they do take great pride in the following: their concern for their group in opposition to other groups; the validity of their word to other members of the group; and their actions, which are in accord with their word. Consequently, they do not snitch; and in those areas where they, as a group, are opposed by another group, they are able to attain a real group unity. In contrast, many blacks and inmates may *say* a great deal about their loyalty to the group and the validity of their word, but their actual behavior is quite different. Most blacks and inmates are more concerned about themselves than about any group. They are not bothered by the obvious hypocrisy between their words and their deeds—that they may privately do just the opposite of what they publicly say. Therefore, since most blacks and inmates are inclined to snitch in order to better their personal position, the group is never able to attain any real unity.

Since these examples of the Chicano-black continuum deal with behavior that generally is characteristic of either the Chicanos or the blacks, it must be kept in mind that exceptions to this behavior are to be found among both groups, with a greater range of behavior manifest among the blacks. Many prisoners from each of the three major ethnic groups agreed with this analysis. Therefore, it can reasonably be stated that the characteristic Chicano behavior is applicable to *almost all*

Chicanos; and, in contrast, that the *majority* of blacks are inclined to engage in the behavior that is characteristic of blacks. With these qualifications in mind, it can be noted that blacks snivel or complain, but Chicanos do not. Chicanos are quiet and reserved, keeping their ideas and emotions inside; and the blacks are quite verbal, often openly displaying their ideas and emotions. The Chicanos are action people; they do not back down on their few words and subtle actions; and when violence comes, it usually is without any apparent warning to outsiders. In contrast, the blacks are vocal people; they are able to verbally back off from almost anything they say; and when violence comes, there has usually been a long public prelude.

The Chicanos' concept of *machismo* and the comparable concept of manliness among blacks are factors that significantly contribute to the behavioral differences that fit into the Chicano-black continuum. It has been shown how the Chicano prisoners' very strong concern for the traditional ideals of *machismo* and the prison environment have led them to an extreme emphasis on *macho* behavior that accords with the very manly behavior of convicts. The range of acceptable manly behavior among Chicanos is tightly constricted by this strong emphasis on *machismo*.

The concept of manliness held by the blacks is quite different. The eclectic and undefined nature of their idea of manliness seems to set few limits on the range of acceptable behavior among black prisoners. For example, two of the very few black convicts hold a personal concept of manliness that is similar to the *machismo* of Chicanos. These same black convicts have discussed the image of manliness that they and others feel is held by the majority of black prisoners. Most blacks take manly pride in the ability to handle themselves well verbally. This includes a pride in the ability to talk oneself out of an undesirable situation. Consequently, there is little concern about being held accountable for what one says; that is, the ability to use words is more important than the validity of any particular words. This ability is directly linked to a second quality from which many blacks take manly pride—the pragmatic ability to personally get ahead of and/or manipulate others. The black convicts recognize that many black prisoners openly make verbal expressions of group unity that are often contradicted by the prisoners' private actions. These conflicting private actions—which stem from the inclination to better one's personal position or condition at almost anyone's expense—prevent the black prisoners from attaining any real group unity. Since these contradictory actions by many black prisoners often involve snitching, it is very difficult for the black convicts to avoid the suspicion of nonblack convicts. And since the behavior of most black prisoners accords with the behavior of inmates, it is hard for the blacks to function as convicts.

Since the Chicano-black continuum brings together the major types of prisoners found in San Quentin and emphasizes the differences between those types of prisoners, it has been used as a conclusion to this chapter on types of prisoners. Additional behavior that fits into the Chicano-black continuum will be treated in the following chapters.

# 5 / Baby Mafia
# or Family

Outsiders are inclined to think that the longer a prisoner stays in prison the better he understands the prisoner culture. This is not true. Most prisoners spend years inside without ever fully understanding their own culture. Views of this culture vary according to the depth to which a prisoner knows his culture. The three levels of the prisoner culture may or may not be perceived by a prisoner, according to the type of prisoner he is. For example, since inmates are not to be trusted, they seldom develop more than a relatively superficial view—primarily based on their knowledge of the first (inmate) level. In contrast, convicts can be trusted and thus are privy to much of the relatively covert activity of their fellow convicts—activity that inmates are never permitted to know. Convicts know both the inmate (first) and the convict (second) levels. However, in order to gain a full comprehension of what really takes place inside San Quentin—as well as in most other California prisons—an understanding of the deeper, third level of the prisoner culture is necessary.

This third level—the Family level—is relatively unknown to most prisoners, because the activities at this level are extremely secret and controlled by a group of Chicano prisoners. Only by comprehending this particular group and its activities can one get a complete picture of the prisoner culture. This group is the real *key* to a full understanding of the prisoner culture, for its activities and influence intrude into most of the major aspects of the prisoner culture. Without this key, one would have to guess how the culture works.

One of the first public acknowledgments of this Chicano group was made by Warden Louis S. Nelson in September 1968. He spoke on television, noting that a "Mexican-American inmate" had been killed by the "Mexican Mafia." He discussed the group, noting that it was composed of Mexican-American gunsels. He concluded by claiming that his staff had "eliminated the Mexican-Mafia." The members of the group were amused by Nelson's statements, for they are not gunsels, they are not the "Mexican Mafia," and they are far from being eliminated.

This Chicano group initially called itself the Baby Mafia. Later they changed the name to Family. Since Baby Mafia is no longer used, I normally will use only the term Family henceforth. Baby Mafia was intentionally included in the title of this chapter to avoid confusion with that basic kinship institution called the family. Family is not family, as will soon be seen. Let us now look into the history of the group—why it was necessary to form the group; why it is valid to insiders.

## HISTORY

Even though most Family members are literate, one must look at the group as one would look at a group in a nonliterate culture. Because of the seriousness of the group's activities and the resulting secrecy, no member has ever written down Family's history, goals, ethics, and bylaws. To be in possession of such material would be extremely dangerous and potentially self-incriminating. Therefore, the history, goals, ethics, and bylaws of Family are found only in oral form. Family members know these well; and they are able to tell them to new members, as they have told me. However, as with oral literature, each version may differ slightly from the others, being colored by the perception of the teller. Nevertheless, members generally agree on the important points.

A major factor that ultimately led to the formation of Family is the Chicanos' feeling that they (as well as other prisoners) are being subjected to physical and mental abuse and manipulation by staff. It should be noted that this factor has been keenly felt by most prisoners—regardless of ethnic background—for many years. The vivid examples presented in Chapter 8 will show why the Chicanos have viewed this abuse and manipulation as being well beyond the recognized needs of the official system. Because of their personal experience and knowledge, Chicano prisoners seriously question the morality of many staff members and administrators. The Chicanos see gross hypocrisy in the system, and their *macho* reaction against it is strong. However, the reaction cannot be overt and still be effective.

In 1964, a Chicano convict was sitting in the "hole" of a California prison. He had time to pose many questions about the powerlessness of prisoners. Why are prisoners so powerless in the face of manipulation by staff? Why are individuals, cliques, and even larger groups always kept off balance, being vulnerable at all times? How can the staff get away with breaking or avoiding the very rules which supposedly govern their actions? Isn't there some way to stop these abuses? How can the staff "rehabilitate" and punish at the same time? Couldn't the prison system be changed so as to eliminate the hypocrisy and abuses of the system? How can the prisoners protect themselves? How can they counter these abuses and give some stability to their lives, avoiding manipulation by staff? How could there be some sort of counteractive force to protect the prisoners? How could a large, acephalous group protect itself when there are so many interest groups that put their own good above the welfare of any larger group?

This Chicano convict reasoned that a counter force of prisoners would be necessary. In order to avoid being picked off as groups or cliques, the prisoners would have to show a strong, united front. Being aware that the entire prison population would be too great a group to unite, he thought it might prove successful if this counter force was started among the Chicano prisoners. Since most Chicano prisoners are either convicts or very convictlike, and since they have an additional strong unity on occasion or in opposition to another group, they would have a distinct advantage from the beginning. Later, in another California prison, he discussed his ideas with two other Chicano convicts. Plans and decisions were made. The Baby Mafia was born. It started as a very small group and experienced many growing pains; however, it soon came to be a very tight counter force which protects its members and the deserving prisoners among the Chicano and convict populations. For many, Family is a force that effectively counters much staff manipulation. Family has had to fight for its survival, but its strong unity has enabled Family to win, to grow, and to prosper.

## GOALS AND ETHICS

The founding members of Family recognized that the subcultural background of the Chicanos normally places them at the bottom of the totem pole in California prisons. They felt that the "typical" Chicano is very undereducated. Also, he is either unskilled or poorly prepared to make a decent living. While on the streets, Anglos and authorities often treat him with contempt, failing to accord him a reasonable amount of human dignity. In prison, the same actions are intensified through maltreatment by many staff members. Chicano prisoners feel that this is a non-*macho* situation for them, that they are not able to live with the pride and dignity deserving of adult males. Therefore, the primary Family goal is to preserve the right of Chicano prisoners to live as human beings, in a *macho* manner.

In several ways convicts bear upon a secondary Family goal. In their past struggle against staff, convicts frequently prevented prison staff and administrators from completely "running" the prisoners' lives in abusive, hypocritical ways. Since they are now a very small minority in comparison with inmates, convicts experience serious difficulties maintaining their unity. Consequently, they are unable to accomplish as much as they would like to. The Chicanos, most of whom are convicts or convictlike, view the efforts of convicts as *macho* and respect them for it. Family members recognize the striking similarities between convict and Family goals. Convicts are deserving of support. Therefore, a secondary Family goal is to help preserve and support convicts, enabling them, too, to live in a *macho* manner.

Family ethics pervade all Family activities and are a principal factor in the attainment of Family goals. To act in an unethical or immoral manner, or to break the convict code, would be hypocritical and non-*macho*; it would be counter to the goals of Family, especially since Family ethics are based on the ideals of *machismo*. As noted in the preceeding chapter, the behavior of Family members probably comes closer to the ideals of *machismo* than the behavior of any group of Chicanos—in prison or on the streets. Family members take great pride in their daily dealings with each other and with other prisoners. They feel that their morality and ideals are above reproach, especially when compared with the immorality or lack of ethics of some staff members and most inmates. Members are fair and trustworthy. If a member says he will do something, there is no questioning by others; for it is done. Group decisions are carefully considered and adjudged moral. Family goes to great effort to be sure that its actions are right; if mistakes are made, they are honest ones. Consequently, when something is "ordered" by Family, there are carefully considered reasons behind the "order" that are understood by members and others who are aware of what Family is trying to do. Family actions accord with the highest ideals of *machismo*; they are honest and moral when viewed from within the prisoner culture.

An example of Family concern for the morality of their behavior can be seen in the pattern of Family violence. It was noted in the preceding chapter that Chicanos have a firmly established reputation for their willingness and ability to engage in violence. With its strong emphasis on the ideals of *machismo*, the seriousness of most of its activities, and the necessity to maintain secrecy, Family has increased that reputation. If someone who is subject to the convict code (that is, all who are allowed to knowingly deal with Family) should be so foolish as to cheat or threaten Family in some way, there is little doubt about the potential consequences. With Family, the pattern of violence is even more extreme than among Chicano prisoners. It only occurs for carefully considered ethical (to them) reasons. However, when it does occur, Family violence does not stop half-way—with the knifing of an opponent; it goes all the way—to the death of the non-Family individual. Those who knowingly deal with Family members are well aware of this reputation and treat members with appropriate respect.

An additional example of the manner in which Family ethics pervade Family activities is evident in the members' extreme emphasis of *machismo* in sexual practices. It was noted in the preceding chapter that the Chicanos' concern for *machismo* led most of them to assume the aggressive, male role; however, a very few assumed the female role, encountering little difficulty from other Chicanos for such actions. Since Family is considered the epitome of *machismo*, there are no broads in Family. As a Family member said, "There is a certain weakness in punks." (One can detect that the claim of other Chicanos, that Chicano broads are respected, might be exaggerated; for there do seem to be some subtle, negative feelings about broads, regardless of their sticking to Chicanos and acting like convicts.) There was a "punk" in Family in the past who was observed in a compromising position (in another institution) by a non-Family convict. "The punk had even been so stupid as to pick a non-Chicano for point man during the act." The point man (lookout) became the accuser. It should be noted that it took a great deal of nerve to approach Family and accuse one of its members; if it had been an unjust accusation, it might have brought about the accuser's untimely death. The convict accuser and the Family member were brought together for a face-to-face accusation. From the accused's reaction, which was observed by several Family members, it was apparent that the accuser was right. Since this was a direct challenge involving the two individuals, Family did nothing. Later the non-*macho* Family member (one of only two "strays" in Family's history) was killed. There had been tacit agreement to allow the accuser to do this, so Family did not retaliate against him.

Members are proud that Family has been able to attain its goals. The conditions of many Chicanos and convicts has been significantly improved. Many Chicanos claim that they are in a better position than any other group inside prison. Family has been able to perfect the natural sense of unity among Chicanos to an extreme degree—and to their immense advantage. Only through such unity can prisoners effectively ameliorate their condition to the degree that Family has. Also, the means to their goals are actually a part of the goal itself, since they have taken great care to reach those ends through highly ethical means. Their activities have furnished additional outlets for their *machismo*. They are able to move through the prisoner culture with pride and dignity, knowing that their actions are *macho* —honest, honorable, and manly. There may be those among the staff who do not accord Family members the human dignity and respect that they deserve as human beings. Members realize that those who treat them in such a manner are ignorant of the reality of much that takes place inside—in the depths of the prisoner culture that are known by relatively few prisoners. However, members can readily draw personal support and security from Family accomplishments.

## FOUR TYPES OF FAMILY

At this point, the term Family should be discussed. Actually, Family may denote any of four types of Family. Members find no need for additional terms; for regardless of the particular type of Family being discussed, the meaning is obvious to an insider from the context of the conversation. One use of Family refers to the overall organization, which includes nearly 300 members throughout the state: on the streets, in jails, and in California prisons. This has been the way the term has been used to this point in the text. However, in order for outsiders to see and understand the distinctions between the four types of Family, further explanation is necessary.

In context, Family may also refer to the Leadership Group. The Leadership Group is the ultimate ruling body in Family affairs. Currently there are 25 members in the Leadership Group; at one time it had 31 members. Its members usually are the most influential and outgoing of the larger group. It is felt that they normally are the sharpest individuals, possessing a great deal of common sense. Additional details about the Leadership Group will be presented later, when treating the power structure of Family.

A third usage of Family can be distinguished when one hears a Family member refer to "my Family," "his Family," "our Family," or "your Family." When used in this manner, a member is referring to one of the smaller units of Family which collectively comprise the larger, nearly 300 member group. Members do not have nor need a term to distinguish these smaller units. However, to facilitate discussion by outsiders, I have taken the liberty of calling these units "sub-Families." Each sub-Family is a type of cell; and the members of these cells have developed very close relations with each other. However, when a sub-Family grows to about twenty members, it splits into two such groups.

A fourth usage of Family is apparent when a member refers to his "Third Family." Members of a Third Family are actually related in the traditional kinship manner. At least 40 percent of Family members have Third Family in Family too. However, Third Family members do not necessarily belong to the same sub-Family. It should be noted that about 10 percent of Third Family members are exceptions—they are *not* related; but, they are individuals who have been so very close to each other in the past that they feel and act like brothers. Regardless, of these exceptions, one can see how Third Family, by drawing on the strong bonds of actual kinship, adds a strong personal element to the feelings of unity held for the larger group.

In normal conversation among Family members, a numerical designation is used only in reference to Third Family. There are First and Second Families too; however, the normal context of a conversation usually makes the use of First and Second unnecessary for insiders. When used, First Family refers to the Leadership Group, and Second Family refers to the larger, nearly 300 member group. The sub-Family unit has no numerical designation.

Family members had never thought of how outsiders would refer to them and discuss the different types of Family, as has been done here. The analysis of the term was interesting to them. They were specially interested in the fact that they do not have or need a numerical designation for what I have called sub-Family, yet it is a fourth type of Family. Henceforth, when referring to the four types of Family discussed above, the following terms will be used: Leadership Group (First Family), Family (Second Family), Third Family, and sub-Family.

At this point, I would like to interject some comments about the use of the term Family. I am aware that Family may seem to become reified or even anthropomorphized. This involves several factors. First, the reification of Family is not unlike that which may take place when other secret organizations are discussed, such as the CIA or the Ku Klux Klan; for since individuals seldom can be named, reference necessarily is made to the formal group. Also, Family members' usage of the term has been followed closely in order to give as much of the reality as possible and avoid the use of unnatural, imposed terminology. Since Family members never preface Family with "the" (the Family), Family lacks the "the" that tends to keep *the* CIA and *the* Ku Klux Klan from becoming anthropomorphized. In addition, Family seems to become anthropomorphized by the very term used, for "family" tends to humanize that reified organization. With these factors in mind, I will continue to refer to Family as members do.

## MEMBERSHIP

Membership has been steadily growing since Family began in 1964. Family secures its necessary protective unity and assures its success through its extremely rigid selection of new members from convicts who have been tested through prior association with members. Either individuals or small groups may be admitted as members, with small groups possibly becoming a sub-Family. Potential members must be unquestionably *macho*. Also, as a Family member expressed,

> We are interested in Chicanos who are sharper than the average—convicts who are acutely conwise. These individuals need not be freewise or worldwise; they might even appear to be dull to freemen or outsiders; but they must really be aware of the prison world, even if they can effectively function *only* in prison.

Family is aware that some of these individuals may be unable to function in an acceptable, conventional manner on the streets. Their enculturation into the larger society of the outside world often has been incomplete and unsuccessful. Since some of these individuals need financial support when they are released to the streets, Family often sends money from inside to help them. In prison though, these individuals are strikingly different, for they excell in their knowledge of, and ability to use the prisoner culture. And since most Family activities take place inside, these individuals are quite useful as members.

Many more Chicano convicts would like to become Family members than are granted the honor. Most who are selected to be members have had a long, close association with Family members, either prior to, or in prison. For example, there are many Chicanos who have never been in prison, yet who have helped Family. These individuals may be friends, relatives, friends of relatives, or relatives of friends. Some may come very close to becoming Family on the streets, but no one does so without coming to prison. However, if they should come to prison, they officially become a Family member. Some Chicano convicts—who have worked closely with Family inside, who feel that they have been tested, and who would like to become a Family member—have difficulty understanding why some Chicano newly arrived from the streets is admitted to Family, while they are not. Obviously, when this happens, the Chicano from the streets has already earned himself a place in Family.

There is an additional prerequisite that must be met in order to become a Family member. It may seem extreme, but it probably has been a key factor in Family's ability to succeed and preserve the tight unity among its members. It also assures that *all* members are truly *macho*—even when it involves "gut level action." The prospective member must have killed someone! A kill, or "hit," does not have to be made inside prison in order to qualify one for membership. However, just because a man has killed is not automatic qualification. If the man has pled guilty to murder, thereby cooperating with and aiding the authorities, the hit does not count. Also, if the man's hit is judged as being non-*macho*, he probably would never be able to become a Family member. Therefore, since all Family members have "made a kill," it is obvious that Family (as an organization) and Family members are not taken lightly. To outsiders this extreme prerequisite may appear quite unreasonable, but to Family members it seems perfectly rational. They know the prisoner culture well enough to realize that severe means are necessary for the survival of Family.

In exceptional cases, an individual may become a member without having met this prerequisite. This could occur when a small group is admitted as members and one of the group had never had reason to make a kill. Or, it might be one of the Chicanos from the streets who is automatically admitted as a member on entry into prison for his past help although he may not have made a kill yet. In either case, the individual is able to prove himself fairly soon—with one of the next "ordered" Family kills.

Some additional details about Family membership should be noted. The majority of the roughly 300 members are quite young. About 90 percent are in their twenties, and there are only seven members older than forty. A mere eleven Anglos constitute the entire non-Chicano membership. There are no blacks in Family; for even though exceptions are recognized, Chicanos normally feel strongly that all blacks are potential snitches. In addition to Family members, there are convicts who are associated with Family and work closely with its members. These non-Family convicts quite effectively swell the number of individuals who are actively engaged in Family activities inside California prisons. Of the 300 members, not more than a third were on the streets in 1972—which was a very low figure. However, there are many people who work closely with Family members on the streets; and these individuals increase the number of persons who are actively involved in Family activities outside the prisons.

There has been little attrition in Family membership. Members feel a very definite sense of responsibility toward Family which is tied in with their own personal pride. If a member should want to change his way of life and retire from Family, he is not denied his request and forced to remain active. However, even though the member is allowed to live his own life, the feeling of responsibility seems to remain. He still is there if Family should ever need to call on him. A member of the Leadership Group commented about the individual who "retires":

> I'm quite sure that he would even jeopardize his personal family or friends, or what have you, in responding to our call, if we requested it. I have never found one that wouldn't, and I don't think anyone else has. Of course, some of them have never been tested. But there's no such thing as you *can't* completely retire; you can if that's what you want to do.

Family would never fear their "retired" members in any way. It is almost beyond members' conception to think of some "retired" member hurting Family by testifying against it. Members are fully aware that such an act would be certain "suicide."

## POWER STRUCTURE

Because of the necessity of secrecy, Family's power structure is almost totally unknown to outsiders—even to those non-Family convicts who are active in Family economic activities. If Family did have a written set of bylaws, they might reveal some of Family's power structure. For example, one bylaw might state that the welfare and unity of Family, as a group, will always be more important than any individual member; therefore, all members are subordinate to the group. A second bylaw might state that all members are equals. And, a third bylaw might state that the Leadership Group is the ultimate authority; but its authority is to be exercised in a benevolent, advisory manner which keeps the goals and ideals of Family, as well as the egalitarian nature of its members, utmost in mind. But, even if Family did have formal bylaws, they would be minimal in number and quite general in essence. Perhaps a Family member was right when he stated,

> When all members of an organization are sincerely devoted to its very highly regarded goals and ideals, then few specific rules are necessary. As long as members generally know how to get things done, then there is a great amount of potential flexibility. There is little need to spell out all actions in specific detail, because all members are devoted to those goals and ideals. They have no reason to quibble over relatively minor particulars as long as things get done.

Family members are not inclined to think of the interrelationship of the various parts of Family (from the individual member to the entire group) in terms of formal rules. Members often find it difficult to be specific regarding Family power structure, which apparently tends to be obscured by the following: the distinctive type of leaders who are very different from the typical leaders manifest among most Chicano groups; the absence of a chain of command; and the egalitarian nature of much Family activity—in which special status is not accorded the leaders, a wide range of potential decisions may be made by each member, and the contingencies of prison lead to flexibility and exceptions in the decision-making process.

The founding members of Family recognized the serious problems and pitfalls of typical leadership among most Chicano groups—both inside prison and on the streets. These problems of leadership have been, and continue to be, extensively discussed among Family members, enabling Family members to know what they want to avoid. They feel that many Chicanos have an aversion for most leaders—whether in prison or on the streets—stemming from the hypocrisy between the words and deeds of many Chicano leaders. Furthermore, they believe most leaders are involved in ego trips and put themselves above those that they would lead; consequently, they lose contact with the real grass roots. Most Chicanos react to this non-*macho* hypocrisy by quietly rejecting the leader. They will not allow the leader to "rule over" them, they refuse to follow the leader, and they usually avoid any further association with the leader.

Acting on their ideas about typical leadership among Chicanos, the founding members of Family set out to avoid the normal pitfalls. Keeping in mind the ideas expressed in the three possible bylaws that were earlier noted, they have been able to set up a successful power structure. The leaders of Family have averted hypocrisy between words and deeds, personal ego trips or personal gains, and loss of contact with the grass roots element of which they are a part. Consequently, Family members have *not* rejected their leaders. In fact, they have voluntarily and enthusiastically subordinated themselves to the group. Members have a great deal of respect for the astute, yet considerate guidance abilities of their leaders and have willingly accorded them permissive authority.

In accord with the emphasis on equality, all Family members are of the same status. There is no hierarchy of prestige or special ranks. All members are judged as being capable of making decisions, and it is recognized that all members have their special abilities. Thus, there are many specialized roles in Family—some of which will be treated in the next chapter, when describing the division of labor among Family members. In order for a member to fill one of the specialized roles, he must possess a particular ability; and he must have exhibited that ability in word and/or deed. Some members have a special ability in the area of leadership; they usually fill one of the three leadership roles in Family—Leadership Group members, "Money Men," and sub-Family heads. It must be stressed, though, that those who fill leadership roles do *not* receive special advantages, honors, or favors.

## Leadership Group

The founding members of Family recognized that "someone was going to have to do some leading"—to make major decisions and coordinate the many Family activities. Therefore, the Leadership Group was established as the ultimate authority in Family. Those who came to fill these roles had their special abilities, too. One member of the Leadership Group described them as the sharpest, most outgoing individuals in Family. They had quietly demon-strated their leadership ability as effective leaders. It just seems that they floated to the top, as a normal thing to do. They know how to advise or ask, *not* tell. They *never* show their power by commanding people or telling them what to do. This is a *very* important thing, because our leaders are not the kind that most other groups have. The members of the Leadership Group have their special abilities; they can do the leadership kind of things best; but *all* Family members have their special abilities, too, all are on the same level, and all are equals. All members of the Leadership Group are *macho* on a very active, physical level, too.

The Leadership Group can be seen as being somewhat like a council of elders in a tribal group. Although age is not a factor, in their actions, members of the Leadership Group have proven that they epitomize the goals and ethics of Family. Members find it difficult to even imagine that these men would do some-thing that would be detrimental to Family. Generally, members of the Leadership Group have a deep understanding and respect for others; they make a conscious effort to avoid hurting the feelings of others, to avoid putting individuals down. Their consideration and understanding have enabled them to subtly settle internal problems without hurting feelings. Through their benevolent, "suggesting" type of leadership, they are able to avoid the potential resentment and hostility that is a danger to the solidarity of most groups.

A further manifestation of the egalitarian nature of Family members is evident in the Leadership Group. All of its 25 members are equals, with no single mem-ber having more influence or power than any other; there are no special ranks or positions. Decisions are made by majority vote. However, the voting often is done in bits and pieces, for not all members of the Leadership Group are ever in any one place at the same time. This means that internal problems may take time to solve, because members are not able to gather for meetings at their will. In the past, this sometimes has led to the acceptance of a minority decision, when the majority failed to come to any agreement. However, communication does take place, and decisions are made. And, once a decision is reached, *all* Family mem-bers follow it without question.

With one out of every twelve Family members being a member of the Leader-ship Group, one can see that it is a highly representative group. It is far from being some remote governing body. When a major decision is made by that group, it is democratically made by equals. Consequently, Family actually is an acepha-lous group, because there is no single chief or leader on whose shoulders final responsibility or authority rests. The Leadership Group needs no coercive power behind it, because its decisions are a collective, democratic opinion (somewhat like a consensus) made by a relatively large group, of which each member has already demonstrated his effective, acceptable leadership ability. The decisions are carried out with almost a total absence of formal administration.

As noted earlier, there is open discussion of the problems of leadership and the ability of individuals to lead. A member of the Leadership Group noted that,

Each sub-Family does not necessarily have a representative in the Leadership Group. If the sub-Family doesn't have a born leader among its members, obviously none will appear from that sub-Family. But nobody feels hurt; they're willing to admit among themselves that none of them have that particular special ability, and they see no reason why they should try to ease into something they can't quite handle.

By way of contrast, he noted a large, 17-member sub-Family, that has three of its members in the Leadership Group.

> None of the three is even a sub-Family head. They're just members of the sub-Family, yet all three of them are among the top. They're not only keen in a general sense; each has a little individual path that they follow that they're double-keen on. If we chose leaders, all three of them would undoubtedly be in the top positions. But you see, they themselves admit one thing. They lack the kind of ego thing involved with typical leaders—of getting up there and communicating in front of a lot of other people. If it was all left to them, without having to think of anyone but themselves, they would choose to be loners. They're really just the antithesis of the glib ego-trippers who have disappointed us too many times in the past. Ours are the only kind of leaders that can succeed and get around the Chicano's individualism and the strong feelings Chicanos have about typical leaders.

Major decisions—those that potentially will have an impact on Family in several prisons—are normally made by the Leadership Group. Most of these decisions are in the areas of recruitment, economic activities, internal problems, and security. In recruitment, for example, the Leadership Group determines whether or not a group is to be admitted to Family as a sub-Family. In economic activities, the Leadership Group makes decisions regarding whether or not to "turn" money (manipulate the value of prisoner money) in a particular prison. Or, the decision whether or not to "back another horse" (get involved with a guard who will become a "runner" and bring contraband goods into prison for Family) is made by the Leadership Group. A detailed treatment of these economic activities will be given in the next chapter. An instance of an internal problem involved two sub-Families, each of which (unknown to the other) was "pushing for the same horse" (trying to get a "runner" established who would do business just with them). Both sub-Families succeeded—but only to a degree. Their investment was not returning what they thought it should, and it became obvious to each that they were in competition with some other group of prisoners. Therefore, they consulted with the Leadership Group—to draw upon its extensive, collective information. The Leadership Group decided that the situation should be openly discussed and settled so that hard feelings between the two sub-Families would be avoided. An additional result of this situation was that Family members came to better realize that such secrecy was not necessary or advisable among themselves.

An example of a major decision concerning Family security is the "ordering" of an execution by the Leadership Group. Most individuals who knowingly deal directly with Family are aware that they are subject to the convict code. If an individual should betray Family's confidence or break the convict code by threatening Family security or activities in some way (such as by snitching), the Leadership Group would judge the case. If determined guilty, the man would be "ordered" killed. The insiders' view should be stressed here. All who are subject to the convict code are aware that, in certain activities, they are virtually at war with staff. It is not unlike the United States being at war. If someone who is privy to secret information that is vital to the security of the United States should sell that information to the enemy, all parties involved are aware that he has committed treason. And, if he should be caught and convicted, all parties fully understand that the traitor will be executed as prescribed by the law. Those individuals who function within the convict code and are subject to it are also aware that if a prisoner sells information to the enemy (snitches to the staff), he, too, is guilty of a treasonous act. Therefore, all parties fully understand that the traitor, if found guilty, will be executed in accordance with the convict code—as prescribed by the convicts' law. Family activities to this date have necessitated 73 "ordered" executions. Most of those have been snitches. Two Family members have met their death in carrying out ordered kills—once this resulted in a second ordered kill; but ultimately all those ordered executed have been killed.

Actually, of all Family decisions, those made by the Leadership Group are relatively few. However, if a major decision is to be made, in most cases it is understood that all, or almost all members of the Leadership Group should be in on the decision—especially in cases such as an ordered execution or the admission of a group to Family. However, due to circumstances such as time limitations, some major decisions may be made by a few members, or even a single member of the Leadership Group. There are no formal rules to guide members. It is understood that each member will reasonably exercise his decision-making ability in accord with the circumstances and his knowledge of the facts, such as information gained from the suggestions or advice of a Money Man (an economic expert-advisor) if the decision deals with economic activities. For example, it is not uncommon that Family in a particular prison needs to have a major decision made almost immediately. Under those circumstances, the members of the Leadership Group in that prison will agree on a decision; and if they feel that most of the other members of the Leadership Group would approve of their decision, they will take immediate action on their decision. It is even possible, in exceptionally rare cases (such as in a small prison or a camp), that a major decision has to be made immediately; and, because of the small number of Family members present, the decision may be made by a single member of the Leadership Group, or a single Money Man, or a single sub-Family head, or even a few of the nonleadership members of Family.

Most Family decisions, although usually important and serious in nature, are not considered major decisions that must be made by the Leadership Group. However, a member of the Leadership Group, a Money Man, or a sub-Family head will frequently be asked for his opinion or advice regarding some of these lesser decisions. Their advice or suggestions are usually followed. As one Family member noted, "After all, why ask their opinion if you just turn around and ignore it?" Family members have learned, often through negative experiences, that "it's *not* foolish to ask about something or mention that you think you have something going, but that you don't want to cut in on the wrong guy—can somebody help me here? It's not really asking permission to do something. It's just using the Leadership Group as a source of knowledge." This is a positive attitude that benefits Family. Members of the Leadership Group (and to lesser degrees the Money Men and the sub-Family heads) have the knowledge that a single individual can never have. What a single member doesn't know, somebody on the Leadership Group will know or be able to find out. Collectively the Leadership Group knows almost everything that is going on. This is a key function of the Leadership Group—the gathering and coordination of vast amounts of knowledge. Family members have learned that members of the Leadership Group, Money Men, and sub-Family heads are men they can consult to obtain informal advice and information regarding the larger Family position.

### Money Men

The leadership role of Money Man differs from the other two Family leadership roles. Members of the Leadership Group and sub-Family heads seem to assume their roles naturally. However, the special abilities of potential Money Men are recognized by the Leadership Group, and they are assigned to their role. Therefore, in economic affairs, it can be seen that the Leadership Group voluntarily shifts to the Money Men some of the permissive authority granted to it by Family members. The Money Men have no formal authority as such, but are highly respected for their special abilities in economic affairs. Their advice and suggestions are followed. Family members would cease to heed a Money Man only if he should fail to lead them well in economic affairs. When not involved in leadership activities, Leadership Group members and sub-Family heads are just Family members. In contrast, because of their exceptional ability and the vast scope and importance of economic activities, Money Men are not allowed to engage in the same routine activities as all other members. Money Men are protected from the hazards of hustling to satisfy their own personal needs; they are kept from engaging in any activities that might "put the heat on them." All of their needs (consumer goods and services available in prison) are supplied by Family. However, this is not viewed as a special favor, because Money Men work very hard.

In 1972 there were 33 Money Men. A member of the Leadership Group said,

> That's much more than we usually have. We have between 9 and 11 more than we really need right now because of the circumstances—where men are placed in different prisons by CDC. There are too many in one place and not enough in another. We have three in one place right now, and there are only 19 members there all together, yet they make decisions that affect Folsom and San Quentin. I personally feel that we're overloaded in that spot right now. These men are specialists in money matters, who are capable of making financial decisions because they know the financial situation behind the scenes in all spots at all times. Money Men essentially are bookkeepers without books. They are super-sharp individuals who are able to keep a fantastic number of financial details in their heads.

From their position of specialized knowledge, Money Men are able to advise Family members—and most frequently members of the Leadership Group—in financial matters. Money Men are highly respected for their special ability—not only in financial matters, but in day-to-day activities inside. In economic activities the Money Men follow a pattern of leadership that is successful among Chicanos and deserving of respect—a pattern of asking, suggesting, or advising, not telling or commanding.

*A guard watching industrial workers on their way to lunch. Mt. Tamalpias in the background.* (*Photograph from the* San Francisco Chronicle)

Sub-Family Heads

A sub-Family head might also be referred to as the leader of a sub-Family. Yet there can be a distinction. A sub-Family head, talking about his role, cautioned, "You have to qualify the term leader. We're really talking more about a drawing together ability than what some people would think of as leadership. There might be somebody in his sub-Family that is much sharper and really runs it by making the decisions on things." This latter individual would probably be a member of the Leadership Group. Later he referred to a sub-Family head as the "father" of the sub-Family, and noted that he would be "the one who brought the sub-Family together; he'd be the founder." Family members recognize that sub-Family heads have a charismatic quality that may be lacking in Leadership Group members. In some instances though, a member of the Leadership Group may also be the head of a sub-Family, having both charismatic qualities and leadership abilities. Sub-Family heads who are not members of the Leadership Group are drawn into considerable interaction with it. Consequently, sub-Family heads are much more knowledgeable of Family's overall situation than the general Family members are. Knowing this, and having strong personal feelings for their charismatic leader, sub-Family members frequently approach their sub-Family head for advice or suggestions regarding nonmajor decisions. Sub-Family heads have no binding authority; their power is only advisory. However, their advice is usually followed.

A member of the Leadership Group noted that Family members do not make the distinction between Family and sub-Family as often as it might seem from their activity. He admitted the difficulty of distinguishing between Family and sub-Family at all times, because Family members "may be talking about Family, but not really thinking about whether it's Family or sub-Family." He gave an example, using a small prison where only a few Family members are present.

> Regardless of whether a man is a Money Man, or a member of the Leadership Group, or happens to be the head of a sub-Family, it might be very likely that you would go to the guy for his suggestions. So we're not talking about a decision being made by a sub-Family; it really is a Family deal.

In a larger prison, where many members of a sub-Family are present, it is quite likely that a sub-Family

> will have something of its own going. Why not? We're all Family. It's just that they are very close to each other and do it together. We're not really talking about sub-Family activities though; we're talking about Family activities.

Distinctions between Family and sub-Family *can* be made, but they are not nearly as important as "who's around that has the ability to make a decision." Family members think of most of their activities as Family activities, without making the sub-Family distinction.

Family members find it difficult to distinguish precisely the power structure below the Leadership Group, because there is no certain point above which sub-Families are prohibited to make decisions. When discussing this, the head of a sub-Family said,

> I could go pretty high without ever thinking that I should consult with somebody else. And some of the members in my own Family could go much higher without ever thinking that they would have to consult with me. We are all individuals when we stand alone, when the rest of us aren't there.

There may be times in a small prison or camp that a member of the Leadership Group, a Money Man, or a sub-Family head may not be present to consult regarding a serious decision. At that time, the few regular Family members who are present make a decision.

> They're men too, and they've got to make a decision when necessary. They can't just put their face to the wall and say they'll just ignore something and be walked over or miss out on a profitable business deal. They have their rights and responsibilities too. And it's this kind of flexibility that makes it difficult to decide how the power structure within Family works.

However Family members do not see this as a confusing situation. Sub-Family members have a close relationship with each other; and it is recognized that "all members have a head on their shoulders, they're sharp, they're intelligent." All members are involved in many nonmajor decisions. Even though they may frequently draw upon the knowledge of others (Leadership Group members, Money Men, and sub-Family heads), all members are personally and actively involved in the decision-making process. For example, admitting an individual to Family is a sub-Family decision. However, if it involves something that might be questionable to other Family members, the decision could go all the way to the Leadership Group. But the decision could be made by a single sub-Family member, too. A member of the Leadership Group stated,

> He'd just say that I want this guy in. It can be quite informal. After all, we're all equals. But, it must be remembered that everybody—from the dullest to the sharpest member—realizes that when this happens, don't make a mistake, because that's the individual's responsibility. We take his word for it, but never have to say it—that's just assumed or understood. It's like the con code—if you break it, all parties know—you don't have to talk about it.

There is no strict chain of command in Family. A member of the Leadership Group noted that a nonleadership member "would probably go to his Family father [sub-Family head], because that's his familiar territory, where he feels comfortable." However if he wishes, he is welcome to go to a member of the Leadership Group or a Money Man. But normally, if he wants the advice of someone who is in command of more information than he, his sub-Family head is the man he will approach. Also, when a decision is made by the Leadership Group, it just filters on down to the members. All members who were in on the decision go to different places, and the decision is spread by word of mouth. A Leadership Group member noted that in a tight situation, such as when money has just been turned,

> We don't want the word to just filter down. I'd tell any member of my Family; and if I saw any Family member that I thought might not have come into contact with somebody who would have told him, I'd say, hey, have you heard that it's all money today. Even then, the word isn't spread through the sub-Family heads. It's still a very open kind of thing; but instead of casually telling, you make a point of telling. You don't care who you tell. In that respect, there's no real chain of command or fixed pattern of communication that must be followed.

Family members understand the absolute necessity to show strict loyalty to all four types of Family. When asked if there are varying degrees of loyalty accorded to the different types of Family, members answered with a definite no. However, when a hypothetical conflict situation between two types of Family was posed (wherein an individual's brother—a member of Third Family—did something *very* serious against Second Family), it was admitted that there is a variance. Their loyalty would be in accord with the highest ethics of the group. The individual's brother would have to be taken care of, even executed if necessary. In such a situation, the man would not be expected to carry out the sanction against his brother; a member of Second Family would do it. However, the individual would not protest Second Family action. He would know that his brother had been judged by First Family and found guilty, and that sanctions against his brother would be necessary for the good of the group. Family does not prey on its members, and there have only been two "strays" in the history of Family. One, the punk noted earlier in this chapter, was allowed to be killed by a nonmember convict. The other was ordered executed. In both cases, there was no question about the validity of the decision. Among members, the general appreciation of the dangers of internal conflict seems to be an effective form of control; consequently, coercive force is not necessary to assure compliance with decisions of First Family.

The use of the kinship term, family, to name this group can be seen as an indication of the grave import that the members accord their group. Traditionally, Chicanos (both inside prison and on the streets) have always held their own kin (family) ties in high regard. Among Chicanos, the greatest loyalty and support is accorded one's own kin, with progressively diminishing degrees granted to friendship ties, *barrio* (neighborhood) ties, and Chicano ethnic identity. Therefore, one can see the choice of the term family (as a name for their group) as an extreme intensification of family loyalty, with Family being given the highest degree of allegiance by members.

## MAJOR ACTIVITIES

The two major types of Family activities are economic and protective. Both are necessary for Family to attain its goals. Family economic activities have successfully provided the funds necessary to enable its members, most nonmember Chicano prisoners, and most convicts to live in a *macho* manner, with the pride and dignity of adult male human beings. Without these funds, Family could not exist and accomplish its goals. Consequently, economic activities must be tightly controlled at all times, and anything that interferes is a serious threat to Family's very existence. Such interference can be a matter of life and death for those involved.

The methods used by Family to control the major aspects of the prisoner economy in all the larger California prisons will be detailed in the next chapter. It will be shown that "legal" prisoner economic activities are of minor importance when compared to the large scale illegal economic activity that is the concern of most prisoners. Family virtually controls the illegal economic activities. Through its control of all major amounts of prisoner illegal money and most major sources of contraband goods, Family is able to function much as banks and governments do. It has the means to regulate the flow of contraband money in all the larger California prisons. It can also control the value of this illegal money. It is the prisoners' bank throughout CDC, because all major loans are made either directly or indirectly through Family. It has an unquestioned stability because it has the power and means to collect and pay legitimate debts from one prison to another (or even on the streets), much as a bank can do from state to state. This makes dealing with Family a very positive, secure, yet serious matter. For example, Family *will* collect or pay a legitimate debt, regardless of where the debtor or debtee might be transferred—even if he is released to the streets. In contrast, if a prisoner has financial dealings with an inmate, there is the constant threat that the inmate will be transferred to a different prison (or even be paroled or discharged to the streets)—which would present serious difficulties in tendering payment or collecting a debt.

Through its protective activities, Family is able to insure the secrecy necessary for its security, to prevent or eliminate threats to its economic enterprises, and to maintain its integrity as a group. These protective activities are absolutely necessary to preclude situations or conditions that ultimately could destroy Family. Although they may surface occasionally in the form of violence and death, such as an "ordered" execution, these activities usually are less extreme and quite subtle. Anyone who consciously deals with Family knows the seriousness with which members regard Family activities and the extent to which they will go to protect Family. Non-Family individuals who function on the lower levels of the prisoner culture understand the rules of the game, and even the extreme act of death to a snitch may seem justifiable to them. The mere possession of this knowledge usually is sufficient to keep prisoners from crossing Family in any way. For someone to snitch on Family, the stakes would have to be *very* high, and the informer would have to feel that he could get away with it. If he is discovered by Family, there would be no subtle reminders; there would be no discussion; there would only be deadly action. Members know very well that their group could never survive without such severe protective measures.

## INTERACTION WITH OTHER PRISONERS

A sizable number of prisoners—which includes almost all Chicano prisoners—are aware of Family and its activities. However, only few of those prisoners have any specific knowledge about Family. Members are extremely cautious to prevent nonmembers from learning details about Family membership and activities. Usually, only the relatively few convicts who associate and work closely with Family are privy to some inside information, and most of them are Chicanos. However, because of the cellular structure of Family, no outsider is ever aware of the actual identity of more than just a few Family members. In contrast to those Chicano convicts who know a considerable amount of general information about Family, there are other Chicanos who know relatively little, having picked up their knowledge in bits and pieces. Some older Chicanos who have served time in California prisons (such as those who have been on parole for several years) may know very little about Family or even have mistaken ideas about Family for several reasons: Family is relatively new, Family has never advertised, and Family activity might have been mistaken for the type of activity in which gunsels have engaged for years. In the next chapter, the detailed explanation of Family economic activities will show how a nonmember could easily make this mistake. Most of the rest of the prisoners either are only vaguely aware that Family exists, or have just a sketchy idea of what Family is. However, there are many inmates in the yard who are totally unaware of Family.

Family members prefer to avoid interaction with inmates in their daily activities. In rare instances though, a member may have direct economic dealings with an inmate who receives large amounts of money from the streets. However, in such cases, the inmate would never know and could never prove that he was dealing with a Family member. The inmate would just know that he had a connection for the contraband goods he desires; and he might not even know whether he is dealing with a gunsel or a convict, and never even suspect that his connection is a Family member. Normally Family members will talk with inmates and engage in the necessary, superficial prison activity that a particular situation might demand; but often their interaction is strikingly tacit. Inmates (as well as most staff members) often view this silence as a manifestation of the mistaken stereotype of Chicanos—that they are very uncommunicative. But Family members recognize that they have little in common with inmates as far as the prisoner culture is concerned. As a member said, "We talk with inmates, but we don't communicate with them." In contrast, members intermingle and communicate with convicts on a daily basis. Most convicts who deal with members are not even aware that they are Family members. Although a convict might suspect that the prisoner is a Family member, he would prefer not to know for certain. That way he would avoid the suspicion of being labeled a snitch if something detrimental should happen to a member or to Family. Convicts agree with Family members that the fewer who know, the better—why run the risk of a slip?

At times, subtle pressure may be necessary to cause an outsider to realize that he should honor his financial commitment to Family. Usually the allusion to an example of someone who crossed Family is sufficient. If the individual is experiencing serious, legitimate financial difficulty, Family will accommodate him, much as a bank will reconcile with a borrower who is not able to make a loan payment on time. Family is realistic, and special arrangements are usually made. However, if the individual does not go along with the special arrangements, and merely tries to beat Family out of the money, extreme measures may be taken; but this seldom is necessary.

Considering Family's reputation, the fear of crossing Family may occasionally give rise to misunderstanding. For example, let us assume a prisoner loans a Family member a few packs of cigarettes. (This is an individual act by the member, because Family activity is on a volume basis only.) Time passes and the debt and interest are not paid. The prisoner, out of fear and ignorance, knowing or suspecting that the Chicano is a Family member, fails to even remind the member of the debt. Being busy with larger, more important economic deals, the member forgets. The prisoner drops the issue; but he emerges from the experience with the impression that Family does not pay its debts. Family would disagree; for it makes great efforts to maintain absolute correctness in its financial transactions. The member would have paid his personal debt had he been reminded, for all members try to be fair and just in their dealings; and Family would never tolerate a member using the threat of the power of the larger group to avoid payment of a personal debt.

## SUPPORT OF CHICANOS

Family is aware of all Chicano activities inside San Quentin and throughout CDC. As an organization, Family never tries to initiate a new group or activity through the *official* prison system. They know the great amount of time, effort, frustration, and luck necessary to officially start anything new with staff approval. Most efforts are doomed to failure, but a few do succeed. Members may be involved as individuals, but not as representatives of Family; therefore, staff and most prisoners would see the participating Family members simply as Chicano prisoners. If the newly instituted program proves to be for the good of the Chicanos in general, then Family may support it. For example, the Basic Education for Mexican-American Class (BEMA Class), discussed in the preceeding chapter, is supported by Family because it is a positive, *macho* program which had been initiated by the Chicano prisoners.

Chicanos inside California prisons are helped in other, informal, often covert ways. The majority of Family's support of other Chicanos is economic in nature, stemming from the use of Family's "Chicano Fund." This fund is normally used to help the less fortunate nonmember Chicanos who are in need and not in a position to be helped by others, or to aid those who have their own economic resources but who are in temporary need of assistance. The Chicano Fund has been just briefly noted here to give an indication of how Family supports Chicanos economically in unseen ways. Details about this fund will be presented in the next chapter.

At times, Family may support Chicanos in other ways, too. For example, assume that a poorly educated, yet deserving Chicano has been gambling with some sharks; he has lost and now owes them a considerable sum. This Chicano has never had any "draw" and has always had to hustle for what little he has. In his lifetime, he would never be able to pay off the debt; he might not even be able to keep up on the interest payments. In such a situation, a *non*-Chicano might request the staff to lock him up in the hole for his own physical protection. With the Chicano it is different, because Family steps in. A Family member explains to the slick creditors that they never should have allowed the Chicano to gamble with them, knowing that he did not have the kind of money or connections needed to pay them off if he lost. The member tells them to forget the debt; and if they are shrewd enough to have enticed the Chicano into gambling for unreasonable stakes, they should have enough common sense to never press the issue again. In this manner, Family makes it possible for one less Chicano to be subject to manipulation by others. According to Family, this type of action is entirely reasonable and necessary in the prison setting; for prisoners (as well as staff) should treat other prisoners with the human dignity which all men deserve.

The following ideas about Chicano unity were expressed by Family members during discussions about Family support of nonmember Chicanos inside. Family members feel that the larger United States culture has forced Chicanos on the streets to stick together in many ways. But there is little Chicano unity on the political level either on the streets or in prison. However, the circumstances inside prison have intensified all preprison harmony and pushed Chicanos into a deep unity that is manifest on economic and emotional levels. Chicano prisoners have learned to help each other maintain their pride and dignity by sticking together in opposition to non-Chicano prisoners as well as staff and by sharing their economic wealth. Chicanos see their solidarity as being very *macho.* Family is the ultimate expression of this Chicano unity. Family members feel that the type of confederation found among Chicanos also could serve the Anglo and, specially, the black prisoners well. However, it does not exist among them, but only among the Chicanos. With the Chicanos there is a "feeling of sameness," stemming from the fact that they have a culture of their own, which is different from the larger United States culture in which they find themselves.

Family members feel that the blacks have no distinct culture of their own to which they have emotional bonds—as the Chicanos do. They contend that this is a major factor in the lack of unity among black prisoners. Members strongly state their view that, "Instead of unity, each black tries to get all he can, on an individual basis." Family members see most black prisoners as being very busy individuals who are trying to get ahead of other prisoners—regardless of whether they are black, Anglo, or Chicano. Regarding Anglo unity, Family members see the Anglo prisoners as not recognizing any need for such solidarity. The Anglo prisoners view the United States culture as their own culture, and feel no cause to unite in opposition to it.

With this background of the history, goals, ethics, membership, power structure, and major activities of Family, it is hoped that the reader will understand why this group has come into existence. As one Family member stated,

> The administration, by pushing on prisoners the way that it does and has been doing, is forcing new ideas and new ways into existence among us. The Baby Mafia just happened to fall into a race thing and fits well into the Chicano background; but if it had not been that, it would have been something else.

Also, even though it may be difficult for outsiders to comprehend, Family could not work or survive without using extreme methods; they are of the utmost necessity. A strong degree of cultural relativity may be necessary for an outsider to understand the following Family view as it pertains to *all* prisoners, "The harm which may be caused at times by Family, or its activities, is *far* outweighed by the good it does."

# 6 / The prisoner economy

It should be reemphasized that this is not an ethnography of the prison culture, but of the prison*er* culture. Therefore, this description of the prisoner economy will not deal with most of the formal financial aspects of the prison, such as budgetary allocations, cost of various programs, staff wages, and so forth. Obviously, the approximately $2,600 per prisoner per year that is used to run and maintain CDC is necessary; but most aspects of how that amount is allocated and used by CDC and San Quentin administrators are beyond the scope of this book. Consequently, this chapter will treat only those things which pertain directly to the prison*er* economy—the prisoners' production, distribution, and consumption or use of goods and services.

It would be convenient to have an existing model to which the prisoner economy could be applied, but such a model does not exist. The major portion of this sub-system of the prisoner culture exists at covert depths. It is complicated; it has intricate sets of relations, both internally and with the rest of their social system. However, at those hidden levels, regularities to which the prisoners attach meaning can be discerned. From the structure and pattern revealed by these regularities, the organizations and rules that make up their economy can be seen. Many of the analytical focuses of economic anthropologists can shed light on the prisoner econ-omy. However, some covert, complicating factors that are unique to the prison setting should be considered first.

These entangling elements are aspects of the illegal and rule-breaking part of their economy. They sharply contrast with the legal aspects. Legal activities are openly acknowledged and obvious. They are known by both staff and prisoners. However, the illegal activities are extensive and complicated. They range from rather trivial rule-breaking to the most serious of felonies—murder. Usually the relative seriousness of these activities corresponds with the level of the prisoner culture on which they occur. The trivial rule-breaking may occur at all levels, but it is more frequent and can be readily observed at the inmate level. The most serious activities are also the most covert. Except for the *use* of goods and services by some inmates, these grave acts take place only at the convict and Family levels.

## FOUR TYPES OF ECONOMIC ACTIVITIES

The *full* details of production, distribution, and consumption or use of *all* prisoner economic goods and services can be attained *only* from the Family level.

101

Consequently, in order to eliminate the overt confusion and come to a full understanding of the prisoner economy, it is necessary to distinguish four types of prisoner economic activities. One type is legal, and three are illegal. Each of the latter corresponds with the level of the prisoner culture at which such activities normally take place. Henceforth, when legal economic activities are being discussed, they will be noted as such. However, since most prisoner economic activities are illegal or rule-breaking, they merely will be noted as being either prisoner, inmate, convict, or Family economic activities.

For comparative purposes, legal prisoner economic activities can be described as follows. They are formal and official, being subject to the laws of the streets and to the prison rules. In many respects they are important, but they are only the superficial, obvious part of the economy. Comprising only a small part of the total prisoner economy, they are known to all members of the staff and all prisoners. However, as will be shown later, they can be used for, or tied into, illegal aspects of the economy. In some instances, certain of these legal activities become an integral part of the illegal economic activities. The major example of this legal type of activity is the use of the canteen.

Turning to the illegal types, inmate economic activities are informal, usually being against the prison rules or sometimes unlawful. If unlawful, they usually do not involve serious crimes and are not considered consequential by staff. As with legal activities, they are important in many respects, often being the most important part of the economy to many inmates. These activities comprise a larger part of the economy than legal activities do; however, they are still a relatively small, yet evident, part of the entire prisoner economy. All prisoners engage in some of these inmate activities, but convicts and Family members do so to a lesser degree. These inmate activities are well known to staff members and prisoners, even though they are done on a covert basis. Normally they are hidden from staff; but little effort is made to conceal them from most other prisoners. An obvious exception would be the well-known snitches. Some staff members may understand the larger aspects of the prison setting and tolerate this activity as being reasonable. This "tolerated" illegal activity would include things such as small-scale, petty stealing of state materials, like food or clothing from their jobs; construction of shelves or cabinets for their cells; having a *very* small store; and fronting a store for a convict.

Convict economic activities are informal, but more serious. They may involve the breach of major prison rules; however, more frequently they involve unlawful acts, ranging through various misdemeanors to serious felonies. These activities comprise a much greater portion of the prisoner economy than either the legal or inmate types do. In general, convicts are the primary producers of these goods and services, with gunsels acting as the primary distributors to inmates. Inmates are the primary consumers or users of convict-produced goods or services, with one major exception—convicts and Family members are the principal users of drugs. Convicts may engage in these activities on an individual basis; however, they usually form a partnership or join a clique. The cliques range from three members to five or six members. At times, for a big deal, three or four cliques may join together temporarily. Convicts always conduct this activity with great efforts to conceal it from inmates and staff. Examples of this type of activity would include wholesale production of home brew, wholesale production of sandwiches in the evening in the cell block, bringing in dope for sale to others, production of hot plates for sale to others, and wholesale supplying goods for inmate retail stores.

Most staff members and inmates are generally aware of convict activities. However, they normally have a partial or confused view, for they are usually ignorant of most individuals and details. At best, some may know of, or suspect, a few details of one or a few convict operations; but since this would represent only a minute fraction of the almost numberless convict operations being conducted simultaneously, their information is not very full or useful. Some staff members become personally involved in these activities when they bring contraband into the prison for convicts; however, their awareness of details usually extends no further than the particular deal and the one or two convict contacts. Inmates become involved as purchasers of convict goods or services, but they usually know little more than the gunsel distributor from whom they purchase the goods or services. Accordingly, gunsels function both as a buffer and a link between convicts and inmates.

Gunsels and convicts usually have been personally involved in a number of these convict enterprises—the convicts as the producers and the gunsels as the distributors. They may have intimate knowledge of many past and present operations; however, they do not know the details of most convict activities, for such activities are too vast in number. No one individual could legitimately be involved with so many convicts. And it would be foolish to dig for additional detailed information of this type without good reason for personal involvement. To do so would be putting oneself in a vulnerable position—of having knowledge of an operation which could lead to suspicion—if someone should snitch on it. In other words, a convict or a gunsel does not want to know the particulars of an operation unless it is necessary for him to know.

At the very depth of the economy, below convict activities, is Family. Collectively, Family members generally know most convicts and some details of their activities. Family often provides the financial backing necessary for certain operations. Except for this financial involvement, Family, as an organized group, does not engage in convict economic activities. However, since Family members are all convicts, too, a member may act as an individual convict—he may engage in these convict activities; but such activity would *not* be Family activity. If a single convict enterprise should become too big and directly interfere with Family activities, Family will buy the convict out and take over the operation; or, if necessary, Family will force the convict out of business. In either case, the operation is turned into Family activity.

Family economic activities are informal in some superficial respects. However, there is a great degree of organization and formality behind them that is not evident to non-Family individuals, for Family business is *big* business. Usually involving a major felony, these activities account for the majority of serious prisoner economic activity. All such activities are financed and directed by Family. Members may engage in these activities either on the Family or sub-Family level;

however, at either level, Family knowledge, organization, and finances are involved. Family members, convicts, and gunsels (as well as inmates) are consumers of these goods and services. Such goods and services may be produced by Family members or convicts. When a convict is the producer, Family finances the operation. In these cases, a gunsel would be the distributor, and on the surface the operation would appear to be no different than serious convict activity. However, there would be two buffers between Family and inmate consumers—a convict and a gunsel. When a Family member is the producer, a convict usually serves as a distributor on a wholesale basis. The convict distributes the goods or services to the gunsels, who serve as retail distributors to the inmates. Again, as before, there are two buffers between Family and the inmates. Often, even the gunsels involved may not be aware that the operation is Family activity. The two most prominent examples of Family economic activities would be "three-for-two" loans and bringing in drugs for sale to others.

The majority of staff is ignorant of Family, as such. Some staff members have heard vague comments about the existence of a "Mexican Mafia." A few staff members—primarily those in the higher positions of custody—are aware that Family exists and are concerned about stopping its activities. However, the extent of staff knowledge is sharply limited to "suspicion" about a few individuals and some details of a *very* small number of operations that are "suspected" of being Family activities. Staff have guessed about Family, but they are ignorant of specifics concerning Family organization, membership, capital, and so forth. No staff members are personally involved in Family activities, except for those few individuals who happen to be "running" contraband (bringing it into prison) for Family. However, even in these instances, the staff member is usually unaware, and never would be certain, that he is involved in Family activities; for such operations superficially appear to be convict activities, with the staff member dealing with a convict, not a Family member. The few details that are "known" by staff are unsubstantiated; for such knowledge is obtained through snitches who are at least once removed, if not twice or thrice removed from Family. Assumptions pieced together from such information are not likely to be too valid.

Generally, inmates are not aware of Family. Occasionally a few may have heard something about Family, but their knowledge is even more limited than that of the staff. When an inmate does hear something about Family, it is quite vague and confused, often being the product of rumor which usually has been passed many times before reaching him. If an inmate is a consumer or user of Family goods or services, he would not even have reason to suspect that they originated with Family. From his position, such operations would appear to be gunsel or convict activities. Even if he were told that Family is behind the activities, his superficial knowledge would lead him to a very mistaken impression of what Family really is; for he would be likely to conclude that Family is nothing more than a few gunsels. It would confuse him even more if he were told that Family is Chicano; for all he encounters is gunsels dealing Family goods or services—and most gunsels are Anglo, not Chicano. From his state of confusion, he would be unable to comprehend the depth and organization below the surface activity.

Many gunsels are cognizant of Family economic activities, but they usually have only a partial knowledge. Being involved in the distribution of such goods and services, they have seen more than the superficial activities which inmates see; but their view is still a limited one. They may know some details about one or a few operations and have a vague knowledge of the scope of, and organization behind, Family activities. Because even they are buffered from direct contact with Family by the convicts involved, the gunsels' information is not very direct.

Most convicts are aware of Family activities, and their knowledge is first-hand, through direct dealings with Family members. Some of these convicts may not be certain if they are dealing with a Family member or with another convict who has connections with Family; however, they realize that it is not necessary to know —for such information could prove to be a serious liability in case someone snitched on the operation. At the other end of the range are a few convicts—usually Chicano—who may have extensive dealings with Family, may know several members, and may possess considerable detail about the organization and scope of Family activities. But even these very close convicts are ignorant of the specifics necessary to fully understand Family. They may know or suspect that certain individuals are Family members and that Family capital and organization are behind certain operations. However, even they are positive of only a relatively few details and individuals; and, as good convicts, they are aware that a more precise knowledge is not necessary or desirable.

Obviously, Family members are quite knowledgeable of all details of their own economic activities, for they take great care to keep accurate records of their operations. Frequently, owing to the extensive nature of Family activities, a member, or perhaps an entire sub-Family will be ignorant of the particulars of some operations, especially those which take place in another prison. However, if they wanted or needed to find out, they could. In addition, members have information about Family organization and operation that is generally withheld from outsiders—with the occasional exception of the very close convict who is privy to a few of these details. Family realizes that both convicts and gunsels serve as buffers between them and inmates and staff. As a result Family operations are obscured from all but a superficial view; so to inmates as well as to staff, Family activities normally appear to be primarily gunsel and occasionally convict activities. Accordingly, one can see that *only* from the Family level is a full understanding of *all* types of prisoner economic activities possible.

Having distinguished four types of prisoner economic activities, a few concluding remarks are in order. These types are quite real to convicts and Family members; and as outsiders come to comprehend the types, they will achieve a fuller understanding of the prisoner economy. Granted, there may be some shortcomings in this approach, but they seem to be few and minor when compared to the insight gained. For example, inmates and staff may see the prisoner economy as something quite different; they may disagree with this analysis. However, all Family members and most convicts would claim that inmates and staff disagree out of ignorance. This classifying of specific prisoner activities into the three illegal types may be open to debate. In general, though, convicts and Family members would agree that when an individual's inmate operation goes beyond the realm of being small-time hustle and becomes a real business enterprise, then it becomes convict activity; and when convict activity becomes big business, it becomes Family activity. Consequently, in the truly significant areas of the prisoner economy, the prisoners on each of the three different levels generally tend to fill different sets of roles—as they pertain to goods and services. Inmates are primarily consumers. Gunsels, who function between the inmate and convict level, are chiefly distributors and consumers. Convicts are producers, distributors, and consumers. Family members are the organizers, leaders, and financiers—as well as being producers, distributors, and consumers.

## LEGAL ECONOMIC ACTIVITIES

Turning from the generalized description above, it now is necessary to analyze and describe the prisoner economy in more detail. As noted earlier, some legal activities can be used for, or tied into, illegal economic activities. Some even become an integral part of illegal activities. Consequently, an understanding of certain of the legal activities is a prerequisite to a comprehension of the prisoners' largely illegal economy.

Technically, in an economic sense, a man requires no money inside prison, for all of his indispensable needs are taken care of by the state. Essential goods and services such as food, clothing, certain toilet articles, religious services, personal counseling, and medical care are produced and distributed by the state. They are not for sale; they are part of the daily routine and programs, to be used when available or necessary. However, the quantity and quality of such goods and services often leave much to be desired. Also, the prisoners have many needs that are not indispensable in a technical sense, but which are quite real to them. These facts are recognized by both prisoners and staff, and both groups have taken steps to alleviate these undesirable conditions.

Staff attempts to reduce these inadequacies have been ineffective and minimal when compared to the extensive efforts of prisoners. Staff activity has been limited to the area of consumer goods. They have long operated a canteen that is open to "qualified" prisoners during certain daytime hours, and offers such items as food, candy, cigarettes, toilet articles, magazines, and a few paperback books. However, the operation of the canteen has created inequities, for in effect it is partial to those prisoners with a legal source of money, and not all prisoners have such sources.

Legally, in order to qualify to purchase items from the canteen, a prisoner must have a privilege card and money "on the books"—in his inmate account. If his balance is sufficient, he is allowed to "draw" up to $45 each month, only on a specified day. If he fails to make his draw on the specified date, he loses the opportunity for that month and must wait until his date the next month. But, at that time, he is allowed to draw only the $45 maximum. Consequently, there is no way to make up for a missed draw, unless he normally draws less than the maximum and can make larger draws during the following months.

When a prisoner signs for his draw, he is issued "canteen ducats." These are pressed paper token money, with 20 nickles on a perforated sheet. The prisoner's number is in a space at the top of the sheet. He must have both an identification card and a privilege card to match the number appearing on the ducats. Then, only the bull in the canteen is supposed to remove the ducats. Consequently, ducats which are not attached to the full ducat sheet are worthless. This supposedly makes the ducats usable only by the prisoner who makes the draw and only at the canteen.

To make canteen purchases, a prisoner must obtain funds for his inmate account. These funds can come from any of several potential sources. One origin is money from outside. This can be from savings a man had prior to his incarceration, but the economic status of most prisoners precludes this from being a source. Money also can be sent in by approved correspondents; but, like the prisoner, their economic status usually prevents this from being a significant or reliable source. Consequently, money from outside is not usually available to most prisoners.

Another source of legal funds for a prisoner's account may be his job inside prison. However, the jobs which pay prisoners are few, so this source is not available to the vast majority of prisoners. Most jobs or assignments are nonpay, or "slave labor" as referred to by many prisoners. These nonpaying jobs are in the following areas: the laundry, inside construction, outside landscaping, yard crew, maintenance men, and most nonindustry jobs. On the few paying jobs, the scale is predetermined on a fixed, hourly basis which ranges from 3 to 16 cents per hour. On the low end, the library clerk, "key" men in the blocks, and cell block janitors would be paid 2 cents an hour. Some of the top paying (16 cents an hour) jobs would include the following: the four or five lead men, the head clerk, the night watchmen in the furniture factory, and the firemen. The powerhouse worker and the head clerk in the captain's office would be paid from 12 to 16 cents an hour. The average pay for those with jobs is about $10 per month—which is not even enough for a pack of cigarettes a day! But some prisoners feel that "something is better than nothing." An exception to this top limit are the six canteen workers who get a double top, 32 cents an hour. This allows them a double draw each month, and it supposedly discourages them from illegally using the goods they handle.

A final source of legal funds for a prisoner's account may involve his art and craft activities. Some have jokingly called this "criminal art" when discussing it with outsiders. However there is validity behind that statement—not because it has been produced by criminals, but because the price is usually criminally low. If a prisoner has money on the books, he is allowed to buy art and/or craft materials from the hobby shop. The prisoner sets the price for a completed work when he sells it; however, the hobby shop manager may veto it if he feels it is priced too high. Hence, low prices prevail on displayed works at the tiny gift shop at the outer gate and at the visitors' waiting room just outside the main wall. In addition, these "criminal" prices are a significant factor in the success of the annual art show, where prisoner art is sold to the public. Prisoners were amused at the results one year, when over half of the checks used to pay for art or craft works were bad. Since that time, all sales have been on a cash basis only.

A few artists produce excellent works and consistently are able to sell most of what they produce. One painter made about $2,000 in one year. Since this amount was well over what he would ever be able to draw and use inside, he

*Nearly half of the upper yard is covered by this tin roof. Mess halls are on the right; the canteen is in front of South Block in the rear; the guard gun rail (catwalk) is supported above the steel beams on the upper left. (Courtesy of California Department of Corrections)*

*A lazy weekend day in the lower yard. Part of the industrial area is in the immediate background. (Courtesy of California Department of Corrections)*

sent most of it home. Another artist sent enough money home to be able to support his teen-age daughter in a private school. These individuals are among the rare exceptions though. Most artists and craftsmen are lucky to make a few dollars a month for canteen, for not all prisoners have the interest or ability necessary to produce works that would prove salable. Occasionally a good artist will not have any money on the books. Legally, this prevents him from purchasing supplies and materials which would enable him to begin producing art or craft work. Consequently, as far as having a significant financial impact on the prisoner population, this final source of legal funds is limited to a relatively small percentage of prisoners.

From the above description of the canteen and the legal "inmate" draw, one can see that the mitigating effects of these additional legal goods are *not* directly or legally felt by many prisoners; for many prisoners never have money on the books. Turning from these details of the few legal aspects of the prisoner economy, the rest of this chapter will treat aspects of the illegal and rule-breaking part of their economy. It will become evident that staff efforts are petty when compared with the vast scope of the prisoners' chiefly illegal production, distribution, and consumption or use of additional goods and services.

## ILLEGAL ECONOMIC ACTIVITIES

Prisoners, being products of the streets, are well aware of the wide variety of goods and services available there. They have developed patterns of human wants and desires that go far beyond the purely indispensable needs acknowledged by the official prison system. Some of these felt needs might appear to be foolish from an economic point of view, yet prisoners feel that they are necessary to their well being. But it is wrong to assume that people's needs are entirely rational, or that people engage in economic activities just for profit. Economic motives extend to considerations far more complicated than the simple desire to fill indispensable needs or to make money. Any of the following additional incentives may often pervade aspects of their economic system: personal security, social status, personal relationships, prestige, creative satisfaction, participation in one's own destiny, avoidance of boredom, personal challenge, and pride of doing something well.

There are many determinants of what goods and services are available through the prisoner economy. Social values held by the various groups prior to their entry into prison may result in certain commodities being preferred over others. And, size or visibility of goods may often limit or preclude availability inside. However, the resourcefulness of prisoners often amazes outsiders. Prisoners admit that they may have to accept substitutes or wait until certain items are available, but the frequent conquest of the seemingly impossible is an accepted fact of economic life. Granted, demand often may exceed supply, and the available supply is accessible only to those with money or connections. However, prisoners feel that if a man has enough money, he can buy almost anything but freedom.

For example, in the area of sexual behavior, it is generally assumed that prisoners must use some substitute for a female partner. However, convicts claim that the following situation developed in 1959 and 1960. A few convicts invested time, effort, and money into a potential business venture. After about nine months, their efforts resulted in the addiction of a nurse in the San Quentin hospital. She could not support her drug habit, so the convicts supported her. In return, however, she was forced to prostitute herself to other convicts. A hospital room was used. Except for a small viewing window, the doors are solid and open into the room. The tall nurse would stand inside, lean back against the door, and put her hair against the window. This would effectively block vision and entry into the room. The temporary displacement of an undergarment allowed the act to rapidly occur—"there was no candlelight and wine; but for $10 it was real." After over a year of such activity, the nurse came under suspicion and was ultimately fired. The convicts who developed this business operation not only realized a fantastic profit from their initial investment, they also made an apparently unobtainable service available to their fellow convicts.

Production of Goods and Services

Now, turning to the actual production of goods and services by prisoners, it should first be briefly noted that the term production not only means the act or process of manufacturing something, but also the making available of goods or services for human wants. The prisoners' production involves various factors, such as needs, materials, technology, capital, and labor, which are interrelated in complex ways. It is the fundamental function of those involved in the production of goods and services to organize the various productive resources. Prisoners, like individuals and institutions on the streets, may act alone or in concert. Their efforts are patterned and organized. On the inmate level of production, patterns are evident, but little organization is manifest. It is only on the Family level that a very high degree of organization and leadership is evident.

Briefly treating prisoner production from the three levels, it should be noted that there is no economic leadership at the inmate level; for inmate activity is individualistic in nature. The meager productive resources are owned by the individual. The inmate producer normally uses his own products—like an individual's home consumption of homemade products on the streets. Inmate production has little impact on the larger prisoner economy. At the convict level of production, there may be some relatively minor manifestations of organization and leadership; however, convict ownership of resources and production of goods and services still are on an individual, a partnership, or at most a clique basis. Products from the convict level usually are for sale to other prisoners, but small amounts may be set aside for personal use. In addition, convicts depend upon profits from their productive activities to enable them to satisfy their own consumer needs. The considerable volume of convict production is similar to that of small businesses on the streets. In contrast, the high degree of Family organization and leadership is comparable to that of large businesses, corporations, and financial institutions on the streets. A brief description of how Family's productive resources are owned and used will serve as an initial basis for this contrast.

All Family resources are held through corporate ownership, not individual ownership. There is a corporate responsibility for liabilities as well as assets. True, an individual member may have control or possession of Family resources, or he may personally obligate Family to an economic commitment; however, Family, as a corporate body, assumes the ultimate responsibility in such matters. A considerable portion of Family resources are normally held in the form of cash. Family's capital cash account is maintained at a minimum level or above at all times. This cash serves as a reserve to insure Family against diverse economic contingencies. The money in the capital cash account is actually held in a wide variety of places, both inside and on the streets.

Whether in prison or on the streets, Family members may draw upon the capital cash account for Family investment purposes. Such investment is always on a short-term basis; upon completion of the business transaction, the members bring back the cash borrowed—plus the profit made. These business transactions normally yield considerable profit. For example, it is understood that if a profit of 150 percent cannot be made on a narcotics deal, it should not be attempted. At times, the business transactions made inside tend to be of a smaller scale than those made on the streets; however, members are active in both places.

Members usually do not need to draw upon the profit of the Family business transactions they conduct. Some exceptions will be noted later, when discussing the division of labor among Family members. However, a member normally will have something steady going which will allow him to meet his day-to-day financial needs. This steady activity is not considered Family activity. It is merely convict economic activity which a Family member is engaged in as an individual convict. The member normally would draw upon Family funds only for a large, Family deal.

The differentiation of organization and leadership indicated above reflects the degree to which the prisoners' economic activity involves specialized statuses corresponding with the three levels of the prisoner culture. Inmates occupy the lowest position of economic rank and leadership. Economically, they are powerless, frequently being used and abused by all other types of prisoners. Convicts are intermediate between inmates and Family. Due to the vital role they play in production and distribution of goods and services, convicts have a small degree of power and normally avoid being economically abused by other prisoners. Family occupies the highest position of economic rank and leadership. Family's status carries not only privileges, but responsibilities. For example, Family takes great care to maintain accurate records of its activities. This is necessary to maintain the integrity of Family's word in an economy where written contracts and documents do not exist. In addition, Family recognizes its responsibility to the convict population and normally deals with convicts in a cooperative, nonabusive manner, allowing them to realize reasonable profits from their efforts. Or, as noted in Chapter 5 (full details will be given later in this chapter), Family assumes the responsibility of maintaining a "Chicano Fund" to be used for worthy Chicano prisoners in need of assistance, regardless of whether they are Family members or not. Consequently, one can see that Family exerts a positive, stabilizing influence over certain aspects of the prisoner culture. In return, Family members enjoy the fruits of their most favored economic position.

*Resources*

The prisoners' production of goods and services draws upon a vast wealth of material resources that are purchased and owned by the state. Prisoners treat most of these state-owned resources much like many hunters and gatherers treat the natural resources of their habitat. Among both, the resources are viewed as given, and potentially exploitable by any individual or group. Usually no strict sense of individual or corporate ownership is exercised over most of the resources; and only after individuals or groups take possession of some of them, through their personal efforts, do the particular resources become owned. Once prisoners establish personal or corporate possession, the resources are recognized as private property by other prisoners. According to the nature of the resources, they can be made available to others, used in production of goods or services, or sold to others for manufacturing purposes. Prisoners frequently are apprehended while privately possessing state-owned resources. At that time, possession of the resources usually reverts back to the state; but they simultaneously again, become part of the vast wealth of given material resources which are potentially exploitable by the prisoners. Even though this type of reversion may occur frequently, the private possession of state-owned resources by prisoners is of such great magnitude that acts of confiscation by staff have little practical impact on this aspect of the prisoner economy.

In order to possess and use these state-owned resources, a prisoner must have access to them. Access can be accomplished in several ways. One's prison assignment can mean legal access to state-owned resources; and, through such an approach, legal goods can be transformed into contraband. If one does not have direct, legal access, his friendship or connection with those who do may allow an indirect pathway to the resources. Or, one may have sufficient knowledge, connections, and ability to gain illegal access to certain state-owned resources that are beyond the legal means of any prisoners.

The state does not supply the prison with the complete range of resources that may be desired by prisoners. Thus, prisoners must draw upon the legal and illegal resources available for purchase on the streets to satisfy their needs; and, regardless of whether the goods originate from legal or illegal sources on the streets, such activity is considered illegal by staff. Not all prisoners have access to resources from the streets; for the lack of two necessary prerequisites—money and connections. At this point, a detailed description of prisoner money is necessary. It will be followed by a description of economic connections.

*Three Types of Money*

There are three types of prisoner money: ducats, cigarettes, and cash. Ducats are the only legal type of money inside. Legally, they are used only for the purchase of goods from the canteen. Ducats are the pressed paper token money that is issued to a prisoner when he makes a draw from his inmate account. But not all prisoners have funds from which to make such a draw. Consequently, not all prisoners are able to use this type of money, nor are they legally able to buy goods which the canteen offers. In addition, since staff carefully control the use of ducats by the prisoner who actually makes the draw, ducats normally can be used only by that prisoner. The exception to this rule would be when a prisoner— through debt or some sort of obligation—gives all or most of his draw to a convict. Often he would be obliged to make numerous purchases of particular canteen items for the convict each month. Rather than be bothered with this, the prisoner might ask the convict if he could arrange to use his (the prisoner's) ducats. The convict will arrange to have a false privilege card made for himself, with the prisoner's number on it, to enable illegal use of the prisoner's ducats. Obviously, the debt or obligation has to be a major, long-term one to warrant this effort. Except for this single illegal use of ducats, it can be seen that ducats are useless as a medium of exchange for the purchase of prisoner-produced goods and servcies.

Inside, except for ducats, all forms of money are illegal and subject to confiscation upon discovery by staff. This is done to discourage all prisoner economic activity other than the legal use of the canteen by qualified prisoners. The prisoners are left without a legal medium of exchange to use as payment for goods and services that are produced by other prisoners. However, this has not discouraged or stopped prisoners, for they have had two types of illegal money to serve their purposes for a long time: cigarettes and cash. In general, cigarettes are used for small-scale economic transactions, and cash is used for large-scale ones.

Normally, the canteen serves as the source of cigarettes used as money by prisoners. In this respect, legal canteen goods are used for illegal ends. In addition, there are illegal means by which a prisoner without funds may obtain legal ducats; hence, he acts as a source of additional cigarette money through the use of the canteen. In these instances, the prisoners make arrangements for "approved" persons on the streets to send money to the prisoner's "inmate" account so that he can make a legal draw on it each month. If a prisoner has legal ducats, regardless of how they have been obtained, he may purchase cigarettes at the canteen.

Cigarettes are sold either by the package or by the carton, and the price is comparable to the price on the streets. A prisoner is legally allowed to smoke the cigarettes; but if he purchases more than a couple of packs at a time, he must take them to his cell as soon as possible. This rule is designed to discourage or stop the prisoners from using cigarettes as money. If a bull should catch a prisoner outside his cell with more than two packs in his possession (an amount considered reasonable for one day of personal use), the prisoner must be able to prove that he has just purchased the cigarettes that day and has not returned to his cell yet. Without a dated canteen receipt for proof, any cigarettes in excess of the limit are considered contraband and are subject to confiscation by staff. The same is true of all cigarettes in excess of the reasonable reserve of three cartons which a prisoner is allowed to have in his cell. Therefore, any time a prisoner is caught with more than the reasonable amounts noted above, staff assume that the cigarettes are being used as money. Although confiscation of excess cigarettes may impose hardship on the individual prisoner, it does little to discourage the use of cigarettes as money because prisoners are seldom caught using them as such. As sold at the canteen, cigarettes have a known value and are generally accepted as a medium of exchange by prisoners. Hence, all cigarettes are potentially usable as money; and cigarettes held in excess of the reasonable volume are obviously money.

Packs of cigarettes are used by prisoners as coins and dollars are used on the streets. Cartons are used much like 5, 10, 20, and 50 dollar bills. Although the denominations of cigarette monetary units do not directly accord with those of United States legal tender, the conversion is easily accomplished by prisoners. Normally, as the size of the transaction reaches about $100 or so, cigarettes are less likely to be used. For example, the sheer bulk of 20 to 25 cartons would make a transaction for that amount unnecessarily risky. Such transactions can be handled on a cash basis with much less chance of being detected by staff.

Possession of cash (legal tender) is illegal inside. Staff have tried to stop or discourage its use. However, they have failed, for cash is brought in through a variety of channels. The majority of it filters in through visitors in small amounts of $50 or $100. This source is quite extensive. For example, if a prisoner has bills to pay, what can he do if he has already used his monthly draw? Instead of letting interest pile up and in order to avoid getting into potential trouble over it, he has someone bring money in to him—assuming he has a friend who can and will do it. A 50 or 100 dollar bill can be folded very small and tied inside a finger stall (the finger tip portion of a rubber glove). It can be passed inconspicuously; and if need be, the prisoner can put it in his mouth, or even swallow it, to get it back in from the visiting room.

Another less frequently used way cash is brought in is by the bulls. When this method is used, the amount tends to be much larger though, ranging up to several thousand dollars. Any bull who is "running" (bringing contraband goods in) for convicts or Family also will bring cash in. Usually, the bull will pick up the money, on the streets, from any of the various sources specified to him by the prisoners. He will bring it in; and when he turns the money over, he gets $50 for every $500 that he brings in. Some bulls don't like to make the actual pickup and want the money sent to them. However, there are negative aspects to having the money sent, for it must be sent by registered mail to protect the interests of those involved. Consequently, a receipt exists after the operation has been completed. There are other methods to get cash in; but, from the examples given, it can be seen that getting cash into prison is not very difficult. If an inmate has money on the outside, but no way to get it in, there are those who will gladly do it for him—for a percentage.

Although it is a bit of a digression, a similar situation should be noted here. If prisoners want money sent out to the streets, the reverse process is possible. When the bull takes the money out, he gets a receipt for delivering it. When he returns the receipt that shows the money has been delivered, he receives $50 for every $300 delivered. His percentage is higher for taking cash out than for bringing it in because of the increased risk involved in making a pickup inside; for once the cash is picked up, the bull is committed to taking it out that day. If the administration should suspect him of "running" for prisoners, it is relatively easy for them to set him up with marked bills and catch him taking the cash out. In contrast, when bringing cash in, he does it on the day of his choosing, avoiding the necessity of bringing it in on any particular day; and since bulls are almost never searched when they come in, this is relatively safe.

The lesser denominations of cash are not necessary inside, since cigarettes function adequately for smaller economic transactions. Normally, if one is going to go to the effort and risk of bringing cash in, he may as well make it worthwhile. After all, a $100 or $50 bill folds up just as small as a one dollar bill. Consequently, the most common bills inside are of 100, 50, and 20 dollar denominations. Occasionally a ten dollar bill might be brought in, but five and one dollar bills are almost nonexistent inside.

Normally, on an average weekend day, there is a great amount of cash money available in the yard. As an illustration, assume that Family, as a group, through great pressure, is pushed to come up with $100,000 cash. On an average Saturday morning, in the yard, Family could probably come up with almost that amount from its own stashes and creditors. If Family happened to be $10,000 or $15,000 short, it could easily borrow the rest at a three-for-two interest rate.

The ability of convicts to get cash is quite limited in comparison. However, a convict with a good credit rating could probably *borrow* $10,000 on a 90-day loan at three for two. To get a loan of this size would probably necessitate some questions being asked by Family and the personal backing of the convict's partner. Without questions and involvement of a convict partner, the convict could probably borrow $6,000 on similar repayment terms. A few convicts have excellent business connections, fine credit ratings, and many business activities going for themselves. On an average Saturday morning, if necessary, one of these convicts could easily pick up from $900 to $1,800 of his own funds from creditors and stashes. If he was really pushed hard, he might be able to get $2,500.

In striking contrast, inmates have *very* little—both in cash and ability to borrow. The average inmate is living on his draw. He might be able to borrow a sum equivalent to his draw. However, any amount above that would have to be insured by some other source of income—such as access to materials at his job. Even in such cases, it would be doubtful that he could ever borrow much over what he would get in two or three draws. These rather strict limitations are based on the fact that inmates are unable to hustle for any significant amount above what they draw. In contrast, convicts (owing to their ability to hustle) are often given credit above their actual resources.

### Economic Connections

Having treated prisoner money, let us now consider the economic connections that allow prisoners indirect access to resources of the streets. An economic connection may consist of a single individual—such as a visitor—who brings in relatively small amounts of goods to a single prisoner. However, the larger, more economically significant connections tend to be more complex in nature. Often, several individuals are involved in a single operation which draws upon illegal resources available on the streets. It should be noted that these connections also are used to bring cash money in, or take it out, as described in the above discussion of money.

The simplest connection is the visitor who, as a friend or relative, brings goods in to a prisoner. Usually a relatively small amount of narcotics for personal use is involved. The visitor puts the narcotics in a finger stall and ties it tightly into a very small package. This is inconspicuously passed to the prisoner while they visit. The prisoner will put the package in his mouth to avoid detection, swallowing it if necessary. If he does swallow it, and if the package contains narcotics, he will force himself to vomit it out as soon as he gets to his cell. Otherwise, there is the possibility that the rubber will be eaten away as it passes through him; and if so, it would probably result in a fatal overdose. When receiving money this way, the vomiting is not a matter of urgency, but merely a convenience; for the money will pass through the prisoner intact if he cannot vomit it out.

Although a variety of numerous economically significant connections exist, a major portion of the contraband brought into the prison is transported by a single type of individual—the "runner." Consequently, by using the runner as an example, the complexity which often exists in large connections and the monetary value which may be involved in these operations will become evident. The runner is merely the bull who brings the contraband into the prison for the prisoners. He is merely one individual who is paid to perform a single task. His task is merely one of several which must be successfully linked to make a complete connection.

A typical connection to bring in a shipment of narcotics might involve a number of people and tasks. An individual on the streets develops a source for purchasing narcotics. Another individual visits a Family member, relating details which will be further developed at a later visit. A Family member is the link to funds that will be used to purchase the narcotics. He also is the link to a convict. This convict is the individual who deals directly with the runner, giving him instructions as to when, where, and how the goods are to be picked up. He also gives the runner Family's cash to buy the goods. The individual on the streets delivers the goods to the runner at a certain place. The runner picks up and pays for the goods. Later the runner brings the goods in, inside his lunch pail. He gives the narcotics to the convict with whom he deals. The convict pays the runner for performing his task and delivers the goods to the Family member with whom he deals. There may be a greater or lesser number of tasks and individuals involved, and fewer or more of the individuals may be Family members. However, when the individuals and tasks listed for this typical connection are compared with the simplicity of the single visitor connection, the possible range of complexity which may exist in an economic connection is apparent.

Many of the things a runner may do are briefly indicated in the above description of a typical narcotics connection. Now, if the money bulls are paid for running contraband is considered, it will be possible to project from that amount to the much larger actual value of the goods that they bring in. This may not be a precise method of valuation; however, it does suggest the volume of contraband that is brought in by the runners—and they account for a major portion of the smuggling. As many as 30 bulls may be running for prisoners at any one time. Usually a bull will net about $10,000 for a year of running. This is always undeclared, tax-free income. After about a year, the possibility of the bull getting busted increases; so a bull usually will back off and quit for three or four years, until he finds himself in a financial pinch or is pressured into resuming such activities by prisoners. The irregular timing of the runs makes this activity relatively safe for about a year. However, roughly 10 percent of the bulls who run do get caught. Those who are actually caught and convicted in court are usually the ones who (through their ignorance) have been dealing with inmates. When pressed, inmates are often willing to testify against the bull in court, in order to further their own ends. However, if the bull is caught running for a convict, staff can never expect to base any part of their case on the testimony of the convict; for convicts will not testify. The one exceptional convict who did testify against a bull in court lost his right to be considered a convict ever again.

Occasionally, a bull who is running will net as much as $50,000 or $60,000 in a year. When this happens, the bull usually quits his job. Once a bull brought in about $300,000 worth of narcotics at one time (a several months supply for the prisoners). He received $60,000 for his effort. He quit a short time later; and if his considerable earnings from earlier that year are included, his running probably netted him close to $100,000 that year.

At times, through the irregularity of the runs and the cessation of activity by some bulls, the supply of drugs and other contraband may become quite slim. Almost every year at about Christmas time, things tighten up; and the supply of drugs diminishes. The staff keep an extra careful watch over things at this time each year. Bulls and visitors are reluctant to run for the prisoners, and the supply normally dries up for about three weeks. During these slim times, those who are addicted may be cramped to maintain their habits; and some may end up shooting some rather strange drugs. The only exception to this is Family; for even though there may be nothing for sale, there is almost always enough available for the personal use of Family members.

In addition to the contraband that is brought in by bulls and visitors, a considerable amount enters in other ways. Let it suffice to note that the numerous other ways are diverse in nature. Some are astonishing in their simplicity, while others are extremely involved. They are the product of human ingenuity and planning at their finest.

Inmates seldom have either connections for access to resources of the streets or much money. Normally their cash is limited and precludes the purchase of goods and services other than those that are produced and distributed by other prisoners.

In those instances where an inmate does have a connection, such as a friend or relative who visits him, the amount of goods brought in is almost always limited to a quantity sufficient for personal use only. Or, the connection may be used just to bring in money from the inmate's outside sources; this enables the inmate to purchase goods and services produced by other prisoners. In rare instances, an inmate without funds may have a connection who will bring some goods in to fulfill reciprocal obligations, but the quantity is usually minimal. Even if an inmate should have adequate funds to purchase goods, the volume usually would still be limited to the personal use level; for inmates are never able to develop a satisfactory mechanism for distributing and selling goods inside. If he should attempt to do so on a retail basis, one, or several, of the inmates with whom he would be forced to deal would probably snitch on him. And, if he should try to wholesale it, through a gunsel, to a more organized dealer on the convict or Family level (who can afford to buy and distribute it), the absence of competitive bidding for the goods would force him to accept a very low offer. His profit would be so small that he would be discouraged from making similar attempts in the future, for the risk would not be worth it. Hence, it can be seen that the inmates' limited ability to draw upon the resources of the streets has little if any impact on the larger prisoner economy.

With convicts, the situation is different. Convicts have, or are able to develop, viable contacts with the streets. They have enough money to purchase the volume of goods that normally is brought in through the larger, more complex connections. It is not worth the effort and risk to bring in small amounts. They have enough convict or convictlike friends or associates (who will not snitch) to be able to make the numerous necessary contacts and coordinate the efforts of the several individuals involved in an operation. The initial establishment of such a connection may involve considerable risks to the individual convict. He may get busted, or he might lose his financial investment. Consequently, smaller shipments are used initially to test a connection. However, such ventures are regarded as legitimate business risks by convicts. These calculated risks are worth it; for after a connection has been tested and firmly established, the element of danger is greatly diminished; and the convict's contact can become a key element in a successful business enterprise. Also, as with small business ventures on the streets, the connection may prove attractive to others who have sufficient funds to purchase and expand or incorporate the venture into big business. Or, if the convict should find himself in a tight financial spot, he might even ask Family to buy the connection. In this respect, a privately developed and owned productive resource can become a marketable asset. However, a convict, or even a clique of convicts, seldom has enough money to develop and fully exploit more than one connection at a time. In fact, perhaps the initial money used to develop a connection or operation was borrowed from Family. Although convicts do adhere strictly to the convict code, they are quite individualistic in their economic enterprises. They do not have the strong, corporatelike unity which would allow them to successfully pool their resources and turn their business ventures into big business.

## Family's Economic Power

As the earlier descriptions of certain aspects of Family's economic affairs have shown, Family's business is truly big business. Family's ability to gain its corporatelike financial strength and economic power has been made possible through its possession of an additional, but indispensable resource—unity. Each member's loyalty and self-subordination to the group is absolutely required. The vital necessity of maintaining this unity is reflected in Family's ultimate sanction against those who would betray it—that sanction being death. And, as seen from within, members realize that Family would not be able to succeed or survive without its extreme unity.

The Chicano convicts who formed Family pooled their resources; and as Family grew in size, its financial strength and economic power also grew. In the prisoner economy, Family is like a single corporate giant among the small business proprietorships and partnerships of inmates and convicts. Its relatively vast collective wealth and contacts enable it to develop or buy, own or control, and fully exploit the majority of existing large economic connections, either directly or indirectly.

As a result, Family has gained both a monopoly over most major sources of contraband goods and an ability to control the price of many goods and services. Family's position and role in the prisoner economy is such that all significant amounts of money ultimately come under Family's control. All major loans, either directly or indirectly, go through Family. Family is the financial institution of the prisoner economy. In fact, Family is somewhat comparable to an international economic power, for it even controls the value of prisoner money. If one does not understand Family's economic role and how Family maintains its apparently invincible position, one will never fully understand the prisoner economy. Family's unity is only one key to that understanding. Another key is Family's ability to control the value of prisoner money.

Since it controls most cash money, cigarette money, and contraband goods, Family is able to manipulate and regulate the value of prisoner money. Since ducats have an actual cash value, their use for the purchase of cigarettes at the canteen establishes an actual cash value for cigarettes too. Normally, there is a definite exchange rate between cash and cigarette money. Either type of money can be used to buy contraband goods at their normal price. For example, $35 worth of goods can be paid for with cash, or with ten cartons of cigarettes worth $3.50 a carton, or with some combination of the two. However, Family is able to set the value of either type of prisoner money. Members refer to this manipulation as the "turning" of money. When Family turns money, it is able to decrease its effective value or purchasing power. For example, Family is able to force prisoners who have only cash money to exchange their cash for cigarettes. This is done by Family's refusal to accept cash money as payment for contraband goods which it controls. All prisoners with cash money, if they want to purchase contraband goods, must pay an inflated exchange rate for cigarette money—as much as twice the normal rate. During this process, the canteen price of cigarettes remains the same—$3.50 worth of ducats for a carton. Also, the price of contraband goods remains the same—$35 worth of goods still costs 10 cartons. The only difference is that cash is not accepted. Prisoners must turn cash into cigarettes; and if the value of cash has been cut in half by Family, it will take $70 in cash to exchange for $35 worth of cigarettes. In effect, a prisoner with cash must really pay double the price for the same goods. Or, seen another way, Family acquires half of the prisoner's money when it exchanges his cash for cigarettes. Since Family controls the exchange process, it is obvious that a considerable amount of cash comes to Family quite rapidly; and the cash reserves held by prisoners are rapidly diminished.

The prisoners who have no cash, just cigarettes to spend, are not affected by this turning of money. For such a prisoner, ten cartons of cigarettes, which normally are worth $35, still buy $35 worth of goods. However, if Family turns money the other way, his ten cartons might exchange for only $17.50 worth of cash money, allowing him to purchase only that amount of contraband goods.

Family turns money when it finds itself in either of the following situations: it needs to rapidly reap enormous profits, or it needs to eliminate a potential economic threat from other prisoners. In order to illustrate the first situation, assume that Family's funds in San Quentin have run low. By turning money, Family can rapidly increase its funds and make in one week as much as it might normally take a month to make. Since Family controls the majority of contraband goods, it tightens up on the release of these goods, even though it may have an abundant supply in stock. When the purchaser approaches his prisoner connection, from whom he buys contraband goods, he is told that there is too much cash on hand, that it is not worth much now, and that only cigarettes can be accepted as payment. The purchaser then goes to a prisoner connection he knows who exchanges money for a small, normal fee of 5 packs for every $10 or $15. When he tries to exchange his cash for cigarettes at the normal rate, he again is told that there is too much cash on hand and that cigarettes are scarce; and if he really wants cigarettes, they will cost him $7 a carton, instead of the normal $3.50. In reality, most of what he is told is not true. Both of his prisoner connections—for purchase of goods and for exchange of money—are working either directly or indirectly for Family; and, as their part in the turning process, they purposely manipulate the purchaser. If cash is not worth much to most prisoners now, it is only because of Family's manipulation. Normal amounts of both cash and cigarettes are on hand among prisoners; it is only Family that is experiencing a shortage of funds. In addition, either type of money could be accepted as payment; but through Family's arbitrary refusal to accept one type, all prisoners who have only that type to use for purchases of Family goods end up paying double for their goods. Each time money is turned, Family acquires half of it in the process. With the passage of time, Family obtains most of the prisoners' cash; and a shortage of cash develops among most prisoners.

Since prisoners have no idea how long this situation will exist, part of their time and effort is devoted to converting any cash they have or receive into cigarette money. However, without any warning, perhaps two days or a week later, Family might reverse the process, turning money the other way. Suddenly prisoners cannot buy anything with cigarette money, because Family will accept only cash money for its contraband goods. Now the cigarette-owning prisoner, who was not affected by the first turning, finds that his cigarette money is virtually cut in half when he turns it into cash money. But the prisoner who had cash money before the first turning is in even worse shape. He has been turning cash into cigarettes in order to make a purchase. Suddenly he finds that a carton of his very costly cigarettes ($7 cash per carton when earlier acquired in exchange) now is worth only $1.75 when exchanged back into cash money. Earlier, his money had been cut in half by the first turning—the turned money having only half of its original purchasing power. Now, all of the money that he has to turn a second time loses half of its purchasing power again, and therefore has only one quarter of its original purchasing power. So, without selling any goods, Family has acquired three quarters of the prisoner's twice-turned money; and when the prisoner does make his purchase, Family will make its normal profit on the sale. Since Family deals in volume business, it is obvious that Family makes an enormous profit every time it turns money.

In exceptional cases, a few special prisoners may be allowed to purchase goods with cash, even though, at that time, cash is not being accepted by Family as payment for goods. Usually these individuals are very steady customers who have a drug habit. Since the exchanging of money is time-consuming and either considerably inconvenient or difficult for these prisoners to accomplish, they are allowed to buy their narcotics with cash. However, they pay for the privilege; they often are charged as much as three times the normal price. At these times, their cash is worth only one-third its face value. But, if money is turned two or more times, even the tripled price is not excessive in comparison with what other prisoners ultimately pay.

The second situation which gives rise to Family's turning of money is when Family needs to eliminate a potential economic threat from other prisoners. The following example will deal with the retail stores that are set up in cells throughout most of the prison. Inmates normally run most of the stores. In a few cases, they may have some funds to invest and may actually supply their own goods from the canteen. However, in these cases, the stores tend to be exceptionally small. Usually the inmate uses his investment to buy goods from a convict wholesale supplier (often on a partial consignment basis), who supplies a number of stores. Or, a convict may actually own many stores and just have inmates fronting them for him. Normally, the stores sell canteen items at inflated prices. Cigarettes almost always are used to pay for the relatively small purchases, and most of the sales are on credit.

Assume that many of the prisoners involved in the operation of stores have begun to set aside bankrolls in either cash or cigarettes. If enough of these prisoners were able to save considerable amounts, they might be able to join together and form a competitive, threatening force. When this situation arises, Family uses the turning of money as a protective economic leveling device. This turning of money will usually wipe out all the savings held by most non-Family prisoners and virtually bankrupt almost all stores. Usually all stores close immediately because those who run or own them know what will happen. If a prisoner should somehow survive the turning of money, his savings will have been so greatly diminished that he will no longer pose any threat to Family. As a result, only Family and a few convicts who work closely with Family are in a position to establish new stores.

To fully understand the actual details of this situation, one first must try to realize how extensively prisoners use credit in their economy. On the streets, free people purchase a vast number of goods and services on credit. Producers, wholesalers, and retailers routinely extend credit to their customers. It is rare when goods from a producer to a wholesaler, or goods from a wholesaler to a retailer are paid for with cash. Most free people budget their income and have a fairly good idea how most of it will be used. In prison, the situation is no different. Producers, wholesalers, and retailers routinely deal in credit. The greatest sales and profits are reaped by giving credit. Individual prisoners carefully budget their income. They know exactly how much will be necessary for things such as loan payments, vital or important goods from Family, and cigarettes and toilet articles for personal consumption. If possible, there will be a bit left over to budget for store goodies. As do many free people, prisoners often will have used credit throughout the month; and when their monthly income is received, most of it is almost immediately paid out to creditors. Accordingly, prisoners will go to great efforts to protect their credit standing; for the ability to purchase goods and services on credit and to borrow money is very important to them.

Let us assume a situation wherein several store owners pose an economic threat to Family. Then suppose that Family turns money so that the value of cigarettes is diminished by one half and only cash is accepted as payment for Family goods. Immediately, all prisoners will scramble to get cigarettes to convert into cash. A shortage of both types of money will develop immediately, for prisoners are aware of this unstable situation. Since the effective purchasing power of prisoners who rely on their draw (turning their ducats into cigarette money) for their income has been cut in half for all noncanteen purchases, they will not have enough net funds to cover the credit items in their budget. Even those who have a cash income are afraid to make any purchases that are not entirely necessary, for they know that money might be turned the other way at any time. Consequently, all prisoners hoard any money they can, as a hedge against present problems and future uncertainties. All unnecessary expenditures are limited, for most prisoners have obligatory payments or purchases to make. All goods and services that have been bought on credit from convicts or Family, as well as all loans made through Family, *must* be paid on time to protect the prisoners' credit standings. Some debts have to go unpaid, so most prisoners just forget about the relatively small amounts they owe to the inmates who run or own the stores, because these inmates pose no real threat to them physically, or to their credit standings.

Prisoners are aware that these things will happen. Therefore, most stores disappear almost overnight. Inmate owners usually save what stock they have on hand for their own use, and they end up owing the convict wholesaler for these and the other goods that have been sold on credit and were to have been paid for upon receipt of the cigarettes from the customers. If, under rare circumstances, an inmate owner has some reserves, he might possibly use them to pay the convict wholesaler. However, the inmate normally is unable to pay much, if anything at all, to the wholesaler. The convict will harass the inmate owner, but the inmate is in no position to collect from all the prisoners who happen to owe him a small amount. However, to the convict wholesaler, the many small amounts add up to a large amount; and he usually loses most of it. The convict who has several inmates fronting stores for him is not in a much better position. He, too, is unable either directly or indirectly to collect most of the cigarettes that are owed to his stores. Both the convict owner and the convict wholesaler (regardless of their inability to collect for the goods that they have sold on credit) still owe Family for those goods—which they, too, purchased on credit. The convicts must protect their credit standings with Family if they want to continue conducting business in the prisoner economy. Therefore, if they have reserves, the convicts use them to pay Family. And, if the reserves are in cigarette money (which has diminished value), they are wiped out twice as fast.

If Family reverses the turning of money, the value of cash is cut in half and only cigarettes can be used to buy contraband. The immediate effect on the operation of stores essentially is the same as discussed above. Due to the scarcity of money which rapidly develops, the cigarette money that is owed to inmates who run or own stores is the first part of a prisoner's budget that gives. Most stores disappear overnight. Convict store owners and wholesalers must pay Family for the goods they bought on credit; even though they cannot collect for them. This time reserves in cash money are wiped out twice as fast as cigarette money reserves.

Theoretically, an outsider might argue that if a prisoner has sufficient reserves to absorb his credit losses when money is turned, he should be able to keep his store open. If money is turned so that the value of cash is cut, it should have a minimal impact on the stores, since retail sales are made in cigarette money and wholesale purchases are made in cigarette money. But if money is turned the other way, with the value of cigarettes being cut in half, the situation would obviously be unprofitable; because the half-valued cigarettes from sales would not be of sufficient value even to restock the store. In practice though, it is a very rare exception when a prisoner's store is able to survive the turning of money without some sort of aid from Family, because *the extent of credit sales is truly great.* If this exception should occur, and if the prisoner should try to raise his prices to offset some of his losses, *many* prisoners would find it profitable to open *very* small stores. Collectively, they would drive the prices down. However, the prisoner probably would not even try to raise his prices, because Family or Family-backed stores would be open, selling goods at the normal rate to a limited number of reliable, large volume customers. Family's small loss of profit involved in backing these stores is more than offset by the profit realized in other business deals with these customers. Also, this helps Family to maintain good business relationships. Of those very few store owners who might possibly survive the turning of money, probably only one in a hundred would even try to stay open. And if he were to succeed, he would have to limit his sales to a very small circle of immediate friends. Also, his success would be costly; his reserves would be so greatly reduced that he would not be economically significant to Family any more. In other words, any large store that manages to survive the turning of money suddenly is small.

Family's power enables it to wipe out almost all stores within less than 24 hours. After the stores have gone bankrupt, Family may aid selected convicts to set up new stores. In some cases, Family will selectively and confidentially pass the word of a forthcoming turning of money to certain close convicts, allowing them to prepare for and survive the money switch. These convicts may do a variety of things, such as quietly closing their businesses and pocketing the immediately available profit. This way, they have their own saved funds, allowing them to open up rapidly when businesses begin to reappear. The sooner they open, the greater their profits. These convicts are not leveled, and they do not have to go to Family for funds to finance a new business. In addition, there even have been times that Family has set up its own stores. Regardless of which method is used, Family is capable of closing all the stores one day, of stocking new stores, and of having them open the next day. It should be noted that the convicts who run the newly opened stores operate at a reduced volume of sales and are very careful. Until things settle down and the majority of prisoners solve their personal budgetary problems, sales are limited to selected, reliable customers. Family does not level the prisoners economically and close the stores as a deliberate show of power. Only once did Family close down prisoner businesses—for about three days—just to prove its power to some who seriously questioned it and threatened Family economically.

Regardless of whether Family turns money to reap rapid, enormous profits or to eliminate a potential economic threat from other prisoners, the effects always are the same: Family both increases its funds dramatically and levels the reserve funds held by most non-Family prisoners to virtually nothing. The two situations related above show some of the results of Family's turning of money. Countless examples and details could further illustrate what occurs, but other considerations preclude their use at this time. Let it be noted though, that all non-Family prisoners who have reserves of goods follow Family's lead. For example, they, too, will accept only cash if Family turns money that way. They would have to be insane to accept cigarettes, when cigarettes effectively are only worth one half their normal value. And, since these prisoners have no idea when Family will reverse the turning of money, they have no way to protect themselves. They soon are caught holding the wrong type of prisoner money.

The manner in which Family controls the value of money may strike many as being a deliberate, brazen abuse of the other prisoners. However, Family members feel that their manipulation of the other prisoners and the prisoner economy is no worse, and no more abusive, than the manipulation by big business of the consumers and the economy on the streets. They think that the greater extent and complexity of the economy of the streets enables big business to conceal its maneuvering more effectively. But just like most people on the streets, inmates are largely unaware of the extent to which they actually are manipulated. For example, most inmates do not understand what is really going on when Family turns money. They have been told that "there is too much cigarette money in the yard," and they believe that explanation. Most inmates have come to accept the turning of money; and their reaction to it is rather mild—stronger than, but comparable to, the way the average person on the streets reacts to the higher prices for many consumer goods during the Christmas shopping season.

As seen from within, Family's economic power is not really abusive in nature. In fact, Family has given great stability to the prisoner economy. Family has increased the routine volume of goods available for all prisoners, making more goods available at lower prices than would be otherwise. Even though the vast number of inmate consumers do pay the price and support convicts and Family, the actual standard of living of *all* prisoners is increased. True, Family may level the prisoners' reserves periodically when it is necessary for its own economic well being; and occasionally a convict, who has tried to become too big economically, will strongly resent being leveled. However, the bulls have always done the same, on a less effective, hit-and-miss basis. Before Family, when a convict was wiped out by being busted by a bull, it would take him a long time to accumulate enough to allow him to go back into business and begin making a reasonable profit to support his personal standard of living. Now, Family's substantial wealth allows it to immediately finance convicts in new business enterprises after they have been leveled. In fact, many convicts who are working for Family actually share in the excessive profit made when money is turned. With Family's extensive activities, there is a vast amount of profit to be made by all of those involved in the many aspects of production and distribution of goods and services—Family, convicts, and gunsels. In its economic decisions, Family exercises a high degree of consideration for convicts; and as long as they do not become an economic threat, Family generously shares the profit with them. Most convicts and gunsels are beholden to Family; for they ultimately are allowed to share in the prosperity brought about by Family's economic strength and stability.

*Division of Labor*  Having discussed Family's unity and its ability to control the value of prisoner money (both of which are keys to understanding Family's economic role and how it maintains its apparently invincible position), let us now consider division of labor among the prisoners. Division of labor involves an allocation of manpower which systematizes various phases of many productive activities. On the streets, division of labor is based on factors such as age, sex, caste, and special skills. In prison, the determinants would include the following: access to materials, or tools, or areas—which might be made possible through classification or job assignment; special abilities or skills of an individual; and the level of the prisoner culture on which such organization of work takes place. The individualistic nature of inmate economic activities precludes any real division of labor on that level. On the convict level though, there may be some grouping into cliques, allowing a small degree of division of labor to exist. However, those possessing a special ability or skill usually are not able to fully develop or exploit it as a full-time specialist in prisoner economic activities, because they also must hustle and do other things in order to maintain a steady income. Consequently, this limited, partial division of labor has little impact on the prisoner economy.

Only Family, by exercising its unity, power, and resources, is able to make full use of specialists—often on a full-time basis. Family's organizational structure enables it to exert authority in the allocation of tasks, making possible the utmost efficiency in the production of goods and services. Certain productive activities demand coordinated efforts and considerable organization according to special ability or skill. In many instances, this has led to a very strict division of labor, with some specialists being required to do nothing but their specialty for Family. In fact, some specialists are so technically skilled and vital to Family operations that they are not even allowed to go out and hustle for their own personal needs. They are protected from the nominal risk involved; all of their needs and desires are more than adequately filled for them by Family. Considering the strong feelings of equality among Family members and the very diplomatic way in which leadership normally has to be exercised among Chicanos, it often is a difficult task to convince a member that he should specialize, or that someone else is better suited to accomplish a particular task. This must be done in a very subtle, low-key manner, so that the individual is asked, not told, to do or not to do something. Fortunately there are those among Family who are able to do this successfully. All Family members realize that these imposed restrictions, or obligations, or tasks are advantageous, for ultimately they are the ones who share the fruits of their greater productivity.

Certain prison jobs are quite important to Family in its production of goods and services; and a prisoner who holds one of these jobs can prove to be a necessary specialist in one of Family's enterprises. Even though they may not be Family members, these prisoners are supported by Family and allowed to contribute their specialty, without having to hustle for most of their own consumer goods. If one of these jobs is filled by a prisoner who cannot be trusted, or who will not cooperate, Family will make a very reasonable offer to buy the prisoner out of the job. If the offer is not accepted (a very rare and unwise decision), other more forceful arrangements will be made to create a vacancy in the position. This allows another prisoner to be assigned to the job—a prisoner who will cooperate and can be trusted.

It must be noted that some of these specialists often are king in their own domain. At the same time, however, they might be a dud in other fields. Occasionally a non-Family convict with a desired specialty becomes a direct part of Family's productive activities, but only if his involvement is not too deep. In this way, Family draws upon the skills of convicts and allows them to be specialists —for Family. Also, some Family members who are excellent hustlers, with an adept ability to think and decide quickly on their feet, may specialize even further —in either buying or selling. For example, some are better loan men than others; for in a system without written contracts or applications, it takes a certain knack and a quick mind to juggle figures, quote alternatives, and still be able to see through an applicant's story if necessary. A number of prisoners are just good at stealing; they possess an ability to walk off with almost anything that is portable. A few weapons procurers specialize in keeping connections established for such purposes. The weapons makers are not only highly skilled, but often quite inventive. Some members are experts at cutting dope. One convict has a truly unique ability as a scorekeeper in a craps game. He is able to keep all scores for up to and including 11 players—in his head! The game can go on for hours, with players coming and going and side bets being placed, but paper to record scores is not necessary. Nor is there any need for money on the floor. The only things necessary are the pair of dice and this man's ability. It should be noted that this "king of scorekeepers" can*not* read!

An additional, necessary element for Family's successful exploitation of its economic resources is its concern for punctuality. It is interesting to note that this concern is exhibited among many Chicano convicts, too. Family and non-Family Chicanos have learned (both on the streets and inside) that being punctual is *very* important in economic activities. It is estimated that roughly 60 percent of the Chicanos inside would be conscious of, and act according to, the need to be punctual. This seems to contrast sharply with some Chicanos on the streets who use, and jokingly refer to, "Chicano time." These latter individuals often are involved in the current social-political movement and are members of various Chicano organizations. In these circles being ten, twenty, or even thirty minutes late is quite acceptable, and often quite normal. In fact, some seem to take pride in their ability to consistently be late. A Family member commented on this disparity. He thought that it is those who think that they are rising above other Chicanos in the outside society that acquire this attitude toward time. He felt that it might be an unconscious attempt at one-upmanship over the Anglos, who often are a few minutes late to social gatherings. However, regardless of what is behind it, this social-political attitude, reflected in "Chicano time," certainly is not based on the economic necessity that governs the attitude of those on the grass-roots level, such as Family members.

*Family Specialties* The complexity of factors that have determined which goods and services are produced in volume, coupled with the unity and organization needed to provide this volume on a routine basis, have led Family to emphasize certain activities over others. Family has become identified with four of these activities, which have come to be regarded as Family specialties. These specialties are drugs, three-for-two loans, financing, and executions.

It must be admitted that convicts may bring in considerable amounts of drugs at times. However, an earlier example of Family's control of most economic connections showed that, through its control of most connections, only Family is able to supply drugs on a somewhat continuing volume basis. It also showed that the value of the drugs is enormous. The huge, irregular shipments are impressive when they arrive. The prisoners who actually know the sources—all Family members, most convicts, and a very few inmates—immediately associate Family with the initial source of drugs.

Family's specialty in drugs and the use of drugs by Chicano prisoners can be seen as a further manifestation of the Chicano-black continuum which was presented in Chapter 4. The majority of convicts who do the wholesale supplying and dealing of drugs are Chicanos—either Family members or non-Family Chicano convicts who work closely with Family. The ability of these Chicano convicts to get and use drugs contrasts sharply with the desire of many black prisoners who would like to be able to do the same, but almost never get narcotics except on a small-scale basis. Because of their reputation for snitching, it is very difficult for blacks to get drugs through the normal channels that supply most other prisoners. Quite naturally, when they do get drugs, blacks want to turn on with their own people. However, that is exactly where things fall apart for them, for their own people often sell them out and inform. Consequently, when a black does get some drugs, he has to be very leery of other blacks. Even bulls have recognized this diversity, and accordingly approach the black user differently than they do a Chicano user. Bulls will bust a black user right away, for they feel that the black is not involved in supplying the drugs. However, the bulls often will let the Chicano user go for long periods of time, in hopes of being able to get to the supplier. As with other displays of the Chicano-black continuum, the Anglos generally occupy a position between the Chicanos and the blacks, so the bulls may treat them either way.

Another manifestation of the Chicano-black continuum can be seen in the past efforts of blacks to get into the drug traffic and set up their own organization—patterned after Family. They called it the black Mafia. Family members claim that they knew that the black Mafia would never succeed—that the blacks would not be able to establish the necessary control and trust, being unable to overcome the black prisoners' pattern of snitching. And, if it should ever look like this might happen, Family would take the economic measures to stop it. Family would wipe out their capital in about three minutes by turning money; for, as detailed earlier,

Family can level the whole yard. The lack of trust in business dealings makes it almost impossible for the blacks to engage in big business in prison. For example, if a black gives another black some money to get something, he almost feels compelled to go right along with the fellow to make sure that things get done as they should; and the necessarily covert nature of many economic transactions would not allow this to take place. If a Family member gives a Chicano or a convict some money to do something with, he does not worry about it; for he knows things will get done as planned. Since Anglos can be either inmates or convicts, they range between the Chicanos of Family and the black inmates who failed to set up the black Mafia.

Family's capital, organization, and activities have allowed it to become identified with, and have exclusive rights over all significant three-for-two loans. The volume from this business may not appear to be as great as that involved in drugs, because three-for-two profit does not come in large, isolated sums as drug profits do. However, the vast sources of daily profit from three-for-two loans create a steady flow to Family; and the volume involved is incredible, being greater than the profit from drugs.

Most prisoners are familiar with loans and credit prior to their incarceration. The only thing that is surprising about the prisoners' use of such services in prison is their extent. About two-thirds of the convicts either directly or indirectly work three for two for Family. The convicts use Family money—either cash or cigarettes. For their efforts, they receive one half of the profit, with the other half going to Family. In addition, many Family members work three for two. The loans they make usually are large ones, being made directly to convicts. With these loans, all the profit goes to Family.

The time allowed for repayment of a loan varies. With smaller loans, the time may range from one or two weeks up to a month—usually according to when the prisoner makes his draw, which allows him to make repayment. The average time for small loans would be about three weeks. With larger loans, longer repayment terms may be worked out.

Repayment of three-for-two loans can be made in cigarettes, cash, or a combination of the two. However, there is prior agreement as to which type of money will be required for repayment—usually the type borrowed. It is interesting to note that repayment of about 60 percent of the large three-for-two loans ($1,000 or more) is made outside prison—from free people to free people. Also, Family makes additional profit on three-for-two loans when it turns money. When Family switches the price of money, a prisoner owing cash may have to pay 200 cartons of cigarettes for what normally is 100 cartons worth of cash. The prisoners will panic to do this in order to protect their credit standings which are very important to them. Consequently, through its control of the price of money, Family is repaid double what it normally would receive.

The size of three-for-two loans varies greatly. Family will go as low as two cartons of cigarettes. However, on their own, convicts will make loans of even smaller, insignificant amounts. In contrast, the largest loan yet made by Family was for $30,000. The circumstances behind the granting of this loan are both interesting and informative. The operation which led to this loan began with a prisoner who had a narcotics deal going outside, prior to getting arrested and sent to prison. He still was in a position to complete the deal, even though he had to do it from inside prison with the help of convicts. In order to have the necessary collective resources to handle this large deal, several convict cliques joined together into a group of about 25 members. Family was approached for a loan of $30,000. Every convict involved guaranteed to assume responsibility for repaying the loan—each by himself if unforeseen circumstances should make it necessary. This was not a situation where the decision could be made immediately; Family had many factors to consider before granting the loan. Where would these narcotics be dealt—just in San Quentin, or in some other prison, too? How much did Family have tied up in drugs at that time? How much did Family have coming in soon? Was the supply of drugs inside low enough at the present time to be able to absorb this shipment and still not have retail prices driven down? The loan was for $30,000, but how much had the convicts collectively pooled from their individual resources? What was the size of the shipment? One-third of the loan would be repaid as soon as the shipment came in; however, it would be four months before all the profit was in from the loan. Was it wise to tie up this amount for such lengthy terms when it could be lent several times in lesser sums? Was Family's current cash position adequate to tie up the money and still be able to make all of the smaller loans, too? Family did lend the money. The shipment arrived. The convicts made at least 150 percent profit. After all expenses for items such as procurement, distribution, and interest were paid, they probably made about $20,000 profit for the group of about 25 convicts. In addition, all those involved in cutting and distribution (many of whom were members of the original group of convicts) made their profit. The bull who picked up the shipment on the streets and brought it in was paid handsomely, too. And, Family made $15,000.

Family's ability to provide funds for convict economic enterprises goes beyond the making of three-for-two loans. Financing is recognized as a third Family specialty. Convicts normally have few reserve funds, for they usually spend most of their profits on consumer goods and services. Some may have relatively small amounts set aside that enable them to join with other convicts and put together sizable deals. However, due to their own expenditures or to Family's turning of money, few have the funds to set themselves up in a steady lucrative business; and none would ever have sufficient funds to set other convicts up in business, also. Convicts are aware that if they want to go into business, Family is the only source of funds. For example, the roughly two-thirds of the convicts who are in three-for-two business are either directly or indirectly financed by Family. The same financing applies to bookies. None of them would have the funds to book the bets they make; Family is either directly or indirectly behind them, too. Many other businesses are run by convicts and financed by Family. If a convict has an idea for a business, but no funds to start it, he may approach Family—much like an entrepreneur on the streets would go to a bank. Unlike a bank, though, if Family agrees to finance the enterprise, it normally will enter into a profit-sharing agreement with the convict, as it does with most of the businesses it finances. In addition, through special arrangements and considerations, Family allows all of the businesses it finances to survive the turning of money.

Executions have come to be regarded as Family's fourth specialty. Family members and convicts often refer to the act itself as either "dusting" or killing. This specialty is a direct outgrowth of the type of tight security and organizational structure that are absolutely necessary for Family's survival. As briefly noted in Chapter 5, "ordered deaths" have always involved an individual who was a threat to Family. Most of those executed by Family have been snitches; and Family members, as well as all other convicts, understand that snitches who give or sell important, secret information to the staff (the enemy) are traitors. Since they are guilty of treason, it is understood by all parties involved that—in compliance with the convict code—these "convicted" traitors deserve to die. True, this "legal" sentence is based on an unwritten law; and, of necessity, the trial and judgment are quite informal and covert, lacking due process. Nevertheless, within the limitations of their informal judicial system, all parties recognize that a convicted snitch rightfully must die. The individual who administers this ultimate penalty is not committing a personal act; his is a social act that is fully sanctioned by the other convicts. Family is so powerful that it has never failed to carry out an intended execution—even if the marked individual is transferred to another prison or released to the streets.

This specialty of execution never is for sale. Other than being used for purposes of Family security, this service is available only to very close convicts as a reciprocal gift—and then only rarely. Even in those cases, the execution has to be legitimate—that is, in compliance with the convict code. If not, Family would never make the gift. Convicts often are able to handle their own dustings; however, they have made some rather clumsy mistakes in the past. And if the marked individual is locked up for protective custody, transferred to another prison, or paroled or discharged to the streets, a convict normally will lack the connections necessary to carry out the act. At those times, it is possible that Family occasionally might administer the penalty for the convict. All convicts and gunsels, and many inmates as well, know that Family never misses. Consequently, Family's business is big and serious to them, too.

### Distribution of Goods and Services

Thus far, this chapter primarily has dealt with general aspects of the prisoner economy and the prisoners' production of goods and services. Now, their methods of distribution will be considered. The three widely recognized processes by which goods and services can be distributed are reciprocity, redistribution, and market exchange. The previous general description correctly indicates that at least a major portion of the goods and services are distributed through a market exchange system. Nevertheless, two relatively small, but very important portions are distributed through the methods of reciprocity and redistribution.

### *Reciprocity*

When the process of reciprocity is employed, goods and services are given between prisoners of somewhat equivalent economic rank. They are not for sale as such, and a dollar value seldom is placed on them. There is, however, an expectation that such a gift will be reciprocated should the need ever arise, but threat of force would never be used to exact payment of that "gift." This reciprocal exchange may be quite uneven, for some prisoners may be fortunate enough to never find themselves in such a position of need. But it is worth their effort to keep this network of reciprocal ties active; when and if the need should arise, these ties can be quite valuable. They serve as a type of social-economic security, or insurance. Some reciprocal exchange is used in very socially rewarding, but not vitally important ways, such as sharing of canteen goodies. However, the majority of exchanges involve more serious circumstances.

Of the goods and services exchanged on a reciprocal basis, considerable portions are given among Family members and among Chicanos. Often the gift aspect of the exchange is more important than any economic considerations, for a high degree of disparity frequently exists in the value of goods and services traded. These exchanges are more important in a social sense—as expressions which reinforce ties of economic rank, ethnic affiliation, kinship, barrio (neighborhood) loyalty, and friendship. For example, when Chicanos share canteen goodies, as they frequently do among small groups, it is the act of sharing that is important, not the value of what is shared. The Chicano gives according to his ability, which may not be on an equal basis with that given by others. And, among Family members, there is no real economic necessity behind most reciprocal exchanges; for if a member should legitimately need something, he can easily draw upon Family's substantial resources. So it can be seen that Family members, those in the best economic position to reciprocate in a substantial manner, do it for social (not economic) reasons.

Some reciprocal exchange occurs between Family and certain convicts who have worked closely with Family in the past. Since these often are Chicano convicts, this type of reciprocal exchange frequently is between Family and Chicano convicts. These exchanges often are more urgent in an economic sense than those which occur among Family members. For example, when a convict's wholesale supply of goods has been wiped out unexpectedly, Family might replenish his supplies without obligation, without expectation of repayment. As another example, if a convict should have a short-term deal that will not draw on Family's funds in any continuing or long-term way, he may be allowed to keep all the profit. This is a reciprocal gesture by Family, because it could be treated as normal financing would in the market exchange system; and under those circumstances, Family would take its percentage. In this situation though, Family maximizes its overall gains at the expense of immediate profits by cementing long-term relationships. Or, as another example, a convict might have very serious trouble with a prisoner who, in compliance with the convict code, quite justly deserves to die. Family might kill the prisoner, allowing the convict to place himself in a position that is beyond suspicion. There are times that Family draws upon convicts for reciprocal help; however, the flow of goods and services in these exchanges primarily goes from Family to the convicts. For convicts, these exchanges often are of great economic necessity. For Family, they seldom are of economic urgency, but they are a time- and effort-saving convenience as well as means of strengthening social ties.

Occasionally, emergency situations arise when a convict cannot meet his payments of considerable amounts to others. At these times, Family does place a dollar value on the goods, services, or funds, and it is expected that the "gift" will be repaid—but at the cost value, not at the much higher retail market price. Also, it is understood that such gifts will be repaid as soon as possible, but without an interest charge. This may not appear to be what is commonly thought of as a gift, but the goods, services, or funds that are given in these emergencies are normally well beyond the resources of the convict at that time. Essentially, the "gift" usually enables the convict to avoid economic disaster or bankruptcy; and bankruptcy in prison can prove to be a deadly thing.

The volume of reciprocal exchange dramatically diminishes as one moves from the Family level to the inmate level. True, there is some reciprocal sharing of goods and services among fellow convicts who are locked up in the Adjustment Center or B Section, and there is some small-scale reciprocation among friends. However, the only other significant reciprocal exchange takes place on a clique basis. A convict clique exchanges goods and services on a much lesser scale than is done on the Family level—only as needed and available within the limitations of their resources. A gunsel clique is so restricted by lack of resources that reciprocal exchange has little if any economic impact. Nevertheless, the limited exchange that does take place serves to reinforce social ties. For example, members derive great pride and a sense of unity from being able to get cigarettes into the hole for a clique member, or being able to provide protection through threat of violence. The members of an inmate clique normally are so poor and so weak that there is little reciprocation other than a minimal sharing of a few canteen goodies.

Recognizing that most blacks are inmates, that most Chicanos are convicts, and that almost every Family member is a Chicano, one can see that there are dramatic differences between the Chicanos and the blacks as far as reciprocal exchange is concerned. Reciprocity is very important to the Chicanos. As inmates, the blacks are in a very low economic position. There is some reciprocal sharing among blacks on a friendship or an inmate clique basis. However, even when they share canteen goodies, it does not approach the scale of Chicano sharing. None of this small-scale reciprocal exchange is of much economic significance. It seems to be just another manifestation of behavioral patterns that fit into the Chicano-black continuum which was set forth earlier.

Many of the services in a reciprocal situation are given free; they have no price tag. It is only when they become part of the market exchange system that they acquire a dollar value. The market value of a few of these services may be almost prohibitive to most who are forced to buy them, thereby precluding many prisoners from ever being able to use them. In addition, the act of marketing these services frequently distorts or destroys them. If they are available for a price, they may not be of the same quality as those given free, on a reciprocal basis. For example, many times inmates will approach a Family member or a convict and ask for protection. The inmate usually offers to buy the convict $10 or $15 worth of canteen items each month if the convict will help protect the rest of his full draw. The inmate usually will get a degree of protection, with the convict or Family member telling the person who was pressuring the inmate to lay off. This normally is effective. However, if the situation should continue, it is doubtful that too much more would be done for the inmate, certainly not the drastic things that would be done in a reciprocal situation. In spite of these limitations, a considerable amount of money filters in to convicts and Family in this manner.

An example of a service that is quite costly on the market is having an individual killed. On the Family and convict levels, this is a free, reciprocal service. However, inmates must buy this service; and only convicts will sell it, not Family. Even then, it usually is available only if there is just cause for the act. This service has to be paid for, in advance, in cash, at the initial contact. If payment is made initially, the inmate is not likely to snitch; but if payment is not made immediately, the convict will back off, afraid of being set up for a bust. If the convict knows that the inmate has rich parents, he may start by asking $8,000. He normally will bargain down to probably about $5,000 to $6,000—which is the average price. A minimum price would be $3,000. Obviously, convicts run the serious risk of being set up and have to be extremely careful. However, inmates are not too sharp in these matters and are vulnerable to being burned by the convict. The convict might just take the money and do nothing, especially if the marked man is a fellow convict; for a convict will never dust another convict for pay—especially for an inmate who would never have any rights under the convict code. The inmate, being too weak to personally do anything about the first prisoner, will not press the convict into a physical confrontation. Also, he will not snitch to the bulls, admitting what he had planned. Consequently, he loses his money.

To close this discussion of reciprocity, a final service will be considered—that of getting contraband goods into the Adjustment Center (AC) or B Section for friends or associates. This is usually done as a reciprocal service for those who are locked up, except among inmates. Family members, convicts, and gunsels are able to get things into B Section without too much planning or ingenuity; for even though it is separated from the mainline, there is considerable movement of prisoners in and out; and when prisoners move, goods can move too. In contrast, AC poses a greater challenge. Family members and convicts (note that gunsels and inmates normally are not locked up in AC) must use a great deal of ingenuity and planning to do this, for AC is truly isolated. Some contraband may be brought into AC by bulls, but the majority comes in other ways. For example, a convict who became involved in some hot activities knew that he probably would be busted by staff and most likely be sent to AC. Since his activities at that time were quite serious in nature, he felt that he might need a knife as a weapon in AC. Therefore, he bought a legal three-pound block of cheese from the canteen and carefully inserted a knife into it lengthwise. He took care to make sure that the width of the blade was horizontal, with the cutting edge facing up. If the cutting edge was facing down, there was the slight possibility that it gradually could have settled on the bottom of the block, exposing the knife. Later, when he was in AC, the bulls quite obligingly brought his knife to him one day—as part of his personal property—without the least suspicion of what was concealed in the cheese.

### Redistribution

The process of redistribution normally involves the movement of productive efforts toward a central location and a dispensing of those goods and services, as they are needed, by those in power. Implicit in this method of distribution is the existence of a heirarchial ranking, with a minority of individuals normally having greater powers than the others. In prison, only Family has the power, resources, and organization necessary to administer and enforce participation in a redistributive system. Also, since it is necessary to keep most of its economic activities concealed, Family does not bring these productive efforts to a central location. Instead, they are held in a variety of locations—to be used as needed.

Family's high economic rank affords its members considerable advantages over other prisoners. However, Family has not abused its power. It has assumed responsibilities, too. For example, Family takes great care to deal fairly with convicts, allowing them to realize a reasonable share of the profits from the extensive prisoner economic activities. In addition, since Family essentially is a Chicano organization, it takes an interest in Chicano activities inside and out. In particular, Family exhibits a keen concern for the well-being of all deserving Chicano prisoners. Therefore, it has expanded its concern and authority to a group much wider than its membership. In a forceful, yet benevolent manner, Family has set up a redistributive system that endeavors to mitigate some of the individual and group needs of worthy Chicano prisoners, with some help being given to nonprison Chicanos and Chicano causes, and occasionally to deserving non-Chicano convicts. This redistributive system is known as the "Chicano Fund."

In order to accumulate money for the Chicano Fund, Family has imposed a type of voluntary taxation on almost all Chicanos who receive a monthly draw or some sort of income. Most Chicanos who enter prison have at least heard of Family. When approached by Family about the Chicano Fund, most Chicanos with some income are glad to voluntarily and routinely contribute a portion of it —such as $5 out of a $35 monthly draw. They understand that the contributors, as well as others covered by the fund, are given protection, goods, and services by Family. Most frequently, this might involve getting cigarettes and essentials to someone locked up in AC or B Section. The Chicano Fund is a communal fund which normally is used to help those deserving Chicanos who have nothing. However, even those with adequate incomes may need to draw upon the fund in emergencies. For example, if one of these individuals is thrown in the hole, he might appreciate Family stepping in for him and taking care of his normally manageable debts and any other emergency items. This enables him to come out of the hole in no worse shape than when he went in. Since some Chicanos feel that they would seldom, if ever, need help from the fund, resentment and misunderstanding can develop. A few of them may refuse to contribute; but, since they are expected to contribute, Family will take the "voluntary contributions" from them if necessary. Nevertheless, 99 percent of the contributors are pleased to do it, and no pressure is needed to collect from them. In addition, Family contributes part of its profits to the fund; and, at times, Family's contributions are considerable. Therefore, it can be seen that this "voluntary" taxation allows the wider group covered by the Chicano Fund to pool the products of its collective efforts and redistribute them as required to meet individual and group needs.

The actual redistribution of the Chicano Fund may be done by any Family member. Any member can draw from the fund, keeping in mind that the fund is not unlimited. Several members, or even the Leadership Group, may be involved in approving the use of large sums. However, there are so many relatively small sums drawn from the fund—for which no accounting is necessary—that they create a steady flow of considerable volume. Most members do not know any particulars about these relatively small sums; for they are too numerous to be noted, except by Family's bookkeepers. Money also comes into the fund in varying amounts from many sources. This money is then distributed and held in a variety of places—as in the Chicano Fund. The Chicano Fund account may be totally depleted or it may go up to considerable sums. Simultaneously, it may be down to nothing in one prison and quite fat in another. However, even if the fund is totally depleted in a prison, it is never obliterated; for Family will borrow if necessary to fill urgent needs. Amazingly, there have been almost no instances of misuse of this fund. Businessmen, and even leaders of church organizations, might legitimately question how the fund could be administered—with the amount of money and the number of people involved—without abuse. As a Family member stated, "Family may work on a small scale compared to the multimillion dollar corporations on the streets, but it does work."

The fund is used quite extensively, often for non-Family Chicanos. On holidays, *all* Chicano convicts that are locked up (in AC or B Section) are taken care of with an additional supply of contraband goods, made possible through a laxness by the bulls at these times. Also, no Chicano does without toilet articles and cigarettes when he "hits the joint." If his friends do not take care of him, Family will. In fact, if the Chicano has no draw and no ability to hustle, Family even may supply toilet articles and cigarettes on a continuing basis. Fortunately this is not necessary for a large number on a sustained basis. It is evident that some of these uses of the Chicano Fund represent a steady outflow, with no return. In addition, the use of this fund extends beyond the prisons. For example, if a Chicano convict's family cannot afford to bury a relative, a coffin and plot will be purchased with money from the fund. In fact, many times Family has been asked to do this so that a convict's relative would not have to be buried in potter's field. At other times the fund has been used to keep relatives of Chicano convicts above a starvation-poverty level. Or, funds have been used to pay medical bills for relatives on the streets. The Chicano Fund also has often been the source of very adequate donations to many Chicano activities on the streets. For example, a group on the streets was attempting to help poor Chicanos get a better education. When they ran out of money, word reached inside California prisons. With the permission of state administrators, the Chicanos inside all California prisons were allowed to collect funds for the outside group. After the funds had been collected, Family matched the amount from the Chicano Fund.

Many of the needs that led to the formation of Family were felt by the entire Chicano prisoner population. Consequently, Family set up the Chicano Fund to answer some of those exigencies for the rest of the Chicano prisoners. The Chicano Fund obviously does not bring all Chicano prisoners up to Family's economic level. However, it does satisfy many of their urgent needs. This is the only system of redistribution inside. For the Chicanos, there is no reason for any other. In contrast, the Anglo and black prisoners have no form of redistribution. And, as Family members point out, the blacks in particular have many of the same serious requirements that led to the formation of Family and later to the Chicano Fund. However, for many earlier-noted reasons that often fit into the Chicano-black continuum, the blacks have no group that could do for them what Family has done for the Chicanos. Drawing on his knowledge of blacks, a Family member speculated that, even if they could set up some redistributive system, the blacks could never agree on who should receive the help.

### Market Exchange System

As previously noted, a major portion of the goods and services are distributed through the prisoners' market exchange system. In this respect, the prisoner economy is not unlike the larger national economy. Earlier descriptions of other aspects of the prisoner economy already have provided considerable detail about their market system. Before giving further details—of how Family, convicts, gunsels, and inmates fit into this distribution system—two things should be noted. First, both credit and money are involved in both wholesale and retail sales, depending on the circumstances. It should be remembered though, the use of credit (even though it often is on very short terms) is extensive. Second, the number of distribution links between the source of goods and the consumer is usually greater than the number between the source of a service and the customer, because the service usually originates or is performed inside prison. Therefore, in order to give the fullest potential patterns of market distribution, the following discussion will tend to emphasize goods more than services.

Family has goods coming into the prison on a continuing basis; but there is no set pattern or schedule. Shipments arrive on an irregular basis. Consequently, when goods arrive, several factors have to be considered before deciding what to do with them. For example, if there is an abundant supply of this particular type of goods in the yard at that time, and if Family is not pressed to turn the goods into cash, the goods may be temporarily warehoused until the supply in the yard diminishes and allows for a normal profit. Or, Family members may be quite busy with other activities at that time and under no pressure to turn the goods into cash. Under these conditions, the goods might be warehoused until members have time to handle them properly. If time and circumstances allow, the goods might be distributed among the members to "pass off to the public." This means that the members would retail the goods directly to convicts in the yard, and all the profit would stay with Family. At times, certain goods are designated for Family use only; these goods never reach the yard, for they are consumed by Family members.

Occasionally Family goes directly to certain non-Family convicts. Family has faith in convicts—in their not snitching. However, Family does not deal directly with all convicts, for it takes a sharp individual to make rapid, final decisions. These selected convicts must have the ability to think and act rapidly, to make extensive computations in their heads and come to a decision—all in a matter of a couple of minutes. In the prisoner market system, goods normally are not warehoused and held while a buyer is found. If they are to be wholesaled out to a convict, the operation is completed rapidly, with the goods often being moved directly from the incoming source to the convict buyer. For example, if Family should need to turn the goods into cash, or its members are too busy to retail the goods, they may be sold to a convict on a wholesale basis. Preferably a single, reliable convict is approached. This eliminates the necessity of breaking up the shipment of goods or of having to find more convicts to enter into the deal. Once the goods are sold, it is up to the convict to determine what price to get for them in the yard. If he is greedy and sets his prices too high, he will have trouble selling them. Even though a single convict will handle the deal with Family, he usually has at least one partner involved behind the scenes. And if the convict cannot handle the deal himself, with his partners, he will bring other convicts in; but this is the convict's concern, not Family's. If the amount involved is small, the convict will pay for the goods right away. When a large amount is involved, the obligation is paid within a reasonable, agreed upon time—usually from 3 or 4 days to a week.

There are times that Family does not want to be bothered by having either to warehouse the goods or to retail them in the yard. It may be at a time when there is a more than abundant supply of these particular goods already available in the yard. If Family tries to wholesale the goods to a convict, he may refuse to buy them, knowing that they would be difficult to sell right away. In this situation, Family might ask him to do it as a favor. If so, he would be asked how long it would take him to get the money. It might be agreed that three weeks would be reasonable. This would end Family's concern for the goods and still allow the convict to make a reasonable profit. However, in return, but with some loss of profit, Family might offer to do a favor for the convict. This could entail something such as bringing in $100 worth of chewing gum for him at cost, or exchanging money for him without a charge. It is evident that there is a degree of reciprocation built into this kind of cooperation, for such favors are remembered.

The convicts' wholesale and retail methods of distributing goods resemble those used by Family. However, convict distribution is on a lesser scale and does differ in some significant ways. For example, some convicts may have their own connections for bringing in goods, but most convicts normally rely on Family to produce the majority of the goods that they distribute either as middleman jobbers or as retailers. When they purchase goods from Family on a wholesale basis, they lose the profit involved in bringing goods in from the streets. Also, convict sales often are on a smaller scale than those of Family. Usually convicts are further down the lines of distribution than Family. Most are at least one step removed from the connection to the source of goods and at least a step closer to the inmate consumers. Those convicts who do directly bring in goods would rarely wholesale the entire shipment out to other convicts as Family does, for they would lose the considerable profit involved in retailing the goods. If convicts do wholesale goods, they are most likely to do it on a smaller scale, working with lesser amounts. They function much like a middleman jobber, being neither the wholesale producer (as Family is) nor the retailer. Also, convicts generally conduct a much higher percentage of retail sales than would ever be found in Family distribution activities. In their retail sales, convicts not only deal with other convicts, they also deal directly with gunsels and a small number of dependable inmates—up to a limit.

And, as Family does, convicts set aside certain goods for their own consumption.

Gunsels play a very important role in the distribution of goods. Except for the canteen goodies that are sold by inmates from stores set up in their cells, gunsels serve as the major link between the convict retailers and most inmate consumers. Because they tend to consume almost everything that they make, gunsels are always broke. Their immature, independent nature, coupled with their incessant, risky hustling, makes them a very poor risk in any long-term operation, especially if credit is involved. These factors preclude gunsels from being able to purchase a volume of wholesale goods to sell on a retail basis. Nevertheless, with their nerve, their guts, their ability to hustle, and their willingness to take risks, they make excellent salesmen. The convict retailers have no retail stores; of necessity they maintain covert markets. The gunsels serve as salesmen for the convicts' secret markets. Instead of working in a store, the gunsels work a territory—the prison. Each gunsel is a kind of traveling salesman who acts as a representative for several convict retail businessmen. The gunsel serves as the link between the covert markets and the inmate customers. The gunsel, not the customer, goes to the market. The gunsel receives no salary from the convict—just a percentage of the money paid for goods or services. He may be able to make more, though, by hustling the inmate to pay a higher price than the convict is asking. Although the gunsel may take advantage of inmates, he is quite proud of the fact that he will never snitch on a convict. Therefore, in a market system where the owner of retail goods or services does not want to be known by the consumer, the gunsel salesmen also serve as effective buffers.

Inmates may not be deemed worthy of being included in the reciprocal or redistributive systems. However, in the market exchange system they are "allowed" to play two roles. The first role involves the relatively small number of inmates who are permitted to run stores in their cells and sell canteen goodies. They, too, form an important link between the convict wholesalers and retailers and the inmate consumers; but the volume of canteen goodies they sell is small when compared with the volume of contraband goods and services sold by gunsels. Even though it is on a lesser scale, a considerable volume of canteen goodies is sold through these stores. The inmate salesmen are allowed to share in a bit of the profit from these sales. And, although considered inferior when compared with gunsels who almost never snitch, these inmates also serve as buffers between the convict wholesalers and retailers and the inmate consumers. Convicts are quite willing to let them fill this role; for inmates, not convicts, are the ones who frequently get busted for running stores.

The second role that inmates are allowed to play is vitally important. In fact, they are not only allowed, they are encouraged to be the retail customers on the end of the line. Since they are the terminus, they cannot distribute goods or services any further. Nevertheless, they are actively persuaded to supply their cigarettes from the canteen to Family and convicts—in the form of cigarette money used to purchase contraband goods and services. The monthly amount most inmates spend may be small, but there are so many inmates that the total sum is great. It is the high prices they pay for retail goods and services that enable the *many* persons involved in the production and distribution of these goods and services to make considerable profit from their efforts. In fact, the total profit is so great that Family members and convicts can consume major portions of certain types of goods and still realize a sizable net profit.

Occasionally an inmate will have a connection which will supply him with goods for personal consumption. These goods are almost never sold to, or used by, other prisoners. However, in rare instances, an inmate will have goods brought in for him to sell. This is done to supplement his draw. Normally, to sell the goods, the inmate will go to the gunsel source from whom he has purchased things in the past. The gunsel will not have enough money to buy the goods; but he will find a buyer—usually a convict, or even a Family member if necessary. Ultimately, the inmate will end up accepting the very low wholesale offer that is made for his goods. Two factors influence his decision. First, he too does not want to retail the goods because of his lack of trust in other inmates. Second, he recognizes his bind of having only one connection, which precludes any sort of competitive bidding for the goods. Usually the small net profit realized from the risky operation is a great disappointment. This discourages him from further attempts to bring goods in for sale.

Some additional details and examples of the extensiveness of the prisoners' market exchange system now are in order. They will show how some of the prisoners fit themselves into it as producers or distributors. They will also give a further indication of what goods and services are available through the prisoners' market system and how much some of these goods and services cost. In addition, it is hoped that these examples and details will supplement the earlier treatment of the prisoner economy in such a way that the reader will gain a deeper sense of what that economy really means to a prisoner.

## Hustle

*Webster's Dictionary* lists two definitions for the verb "hustle." It may mean "to sell something to or obtain something from by energetic and especially under-handed activity." Or, it may mean "to make strenuous efforts to secure often illicit money or business." It has corresponding nouns: hustle and hustler. Prisoners frequently use these words in reference to their prisoner economic activities. For example, the staff may have assigned them to a prison job; but, as they say, "There is not a job that doesn't have some sort of hustle to it." Therefore, they would not call their prisoner occupation (or occupations) their job. Instead, they call it their hustle. For prisoners, as insiders, hustle does not carry the negative denotations which normally are indicated to outsiders by "underhanded" and "illicit." Prisoners use the term to distinguish between their prison and prisoner economic activities; and, owing to their experience and background, hustle has acquired positive connotations for them. They are proud of their ability to hustle. And those who are unable to hustle effectively are often negatively regarded, as a man who had failed in business might be considered on the streets.

For prisoners, hustling means being able to make something out of—or to do something with—nothing. However, this "nothing" is just that if the prisoner abides by the laws and rules. As noted above, "There is not a job that doesn't have some sort of hustle to it." The hustle is obvious in any job that puts a prisoner in contact with usable, stealable items that are in demand, such as clothing, soap, towels, food, or even information if nothing else is available. With clothing for example, state-issued sweatshirts that are stolen from the gym department sell for 5 packs of cigarettes apiece, and there is a heavy demand for them in the late fall and winter. And, if a prisoner gets tired of the ill-fitting clothes he routinely has to pick out of the freshly laundered pile that supposedly is his size, he may arrange to have some tailored blues of his own. First, he buys shirts and pants for one package of cigarettes each. Then he has them tailored to fit by a prisoner who works in the clothing factory. The charge for this service is 2 packs for each shirt and 3 packs for a pair of pants. Usually a prisoner will buy 3 or 4 sets so that he can rotate them while they are being "bonarooed"—given special starching and pressing service at the laundry. The charge for this service is one pack for each garment. The many prisoners involved in this extensively used service all get their cut of the money. The prisoner will not be bothered by bulls simply because he is wearing bonarooed blues. Trouble would occur only if a prisoner who is engaged in this service is caught bringing them from the laundry.

The hustle resulting from some prison jobs may be in direct competition with state-offered services. Even though the prisoners who do the hustling charge for their services, the superior quality of the prisoner services allow them to compete successfully with the state's free services. The bonarooing of clothing, noted above, is a good example of this type of competition. Another example would be the state's free shoe repair service. The drawback is that not only is there a 4- or 5-day wait, but there is no guarantee that a prisoner will ever get his shoes back. The prisoners offer a personalized service. One-day service is available for 5 packs of cigarettes; and, for a little more, one can have leather soles and heels put on. Also, routine haircuts are free. However, prisoner barbers sell special haircuts and talcum, and the large volume of their special business is not really surprising. The situation is not unlike that of the soldier who passes up a free scalping by an army barber to pay a civilian barber to give him a decent haircut. The vintage quality and lack of relevance of the majority of the books available in the library has led to another successful hustle. Prisoners who are attending school are required to read certain books for their classes, but other prisoners have discovered and profited from the relevancy and popularity of many of the books that are stocked in the education department's book room. In addition to the above examples, there are those prisoners who have a personal interest or ability (not necessarily from a prison job) that allows them to hustle and compete with state-offered services. For example, there are a few highly competent jailhouse lawyers who are in competititon with, and much more effective than, the poor quality law library that is offered to prisoners for their assistance in legal matters.

Some prisoners have hustles that capitalize on the desire of many prisoners to fix up their cells. For example, a job in the paint shop allows a prisoner to prepare special cans of paint. These are sold to others who want to paint their cells. And a job in the woodworking shop enables the prisoner employees to make and sell many small items that prisoners use in their cells—such as small shelves, covered boxes, and toilet paper dispensers. A few gifted prisoners sell their art works to prisoners who want a painting on the wall of their cell. At times these prisoners are even commissioned to do a portrait of a prisoner's wife, girlfriend, or children. For some artists, this hustle may supplement their income from the legal sale of their paintings. However, a few may not even have money for a legal draw; and consequently, they are unable to legally purchase supplies from the hobby shop. They must use the supplies of other prisoners, and therefore their paintings can never be sold to the public through legal channels.

A wide variety of hustles cater to the thirst and hunger of the prisoners. For example, some prisoners just steal certain food items from the mess hall and wholesale them to other prisoners who cook or combine the ingredients into consumable products. Additional prisoners usually are involved in the retail distribution of this food. Or, other prisoners may be able to manufacture equipment that is used in the preparation of food or drinks. For example, instant coffee is sold at the canteen, but there is no hot water in the cells. Even the "hot" water that is passed around in the evening is not very hot. Therefore, many prisoners make and sell "stingers"—small electrical coil immersion heaters that are used to heat a single cup of water. The stingers enable prisoners to make hot coffee almost any time they wish. However, there is one drawback from which stingers get their name. Those who use them must take care to avoid getting "stung" by an electrical shock. At one time, the prisoners who worked in the office machinery repair shop actually had an assembly line set up to produce them. Also, the hot plates that prisoners produce are popular. They enable prisoners to cook a surprisingly wide variety of things. Since sandwiches and home brew are quite popular and plentiful, they will be considered in more detail.

In the evening, prisoners often buy sandwiches from someone in the block who is making them in volume from food that has been stolen from the mess hall. Several prisoners normally are involved in the collection of contraband that is necessary to make a sandwich. For example, a grilled cheese sandwich requires the following: a hot plate, butter for grilling (stolen by the pound), cheese (stolen from 5-pound blocks or wheels), bread (often many prisoners filch their uneaten bread from the mess hall, although all food is supposed to be consumed there), and mustard, mayonnaise or catsup. Sometimes sandwiches are made with ingredients such as steak, cheese, lunch meat, and occasionally even bacon and tomato. Regardless of the ingredients, sandwiches normally sell for one pack each. The buyer usually has little choice, having to accept the offering of the evening. The fragrant aroma of the sandwiches being prepared often is sufficient advertisement to let the prisoners in at least part of the block know that a certain item is for sale that evening. At such times, the shouts of prisoners may be heard as they place their order by yelling out the number of sandwiches wanted and their cell number. If a convict has a large number of sandwiches to make, he tries to sell all of his stock in one night. Otherwise, he is too vulnerable to snitches. He usually waits for a couple of weeks before repeating the process.

The production of home brew is extensive. Frequently small groups will make it during the day at their job for their collective use. However, most home brew is produced for sale to others. Normally a basic ingredient, such as orange juice, tomato puree, potatoes, or raisins, is mixed with water, sugar, and yeast. Then the mixture is allowed to ferment. Tomato puree is the fastest and most powerful. However, powdered orange juice, which can be purchased in the canteen, is the most convenient. A prisoner can even make successive small batches for his own personal use. If potatoes or raisins are used, the prisoners usually put some powdered soft drink in to give it a better flavor. The odors from these fermenting mixtures are very strong, but the prisoners have a trick which eliminates the odor and much of the possibility of getting caught by a bull. They put a plastic cover over the mixture, with a tube coming out of the top of the cover. The other end of the tube is put in the bottom of a cup of disinfectant. The fermenting odors are destroyed as they pass through the disinfectant. Some prisoners will take the fermented potatoes one step further by distilling the mixture. The resulting "white lightning" is then bottled in empty lotion bottles that have been saved for this purpose. White lightning is a hot item, for it is very potent.

Just like the convict with a large number of sandwiches to sell, a convict who has a batch of home brew tries to retail the entire lot in one night to avoid the risk of snitches. Or, a convict might just wholesale home brew, having some other prisoner keep the batch for him while it is brewing and give it to a designated buyer when it is ready. Then it would be the buyer's responsibility to retail it. In this manner the convict does not even see the completed batch. The convict would give the buyer his identification card so that the pickup person could show it to the prisoner who is holding the brew. The ID card is proof that the possessor is entitled to pick up the batch. Using this method, one convict can have many batches, in successive stages of completion, brewing at the same time.

In the nonhonor blocks, where evening movement of most prisoners is restricted, much of the distribution of retail sales is handled by the prisoner tier tenders. Regardless of whether they are distributing sandwiches, home brew, or canteen goodies from a store, they receive 1 out of every 3 packs for the vital service they perform. Perhaps the extent of retail sales that are connected with thirst and hunger is more understandable if one remembers that the prisoners eat their last meal of the day between 5:30 and 6:30 P.M. How many readers, at least occasionally, partake of a late evening snack or drink?

By now, some of the variety of potential hustles should be evident. It often takes considerable ingenuity to develop a hustle by making something out of, or doing something with, "nothing." For example, a hospital worker may hustle pills from patients to sell to other prisoners who use them to turn on. Or a patient may endure or feign considerable pain in order to get pills to save and sell to others. Perhaps a prisoner is unable to establish a heavy connection to the streets with a bull, but is able to hustle him to bring in small items. One time a bull brought in some pretty good perfume to a prisoner who had been hustling him. All the broads went wild over the perfume. Actually, even though it was not an expensive item, it made a great deal of profit for many, being cut and recut many times. If perfume were supplied on a routine basis, it probably would not yield too much profit; it was just a fad. One can see that a good hustler has to be on his toes at all times, for there seems to be some sort of hustle possible in almost any situation.

An interesting hustle developed by a few prisoners is a type of pawnshop operation. As illustration, if a prisoner should have money and buy a good pair of shoes (these can legally be ordered), he can still use the shoes as money. He can give them to one of these hustlers to hold for him, in exchange for so many packs of cigarettes. If he does not get the money to pay back, he loses the shoes. The hustler who holds the shoes does so without interest, for he realizes that he may end up with the goods, rather than repayment; and his profits come from the sale of such unclaimed goods. This type of barter keeps a considerable amount of personal property on the move. Actually, it supplements the three types of prisoner money and serves as a source of profit for those who work this hustle.

### Prices

In the market exchange system, the sale of drugs is extensive. The price of drugs (commonly called dope by prisoners) may vary at any particular time owing to supply and demand. However, the following examples would be considered normal prices inside. Several types of "uppers" (stimulants) are available: one Benzedrene pill costs a "box" (a 10 package carton of cigarettes); or, a single Dexamyl pill sells for 15 packs. Wyamine and Dristan inhalers ("tubes") also are used for uppers; and since they cost only about 79 cents on the streets, there is considerable profit when they are sold for 5 boxes inside. The prisoners use the treated cotton from inside these tubes for their high. In the past, a wide variety of these tubes were available. However, regulatory efforts by the federal government have limited the number to the two brands mentioned above. One bull has brought in a single tube every day for many years. He inserts the tube like a rectal suppository, secreting it internally so as to avoid detection if he should ever be suspected and searched. Once in his work area, a short trip to the toilet and wash basin produces a clean tube for his convict connection. At times he even steals some of his wife's doctor-prescribed pills and brings them in, inside an empty tube. This bull is not greedy; but, through his sustained efforts, he has probably netted a considerable amount over the years.

Marijuana is available, but the price might vary from 35 packs to 2 boxes for a joint, depending on the quality. Mace and nutmeg give the user a marijuanalike experience; and either spice sells for about 5 packs per teaspoonful. The prisoners drink it down with water and then follow it with some hot coffee. The resulting trip lasts for about 10 hours. Prisoners claim that Schilling brand gives the best trip. A bull can buy either of these spices in bulk on the streets. Then, with 2 to 3 ounces in a loosely packed plastic bag, in the bottom of each shoe, he is able to bring 4 to 6 ounces in every day.

Hard narcotics and pills come into the prison in a steady supply, and in a vast number of ways. A $10 "paper" (a shot of heroin, cocaine, or other hard narcotic) from the streets will be cut into three or four $10 papers inside. Hence, a paper sells for $10 inside, but it is only one third or one fourth the strength of papers on the streets. A single "yellow jacket" pill (Nembutal, used as a "downer" or sedative) can be bought for 5 packs. Artane is rapidly becoming the most popular pill inside. It gives the user a kind of marijuana trip, and time passes without the user knowing it. On the streets Artane is used to treat Parkinson's disease; and, at times, it is used with mental patients who develop a similar type of disease of the central nervous system. Inside, however, prisoners have discovered that it builds up in the body to a point where half of a pill in the morning and half in the afternoon gives a sustained high. During this high, one's reading may become blurry at times, but otherwise one is able to function normally. With Artane, a man can trip through 29 days in the hole without much effort. A few prisoners, using their monthly draw of $45, now do their time by purchasing a jar of instant coffee, 3 cartons of cigarettes, and the rest in Artane.

Since the inmate stores serve as a significant part of the market exchange system, some additional details about them now are in order. An outsider might wonder why the prisoners use these stores when the canteen goodies are usually sold there at about double the price charged at the canteen. For example, three 5-cent canteen candies sell in the stores for a pack of cigarettes (35 cents). Or, three 10-cent candies sell for 2 packs (70 cents) in the stores. The prisoners are not irrational; there are three valid reasons why prisoners buy from the stores.

First, as noted earlier, not all prisoners are able to use the canteen; and some of those men might like to have such goodies, too, from time to time. In addition, the state ration of certain items (which also are sold in the canteen) is less than adequate. And, the normal routine of prison life often makes some canteen articles almost indispensable for some prisoners. For example, the state rations each prisoner one bar of soap, and four razor blades each month. In addition, the state provides tooth powder for them. Consider just these three items. How many bars of soap does the advertisement-indoctrinated American use each month? Even though the prisoners do not think the soap is the best, they admit that it does get them clean. However, if they shower frequently (if their job assignment allows it), they must buy more soap and/or deodorant. Most Americans consider deodorant a necessity, but it certainly is imperative for those prisoners who are able to shower only once a week. The razor blades are poor quality. Prisoners claim that after they are used once, they are useless; they think that the blades are rejects from the streets. In any case, prisoners need more than four each month, so they have to buy them. As for the tooth powder, prisoners claim that it tastes like cleaning powder. No one uses it for his teeth, but uses it effectively to polish dominoes, to clean sinks and toilets in the cells, and the like. Accordingly, prisoners also must buy toothpaste. These items are for sale at the canteen. However, if a prisoner cannot legally use the canteen, he must buy these necessities from a store.

A second reason why prisoners use the stores is that not all of the store prices are inflated over the canteen prices. The stores are in direct competition with the canteen on many items. For example, soap is for sale in the canteen and the stores. In the canteen, the price is 25 cents a bar. At a store a prisoner can get 4 or 5 bars for a pack of cigarettes (35 cents). The soap is identical in both places, because the prisoners steal their stock from the state's supply. There is an even greater bargain on razor blades. In the canteen a package of 10 blades sells for 70 cents. At the stores, three packages of 10 blades (a total of 30 blades) sells for a pack of cigarettes. Therefore, with 70 cents (2 packs of cigarettes) a prisoner can buy a total of 60 blades from a store. And, as with the soap, the blades are identical in both places. These and similar bargains are the explanation for the canteen's poor sales of certain items. Prisoners think that a man would be idiotic not to buy certain contraband items from the stores.

Even if a prisoner did not use the stores for either of the above reasons, he might at least use it to buy goods when he has no money. Knowing that a prisoner has a monthly income, a store owner is glad to extend a reasonable amount of credit to the prisoner. Since most of the store items sell at double the canteen price, the prisoner may buy a list of goods from the canteen for the store owner to repay the amount of money he owes the store. He may do this instead of paying off the debt in cigarettes. He is not charged interest because the store owner makes a profit on the value of the goods brought to him. In addition, this arrangement not only helps him restock his store, it also effectively hooks the prisoner on credit purchases.

## Consumption or Use of Goods and Services

The most salient characteristics of consumption or use have already been presented as an integral part of the earlier description and explanation of the prisoners' production and distribution of goods and services. The only additional material that should be added at this point is a brief treatment of the way the prisoners on the three different levels generally use their income.

Family sets aside a sizable portion of certain goods that it brings into prison for the personal use of its members. These consumer goods actually are a part of Family's income. Most of the rest of Family's income is used in the following ways: to support those Family specialists who are not allowed to hustle for their own needs; to help out individual members who temporarily need assistance in their personal affairs; to support reciprocal acts (the financial flow normally is away from Family); to support the Chicano Fund; and to reinvest in additional business activities.

Convicts (including Family members, as individual convicts hustling for their own personal needs and not engaged in Family business as such) also set aside portions of certain goods for their own personal use. Usually this just reduces their net profit which is primarily used for the consumption or use of goods and services. Some profit is reinvested in additional business activities. On the convict level, however, the scale of business and the total income is much smaller than on the Family level. Consequently, convicts seldom have enough net profit to allow them to become too large. If they should, Family would soon wipe them out by turning money.

Inmates normally derive their incomes from outside sources, the majority of which comes through their legal draw. Less frequently, some have income from a prison job. Also, there are those who illegally receive income from outside sources, and occasionally this income is considerable. However, inmates are not able to hustle and make any significant amount through prisoner economic activities. Virtually all inmate income, regardless of source, is used to purchase consumer goods and services.

Gunsels, even though they do not fit on either the convict or inmate level, serve as important links and buffers between the two levels. Gunsels are poor. Unlike inmates, they have no source of outside funds. Due to their unpredictability, they almost never have a paying prison job. Consequently, they have no legal source of funds. However, they do have an ability to hustle. Although their profits are much smaller than those of convicts, gunsels do make a lot through their hustling. However, unlike convicts, they are never able to save anything to invest in a business enterprise, because they use all of their income to purchase consumer goods and services.

Since drugs are the principal goods in the prisoner economy, and since they form the majority of income set aside for personal use by Family and convicts, drugs will be used as an important illustration of the types of differences that exist in the use of incomes by prisoners on the three levels of the prisoner culture. Some Family members and convicts have and are able to support drug habits. However, many of them are just on-and-off users; but as such, they consume a considerable volume of drugs. The percentage of drugs set aside for personal use by Family members and convicts has very roughly been estimated at about 50 percent. Accordingly, one can see that the wholesale and retail markup is great, in that Family and convicts still make a reasonable net profit on their drug sales. In contrast, gunsels would never have enough money to support a habit; and they are in and out of the hole so often that it would prevent them from sustaining one. At the most, gunsels use a relatively small portion of their income for occasional purchases of drugs. Since the income of inmates is limited, few of them are able to support drug habits. The many who do buy drugs, merely do it on an occasional basis; but, even though the monthly purchase of each is not great, collectively they buy a considerable volume. Relatively few inmates have an illegal source of funds that is adequate to allow them to support a habit; however, the steady, exceptionally high retail prices those few pay for their drugs adds up to a considerable amount, too. It is obvious that collectively the inmates more than adequately support the drug use of Family members and convicts.

The previous chapters were necessary prerequisites to this chapter, which by detailing the various levels of prisoner economic activity, hopefully has developed a fuller understanding of the whole prisoner culture. It has become evident that the real key to the prisoner culture lies in a comprehension of Family's economic role. Although the next chapter discusses the sociopolitical prisoner leadership, it should be noted that the only truly significant leadership for the majority of prisoners is the economic leadership that is covertly exercised by a relatively small group of Chicano convicts—Family's members. Of necessity, sociopolitical leadership generally is open and public in nature. But in prison, with the opposition between the prisoner culture and the staff, the only activities truly meaningful to prisoners are, of necessity, covert in nature.

Family members think that prison administrators and staff, by abusing and manipulating prisoners, are forcing new ideas and practices into existence. As a result of that maltreatment, the formation of Family happened to parallel ethnic lines and fit well with the Chicanos' subcultural background. However, had it not been Family, members think that something else would have been organized. The constant potential for use of violence by Family as a protective mechanism enables Family to function and survive. Serious, abusive, and even violent activity would take place inside a large prison, regardless of whether Family or convicts were there. There would always be those who would hustle, and their hustling would lead to those serious, violent activities. Inmate types would always fall prey to the convict types. In California prisons, Family's existence has allowed a counter force to develop and function in an atmosphere of relative security, regardless of staff pressures. Even though inmates are mistreated by convicts and Family, they ultimately are better off under the relative stability and welfare brought about by Family's activities. Convicts and Family members enjoy a much greater prosperity and more personal security; for without Family, these prisoners would be continually vulnerable to staff abuse and manipulation.

This comparatively small number of Chicano prisoners in California prisons has quietly attained some remarkable objectives. Family's ability to control and use parts of the prison system is impressive to some and amazing to many. Family's position and power rests on its rigid unity. In addition, the supportive solidarity of almost all Chicano prisoners further increases the strength of Family. However, this very unity also precludes outsiders from viewing or understanding the Chicanos, except superficially. On the surface, the Chicano prisoners normally appear to be an acephalous group; but, in reality, they are not. There is a great deal of Chicano leadership at this hidden level where the most important part of the prisoner economy functions. Most outsiders have never understood the prisoner culture in enough depth to even make a definite distinction between the inmate and convict levels. Usually inmates and convicts are lumped together and discussed as "inmates." Observers and writers normally treat all prisoner economic activity as one type. If a further distinction is made, it only is between legal and illegal activities. In fact, some studies of prison economic activities deal only with the legal economic pursuits of prisoners; and, as can be seen from this chapter, those are a rather insignificant part of the prisoner economy. Obviously the prisoner economy can be understood only as it relates to all three levels of the prisoner culture. And, only by examining Family's vast, corporatelike activities can an outsider ever really begin to comprehend the full extent of prisoner economic activities.

# 7 / Sociopolitical
# prisoner leadership

According to the traditional functions of control and confinement, prison systems are designed so that the staff exercises considerable authority over the prisoners. Most activities that would normally require sociopolitical leadership on the streets are directly or indirectly controlled by the staff inside prison. Staff does allow a formal sociopolitical leadership to exist among the prisoners in the form of elected prisoner leaders. However, prisoners recognize that this is a rather ineffective and meaningless front, since the staff normally has veto power over prisoners. Actually, significant sociopolitical leadership usually is not tolerated or permitted by the staff. Prisoners know that those who do attempt leadership in truly significant areas of activity are usually singled out and punished by the staff.

### POWERLESS LEADERS

The prisoners at San Quentin are allowed to have their own governing body—the Inmate Advisory Council (IAC). The IAC is the formal manifestation of the prisoners' sociopolitical leadership. The officers and members are democratically elected by the prisoners who wish to vote; however, they usually are inmates who have virtually no *real* influence over other prisoners. The IAC is allowed to deal with superficial problems; but it has no real power to govern, because the staff has the power to disregard all "advice" from the Inmate *Advisory* Council. Prisoners realize that the IAC, created and recognized by staff, is not part of the reality of the prisoner culture and that it has little practical effect on their lives. A Chicano prisoner's comment about two Chicanos who were on the IAC (one as the president and one as a member) is representative of the general prisoner attitude toward those on the IAC. He said, "If all of us were on the streets, I'd never go to either of them for help in settling a problem or getting something done."

### REAL LEADERS

Let us turn from the formal, or official, sociopolitical prisoner leadership, which merely is a tolerated manifestation of what the staff thinks should be allowed to

148

exist among the prisoners, to the *real* sociopolitical prisoner leadership. Unfortunately, the prisoners haven't the sense of unity as an entire group that would lead them to select real leaders, on a prisonwide basis, to treat really meaningful sociopolitical issues. Prisoners are aware that even if it were possible to form such a representative body, their efforts would be doomed to failure. If prisoners approach truly relevant issues in the traditional sociopolitical manner (such as trying to legitimately express their concern about how the Adult Authority abuses the indeterminate sentence system), the leaders have to be open in many of their actions. And, as soon as they do this, the leaders usually are singled out, isolated from the other prisoners, and punished by the staff. Although they may be able to start something significant, the prisoners know they will never be able to sustain it in the traditional sociopolitical manner.

Occasionally sociopolitical leadership does become apparent on a prisonwide basis, but it always is temporary in nature. Such leadership and the resultant sociopolitical action normally arises from issues that are extremely important to the prisoners involved. Historically, the things of major concern to prisoners have been the quality of food, staff brutality, living conditions, and even the elimination of prison walls. Today the issues that prisoners would judge as being extremely important to them have become quite sophisticated. For several years, the main topics that have been the object of sociopolitical action by California prisoners could very well form the checklist of legislators or attorneys who are interested in bringing about some legitimately needed reform in the prison system.

Prisoners have learned through bitter experience that, when a major issue is involved, their efforts to effect change by normal sociopolitical methods will be aborted by the staff. Consequently, prisoners rarely take action; but when they do, crucially important issues must be involved. At these times, since normal or moderate means will be thwarted by the staff, the prisoners must use more extreme methods if they are to have any chance to succeed. Prisoners feel that the only effective way open to them is protest—usually in the form of a peaceful work strike, a sit-down, or the like. However, these pacific dissents can easily erupt into violence. And, if the protest is generally or totally frustrated by the staff, it may turn into a riot.

If these sociopolitical protests are to be successful on a prisonwide basis, they must have support and force from the convict and Family levels, from those who have gained real power through covert economic activities. Since between two-thirds and three-fourths of all convicts are Chicanos and since almost all Family members are Chicanos, perhaps it is evident why the Chicanos are the only ethnic group that has that much power. Normally, most Chicano prisoners have little interest in sociopolitical activities. For example, Family members believe that politics are not really very important, that very little seems to get done in this area—either inside prison or on the streets. Their lack of interest appears to be quite pragmatic, being based on what they consider to be a dearth of truly significant results from political efforts. In contrast, the economic efforts of Chicanos do show results, even though they often may be less than ideal. Inside prison, Family's economic endeavors have yielded impressive fruits that never could have been attained through open sociopolitical means.

There are times, however, that Chicanos or Family members will covertly (from the staff perspective) use the power and authority they have acquired through economic activities to influence and lead sociopolitical activities inside. Recognizing this, many prisoners claim that a protest inside could not succeed on a prisonwide basis without the support of the Chicanos. And, without Family backing, Chicanos probably would not even press for a protest. The Chicanos' ability to pressure other prisoners into protest lies in the fact that most other prisoners have a fearful respect of Family (if they are aware of its existence), of convicts, and of the potential violence of Chicanos. Few prisoners actually know which Chicanos are Family members or convicts; so all Chicanos are regarded solicitously by most prisoners—especially if the Chicanos are actively exerting pressure in support of a protest. Occasionally non-Chicanos may start sociopolitical action over a particular issue, and situational leaders may rise to fill the temporary need to front the prisoners' action to the staff. However, these leaders are not the real leaders. The real power lies hidden with the Chicanos and convicts; and without the active support of this real power, the protest action would never become prisonwide.

Except for the occasional, temporary, issue-oriented sociopolitical leadership and activity displayed on a prisonwide basis, the only other real sociopolitical leadership in prison occurs among smaller groups of prisoners. Generally having little if any impact on the general prisoner population, this type of leadership can best be understood by examining its manifestations among each of the three major ethnic groups.

## ANGLO LEADERS

The Anglos essentially are leaderless. Anglo convicts generally agree with Chicano and black prisoners who observe that the Anglos seem to feel that they own this country, that the culture is theirs, that they are the majority, and that there is no reason for them to organize or stick together as a united group. Generally, their only form of leadership is found among small informal cliques, where a few prisoners with like interests will group together for pleasure, diversion, or even protection. Normally, those who lead cliques do so in a very informal manner, and the actions of the cliques have very little if any significant influence on the general prisoner population. The one limited exception among the Anglos is a relatively large, tightly knit clique that has been successfully formed by men who have experienced enough persecution from the larger Anglo culture to feel a strong sense of group unity. Except for Chicanos, these men form the tightest knit group of convicts inside prison. They take pride in being Okies and in being very righteous convicts. However, even the Okies' unity is only on a large clique basis, with relatively little sociopolitical influence or impact on the general prisoner population. Their unity is effective merely as a protective mechanism (other prisoners know that it is unwise to try to pressure an Okie) and in their economic dealings.

## BLACK LEADERS

In order to analyze the sociopolitical leadership among the blacks, it should be noted that the black prisoners seem to be broken up into four major segments of about equal size. The prisoners in three of these segments have formed into loose groups that are led by quiet, relatively powerful leaders. The fourth segment is leaderless, with no general unity seen among the prisoners in it. With the three former groups, each of the leaders is informally chosen by the influential prisoners among the group and pushed into the position of power. These leaders are real leaders in the full sense of the term while they are in power, and they continue in this capacity as long as the influential prisoners support them. Although it rarely happens, when one of these leaders loses his position of leadership, he usually leaves the group with ill feelings and bitter words. The deposed leader will end up in the leaderless segment. Each of these three leaders has the power to get many things done for those in his group by using the system to advantage and coordinating the collective manipulative ability of the members of the group. However, these leaders have no real influence on major sociopolitical issues or in areas of activity that are below the inmate level of the prisoner culture. Even if these leaders were to try to exercise power on major issues, few prisoners from outside their groups would follow them; and the staff would almost immediately isolate and punish them. Consequently, they have little significant effect on the general prisoner population or even on the black prisoners in general. Economically, the power or influence of these leaders is minimal, being limited to the inmate level.

The leaderless nature of the fourth segment of the black prisoner population is much like the absence of leadership described among Anglo prisoners, with the only leadership found among the small cliques that group together for pleasure, diversion, or even protection. Although some larger cliques have formed among the prisoners in this segment in the past, their influence generally has been minimal. For example, for several years the Black Muslims have received a great deal of attention by CDC. However, even though the Black Muslims are a very tightly knit group in some ways, their group is little more than a large clique. The Black Muslims have a minimal impact on the rest of the prisoners; they have no significant economic power. Much like a small Nazi group that persists among the Anglos, the Black Muslims are largely ignored by other prisoners. The Muslims are concerned about their own ideas, not about issues that are important to the prisoners in general.

## CHICANO LEADERS

As an ethnic group, the Chicano prisoners do not have sociopolitical leaders who work in what most people would consider to be a *typical*, overt manner, dealing with issues that are significant to all Chicano prisoners. In contrast to this type of leadership (which I will refer to as "typical leadership"), there does exist *real* leadership that takes action on significant sociopolitical issues on rare occasions. This "real leadership" will be discussed presently. First, however, the reasons for the failure of the typical sociopolitical leadership should be considered, because some of those reasons will add to our understanding of the real leadership among Chicano prisoners.

## TYPICAL LEADERSHIP

In the first place, any attempt to treat significant issues through typical leadership would not be tolerated by the staff. To be successful, such leadership must involve power; and real power among the prisoners can potentially lead to prisoner unity—which is a threat to staff authority and power over the prisoners. Since typical leadership is overt in nature, it would not be tolerated; the staff would effectively eliminate it by isolating the leaders. Chicano prisoners are fully aware that important activities must be carried out in a covert manner—as Family has done in the economic area.

Even if the staff would not interfere, the typical form of open sociopolitical leadership would fail among Chicano prisoners, who have a very negative attitude toward typical leaders. This attitude is a reflection of certain aspects of the Chicano subcultural traditions, ideals, and experience on the streets. And, the size and nature of the prisoner culture seems to have led to an intensity of that negative attitude among Chicano prisoners. In prison, the Chicanos are able to isolate themselves and maintain their identity as a subcultural group to a greater degree than Chicanos on the streets are able to do. Outside prison, Chicanos are usually drawn into the larger national culture by the necessity of earning a living. This entails considerable time and interaction outside of the Chicano subculture and tends to weaken or dilute that subculture. Inside prison, though, it is the illegal and rule-breaking economic activity of Chicanos that has greatly added to their sense of identity and unity as a subcultural group. With their emphasis on economic activities (which they, not the Anglos, control), they have a greater sense of shared interests. In addition, being fewer in number than on the streets, their relations often are more direct. Also, since there are fewer of the highly acculturated (Anglolike) Chicanos among them, they are able to see themselves ideally as equals. Accordingly, if a Chicano prisoner were to attempt to assume a typical leadership role, reaction against him would be more intense than on the streets. In prison, such an act almost would place the individual outside the group; and most Chicano prisoners would see him as being in opposition to the group in many ways—much as staff members and inmates are antagonistic to convicts.

It appears that the negative attitude toward typical leaders arises from both subcultural experience in the United States and traditional village life in Mexico. A Chicano prisoner exemplified an idea that was frequently expressed by others when he said, "Anyone in a position of authority has always abused it when dealing with the Mexican villagers or with Chicanos." Another prisoner typically claimed, "We are so used to being abused by people in positions of authority that we don't trust Chicanos who attain those positions." Being aware that the villagers in Mexico are abused by those outside (nonvillage) authorities, and having experienced a similar situation on the streets, Chicano prisoners are not willing to let one from their midst do the same to them—to have *real* power over them in the typical way, to be able to manipulate and maltreat them. Chicano prisoners see themselves as equals—as members of the Chicano group; and when someone assumes a formal leadership role, it is seen as stepping out of the group and joining the other side—the side that traditionally has been abusive of Chicanos and Mexican villagers.

Chicano prisoners feel that most of the Chicanos who do assume a typical leadership role on the streets seem to not only step out of the real grass-roots element and join the Anglo side, but they also enjoy personal gain and profit—often at the expense of the grass-roots Chicanos. Some Chicano prisoners agree that this may be merely an extension of a traditional pattern that still exists in Mexico, where those who do reach a position of influence also are prone to use their position for personal economic gain. For example, these Chicano prisoners realize that many public officials in Mexico are so poorly paid that it is expected that they will take their *mordida* (bite)—cut or bribe—before doing what they are hired and paid by the government to do. Projecting from that traditional pattern, the prisoners have reason to believe that many Chicanos who attain positions of influence or power on the streets are prone to use their position for personal economic gain too. This feeling is so strong that even those leaders who would not take personal economic advantage of their leadership position find it difficult to overcome the suspicion of doing so. Chicano prisoners are aware that there are some individuals who are exceptions to this pattern—the most well known being Cesar Chavez—who have refused to accept the financial reward that others might demand. Likewise inside prison, if a Chicano prisoner were to attempt to assume a typical leadership role, the other Chicano prisoners would see him as not only stepping out of their group and joining the staff side, but also as doing so for personal advantage. Although the personal profit involved might not be economic in nature, it certainly would be seen as potentially being at the expense of his fellow Chicano prisoners. Thus, it can be seen that such a step would also be breaking the convict code—against fellow Chicanos (the majority of whom are either convicts or convictlike).

For further insight into the Chicanos' negative attitude toward typical leaders, let us consider certain aspects of three roles: the ideal role of the Chicano, the ideal role of the Chicano leader, and the actual role of the typical leader in the larger United States culture. The ideal role of the Chicano and the ideal role of the Chicano leader both involve living up to the ideals of *machismo*, including the following: one should always keep one's word, one should reject and never engage in hypocrisy, and one should remain loyal to the group of which he is a member. Some of the actual necessities involved in the role of the typical leader in the larger culture seem to be in direct conflict. Typical leadership in the large, complex United States culture involves compromise, which usually means backing down on one's word at times. The realities of the situation often preclude a leader from being able to deliver on his word at all times; consequently his word no longer can be depended on. Chicanos view this compromise as hypocritical and reject the typical leader who, of necessity, engages in compromise. He is not deemed worthy of being supported or followed. The Chicano himself would not be *macho* if he followed the non-*macho* leader.

From discussions with Chicanos—prisoners and freemen—it appears that this role conflict generally has not been adequately resolved by Chicanos. As an outside Chicano leader said, "Chicanos always end up stabbing someone who assumes a position of leadership in the back—failing to give that person support." Chicanos view a man who does not keep his word as one who would misuse others. And, as a Chicano prisoner stated, "Our cultural experience has taught us to be proud; and anyone who tries to manipulate us must be rejected. We rebel against abusive leaders in a passive, introverted way—we refuse to follow." Another Chicano prisoner suggests a reason for the general failure of Chicanos to resolve this conflict: many Chicanos may not be fully aware of this role conflict. He stated that "Chicano leaders don't take the time to explain their position to the masses of Chicanos. They assume that we understand without explanation." Later, this prisoner agreed with several who thought that some of the leaders themselves may not recognize the incompatibility of the actual role of the typical leader with the two ideal Chicano roles.

## REAL LEADERSHIP

The real leadership that exists among the Chicano prisoners is quite different from the typical leadership that has been discussed above. The real Chicano leaders do not assume the typical role of leader, so they avoid the conflict that exists between that role and the ideals of *machismo*. On a sociopolitical basis, this real leadership normally functions only among smaller units of social organization, such as cliques or *barrio* groups. Among these smaller groups, the leadership deals with things that are important to members of these groups, but are not of significance on a prisonwide basis. To an outsider, this type of leadership is obscure. The actual leaders do not fit the form, or assume the outward role that most people in the United States culture expect.

When a decision needs to be made among these smaller groups, the issue usually is extensively discussed by members of the group. When a consensus is reached, all members of the group act upon that decision; and there is no need to have a formal leader as such. The closest thing to typical leaders are those individuals who are respected for their wisdom, intuition, and good advice. At the most, they talk persuasively and perhaps give positively stated advice; but they do not command or order anyone to do anything. Actually, they are the real leaders. Their friendly, advising type of leadership takes into account the strong individualism found in the Chicano subculture, where all men ideally are recognized as having a head on their shoulders. It allows all the men involved to feel that they personally took part in making the decision.

Normally there are several real leaders in any group. Although they are viewed as equals in the group, the members also recognize them as having the best ability to make decisions and give advice. Consequently, their advice and suggestions are followed. In this way, the influential among the group actually do lead the group. To an outside observer, however, it would appear that decisions are made and things accomplished without leaders. Even some Chicanos do not think of those who are the real leaders of their group as leaders, because they do not act like typical leaders. For example, a member of the El Paso, Texas, group said that his group "actually is ruled by consensus, not even by influential people. I've never seen anyone give an order or even make a suggestion that could be construed as an order. The most orderlike thing would be someone saying 'Let's go down to the lower yard and have some sweet rolls.' " Some of those who are influential and actually are among the real leaders would never consider themselves as leaders.

A Chicano convict commented,

> Chicano leaders are more subtle than Anglo leaders. Our leaders don't get up in front and talk. They lead in a friendly, asking way—such as saying to you, 'Hey, what are you doing tonight? Could you go over to such and such a place to help this guy out?' The real leaders are never in an open position where they can be openly recognized and picked off by the staff. This is not to say that the real leaders would not stand up and be counted and do things if necessary.

It is the covert nature of this real leadership among Chicano prisoners that assures its success in prison. In addition to its success on a sociopolitical basis among smaller groups, it has been developed and used to a much greater degree by Family—in activities that are primarily economic in nature.

As noted earlier, there are rare occasions when the real Chicano leadership may decide to take action on sociopolitical issues that are of utmost significance on a prisonwide basis. In such instances, a consensus first would be reached informally among many smaller Chicano groups that the issues warrant their support. Later, if the influential members from most of those groups collectively arrive at a similar informal accord, there will be general, prisonwide agreement among the Chicanos that they will back the action with all of their influence and power— which is considerable. Only with the support of the Chicanos will action, such as a peaceful work strike, succeed. This support by the Chicanos may be entirely beneath the surface, with no open action by them. In fact, prisoner spokesmen from other ethnic groups may be allowed to openly front for all the prisoners— including the Chicanos. During or after the protest, these spokesmen usually are singled out and punished by the staff. These spokesmen are not the *real* leaders though.

During these rare instances, when the real Chicano leadership decides to support prisonwide sociopolitical action, one or a few Chicanos may rise to a position of overt sociopolitical leadership. I call these individuals "situational leaders." To the staff and other outsiders, these situational leaders appear to have power and to be the leaders of the Chicanos; in fact, they themselves may think so. However, they actually are merely allowed to front as leaders in this sociopolitical situation by the real leaders who remain behind the scenes—before, during, and after the situation. The situational leaders have no more power or authority over the Chicano prisoners than the overt spokesmen from other ethnic groups would have when the Chicanos allow them to front for all prisoners. In other words, the situational leaders merely fill a temporary need. They play one part of the role of a typical leader—as the spokesman to the staff and the outside sociopolitical system if necessary. As long as the situational leaders are in accord with the informal consensus of the *real* leaders, and as long as the temporary situation exists, the

Chicanos will follow. But, if the situational leaders stray and fail to lead in the proper direction, the Chicanos will not follow. And, when the situation has passed, when the Chicanos no longer need them as fronts, the situational leaders lose the power that they only appeared to have.

These situational leaders tend to come from among the most highly acculturated Chicano prisoners. Usually they have had considerable interaction with the Anglo culture in comparison with the other Chicano prisoners. They are better able to verbally and socially interact with the staff. When a pressing occasion arises that requires someone to interact with the staff on the Chicanos' behalf, their ability is recognized and respected as such. However, under normal circumstances, many Chicanos may have negative feelings about these men—that they are only "on an ego kick" or that they are so acculturated that they have "lost their Chicanoness." Some of the situational leaders may also be among the few Chicanos who do fill typical prisoner leadership roles inside prison. From their staff-sanctioned positions of leadership, they have a limited impact on, or influence over, most Chicano prisoners. Granted, some of them may have personal or charismatic qualities that would entice others to follow, but the followers are relatively few in number. Usually these typical leaders are not very highly respected by many other Chicanos because of their association and interaction with the hypocrisy of the prison system. Nevertheless, in a tight situation the real leaders allow these highly acculturated Chicanos to use their special ability to the advantage of all the Chicanos, and any negative feelings about these men are temporarily suspended while the situation exists. Ordinarily, by the end of the prisoners' protest, these situational leaders have been identified by the staff; and since they are mistakenly assumed to be the real leaders, they normally are isolated and punished by the staff.

To conclude this chapter, it should be noted that those real leaders who have a covert, yet prisonwide influence are well aware that all prisoners who openly act on truly significant sociopolitical issues are susceptible to severe punishment by the staff. This discipline, or social control, by the staff is intended to discourage meaningful sociopolitical action by prisoners on issues that may challenge the position or authority of the staff, CDC, or the Adult Authority. Under normal circumstances, the threat of severe social control successfully discourages such action by the prisoners. This is why the real leaders who are able to exercise prisonwide power undetected normally devote their efforts to economic activities, only rarely using their power for sociopolitical ends. As shown in Chapter 6, the economic activities of these real leaders are extremely successful and can be sustained on a permanent basis. In addition, those who control these covert economic activities can generally avoid the formal and informal social control of the staff—which the prisoners contend is often excessive and/or abusive.

# 8 / Social control

A detailed description of the official social control inside prison might include a review of the numerous laws and rules that pertain to CDC, the prison staff, and the prisoners. These laws and rules are designed to set behavioral limits which enable the staff to maintain proper custody over, and assure a reasonable degree of peace and security among, the prisoners. In many respects, the staff is able to accomplish those ends, maintaining some social order among the prisoners. Consequently, it cannot be denied that this official type of social control does have an important impact on the prisoners' lives. However, there is a considerable amount of unofficial social control which is either semicovert or entirely surreptitious in nature. This unofficial social control often is of greater consequence to prisoners than the official type; and, for a full understanding of the reality of the prisoner culture, its significance should not be overlooked. Accordingly, for our purposes, a description of how unofficial social control is exercised *by both the staff and the prisoners* is more important than a detailed review of the above mentioned laws and rules. However, before delving into that study, let us just briefly consider a few aspects of the official type of social control.

## OFFICIAL, LEGAL: STAFF OVER PRISONERS

Officially, only the staff has the legal authority to dominate the lives of the prisoners. Being entrusted with the custody of the prisoners, the staff makes use of laws, rules, walls, guns, and the like to maintain control over the prisoners. The staff endeavors to enforce compliance with the laws and rules by disciplining those prisoners who they have reason to believe are guilty of breaking laws or rules. Let us briefly outline some of the basic steps of the disciplinary procedure. Normally, the staff member who learns of a serious violation is required to make a written report. This serves as the legal basis for placing the prisoner in isolation until the prison's disciplinary committee holds disciplinary court—usually within two days. In most cases, the prisoner is found guilty as charged and subjected to punishment. The punishment ranges in severity from a warning, reprimand, or temporary loss of privileges to confinement in isolation, in either "the hole" or the Adjustment Center. However, if a serious felony is involved (such as assaulting a prisoner or staff member, or possessing a deadly weapon or narcotics), and if the staff has enough evidence for a legal case against the prisoner, he may be prose-cuted for the crime in an outside court of law. If convicted, the prisoner will be subject to an additional sentence for the crime that was committed in prison. These steps in the disciplinary procedure are overt, being clearly based on laws and rules. If the staff were to prepare a description of this procedure for general release to the public, it would probably include at least these basic steps.

In contrast, if the prisoners were allowed to prepare a description of the disci-plinary procedure without staff interference or pressure, it would go into much greater depth than the staff description. The prisoners' report—certainly not a public relations effort—would attempt to show the public the reality they face. The prisoners would present certain aspects and implications of the formal disciplinary procedure that normally are semicovert in nature and somewhat obscured from outsiders. Actually these additional details might be considered official, because they, too, technically are based on laws or rules. However, the staff would not voluntarily include them in its description. If an outsider should be knowledgeable of these additional details, and if the outsider should ask about them, the officials

*A guard on the gun rail, looking down at the entrance to the printing, bookbinding, and cobbler shops. (Photograph from the* San Francisco Chronicle)

would admit that they exist and point out that they are entirely within the law—
*as they see it*. In a strict sense, these additional aspects and implications might be
considered as part of the official social control. Even the prisoners would admit
that they technically are legal. However, since the public generally is ignorant of
them, and since the prisoners have long contended and legally protested that they
are abusive and of questionable legality, I will treat them under unofficial social
control.

## UNOFFICIAL:  STAFF OVER PRISONERS

The unofficial social control exercised by the staff goes beyond the publicly
acknowledged official means of control. Technically, some of it may be legal, but
much of it is illegal. In order to avoid public criticism or legal action, the staff
tries to keep its unofficial disciplinary measures semicovert or secret. The prisoners
acknowledge that much of this unofficial punishment is not physically abusive.
However, through bitter personal experience, most prisoners have come to realize
that mental brutality may be much more severe than the physical type. If all the
manifestations of the unofficial staff control were presented in detail, the treatment
would be so lengthy that it probably would prove quite depressive and wearisome
to the reader. I have seen such a reaction when outsiders were overwhelmed by
a prisoner's presentation of a 15-page listing (without descriptive details) of some
of these usurpations of power. For our purposes, several selected examples of the
staff's unofficial social control over the prisoners will indicate the possible degree of
this control and reveal some of the major abuses felt by the prisoners. First, let
us consider two closely related examples that technically have remained legal to
the time of this writing: the intrinsic abuse of due process of law by the disciplinary committee and "facing the board with a dirty jacket."

### Legal, Yet Abusive

The formal prison discipline is administered by the disciplinary committee, which
normally is composed of four staff members: the associate warden custody, the
associate warden care and treatment, and representatives from the counseling and
psychiatric departments.The committee holds disciplinary court in the Adjustment
Center and in B Section; the prisoner usually is brought before the committee while
it hears his case. The committee faces the difficult task of helping to maintain custody by trying fairly and expeditiously to punish prisoners who have formally been
"beefed" (written up) by a staff member for committing a serious violation of the
laws or rules that govern the prisoners. Unfortunately, considerations of time and
fairness are not compatible in this situation. Regrettably, a dilemma exists from
which expediency prevails. If full due process of law was allowed in disciplinary
court, the procedural formality probably would become so elaborate and time con-
suming that the committee could never accomplish its task. As illustration, on a typical day of hearings, the committee reviewed and made decisions as to the punishment of beefs allegedly committed by 42 prisoners. The most severe violation con-

sidered that day was murder; three prisoners were formally advised of their legal rights and were being held as suspects in the Adjustment Center while the murder was under investigation. The other beefs ranged down the scale of severity to being found in a compromising sexual position with another prisoner, and refusing to move out of the mess hall promptly when requested by a guard. At the end of the day, an outside observer probably would conclude that the disciplinary committee had sincerely tried to be fair and that the punishment generally seemed just.

From the prisoners' perspective, the disciplinary court is a kangaroo court. The prisoners feel that the principles of law and justice are disregarded or perverted by the disciplinary court. They believe the hearings tend to mock the ideals of due process of law as known in the United States. Prisoners are not allowed legal counsel, cannot confront or question their accusers, and cannot bring witnesses in their own defense. An example of a beef considered by the committee will show that a prisoner may not even be given the identity of his accusers. A prisoner who had been transferred from Folsom Prison had been assigned to work in the mess hall. After two weeks, he had been reported for "pressuring" (using the threat of physical force to attain ends that could not be achieved through legal means). Apparently a prisoner (who was allowed to remain anonymous) had merely told the guard this, and the guard wrote up the new prisoner. The accused prisoner protested that he had just arrived at San Quentin, that he had not even settled into things yet, and that he had no idea who would wrongfully accuse him. The committee pondered whether he was guilty or not. The reasoning behind the committee's decision was interesting. It was recognized that the prisoner might not be guilty; but if no action was taken, it would tend to undermine the authority of the guards; and to do this frequently would be demoralizing to the guards. Therefore, the prisoner was found guilty and sentenced to punishment. However, realizing that the prisoner might be innocent, the committee suspended the sentence. Even though due process of law was misused, justice appears to have prevailed.

If in-prison punishment was all that was involved in the committee's verdict, most prisoners might overlook the absence of due process of law and realize that the disciplinary committee faces a dilemma. Unfortunately, the prisoners often are subjected to additional punishment. Regardless of whether a prisoner actually is punished or whether he receives a suspended sentence, the fact that he has been judged guilty of a disciplinary infraction is recorded in his record, resulting in a "dirty jacket." From these dirty jackets arise an unofficial abuse that is keenly felt by the prisoners. They frequently are subjected to additional punishment by the Adult Authority for having a dirty disciplinary record. This is double jeopardy; and its impact is felt even more intensely by those prisoners who have had a dirty jacket unjustly imposed on them by the disciplinary committee.

After a prisoner has served the median time for his particular felony, there is a strong probability that he will be granted a parole at his next parole board hearing. However, if the prisoner's disciplinary record shows infractions within the preceding year, he knows that he will be subjected to double jeopardy. When "facing the board with a dirty jacket," a prisoner is likely to be told to clean up his jacket for a year if he wants to be seriously considered for parole. The Adult Authority usually regards a disciplinary infraction as an indication that the prisoner is not yet rehabilitated. Regardless of whether the prisoner received a suspended sentence or was punished, and regardless of whether or not he actually was guilty of the infraction, as long as the record shows that he was judged guilty, he is most likely to serve at least an additional year beyond his current board appearance.

(As an aside, it should be noted that all prisoners are guilty of committing disciplinary infractions on a routine basis. Only a minute portion of those infractions are ever detected by the staff, however. Many of those prisoners who are caught are not written up because the staff tends to overlook many infractions committed by prisoners who display the proper submissive attitude. In contrast, the prisoner who refuses to be cowed by the guards and remains arrogant is apt to be beefed frequently. In addition, many of those prisoners who are involved in some of the most serious infractions—often pertaining to economic activities—seldom are caught or beefed for infractions. Prisoners strongly contend that a man's behavior in prison is not directly related to, nor is it a valid indication of, what a prisoner will do when he is released to the streets. The prison is one world; the streets are another. It is not unlike entering the world of war. A battlefront hero may learn to be an efficient killer of men; but he will not continue his killing when he returns to his own culture; and few, if any people in his own culture would consider him a killer.)

Having briefly questioned the validity of the disciplinary record as a basis for the action by the Adult Authority, let us return to the topic of double jeopardy that faces a prisoner who is judged guilty of disciplinary infractions. Although the prisoner is subjected to multiple punishment for the same act, and even though there may be no due process of law in the disciplinary hearings that may have unjustly convicted him of the disciplinary infraction, outside courts of law have been reluctant to interfere with prison discipline or the actions of the Adult Authority that are based on verdicts of the disciplinary committee. It can be seen that a prisoner who is repeatedly beefed and convicted of disciplinary infractions may not only be subjected to in-prison punishment, he also may serve many years beyond the median time that normally is served for his crime. If a prisoner should overtly react against abuses in the prison system or try to bring about changes from within, he may be branded as a habitual troublemaker or "revolutionary" and be made to serve his maximum sentence in prison—much of that time probably being served in the Adjustment Center. Prisoners contend that they will have to continue to endure this unofficial, yet legal abuse until the California legislature changes the laws or until the courts intercede.

Illegal

Now let us consider two examples of the illegal type of unofficial staff social control that is acutely felt by prisoners: "silent beefs" to which individual prisoners are subjected; and the intentional manipulation of large numbers of prisoners for ulterior motives. Neither of these examples would be able to survive an open legal test; they are illegal in spirit, if not in fact. However, they also are surreptitious in nature. Consequently, a prisoner or an outsider usually is unable to prove that this type of activity does in fact take place. Under normal circumstances, the very evidence necessary for that proof has either been destroyed or purposely remains hidden in the minds of those who are responsible for the activity and who have reasons for keeping the activity covert.

*Silent Beefs*

When the staff suspects that a prisoner is guilty of committing a crime in prison, but when there is insufficient evidence to legally convict the prisoner in a court of law, the staff may decide to subject the prisoner to a "silent beef." When this occurs, the staff is careful never to formally charge the prisoner with committing the crime. However, some staff members know (and the prisoner soon comes to realize) that he will end up serving the median time normally served for the felony that originally sent him to prison *plus* the median time normally served for the crime behind the silent beef. This usually is possible under the indeterminate sentence system, because the maximum sentences are long enough to allow the median times for two crimes still to be within the maximum time of the original conviction. For example, assume that a prisoner is in prison for a crime that carries a 1-to-15 year sentence, with the median time served inside prison being 3 years. If the staff were to strongly suspect that he committed another felony inside prison, yet if they did not have sufficient evidence to convict him in court, the prisoner might be subjected to a silent beef. If the median time for the in-prison crime was 6 years, he would serve those 6 years in addition to 3 for the original conviction. Only after serving 9 years would the prisoner seriously be considered for possible parole. In this case, the 15-year maximum sentence for the original crime would be long enough to cover the median times for both crimes.

A young prisoner's comments about the silent beef are representative of the feelings expressed by many other prisoners. Without committing himself as to his innocence or guilt, he noted:

> The bulls think I stabbed another inmate. They don't have any evidence for a conviction; but since they think I'm guilty, I'll serve the time for that beef too. These so-called defenders of the peace, these so-called good guys, set themselves up as God, judge, and jury. They're able to get away with convicting a man of a crime merely on a hunch, or on the word of a snitch, or on some other sort of invalid evidence. You can't fight the board on this either, because they're in cahoots with the bulls and they'll always be able to come up with something other than the real reason why they're keeping you in—why they think you aren't rehabilitated yet. You can't protest, because it's just your word against theirs; and they always win.

A sergeant's account of a sequence of events that could have led to a prisoner being subjected to a silent beef will add to an understanding of what a silent beef is. On August 31, 1966, a sergeant who was in charge of investigating crimes committed inside San Quentin quite proudly told me how he had recently obtained a confession to a murder that occurred in the latter part of 1965. A snitch had indicated to the sergeant that a "Mexican-American" prisoner had been killed by a certain Anglo prisoner. The sergeant noted the problems he faced in getting around the *Escobedo*, *Miranda*, and *Dorado* court decisions which pertain to an accused suspect's legal rights to counsel and to remain silent. To avoid the legal implications of those court decisions, he had to take great care to avoid accusing the named prisoner. Any pressure applied on the prisoner would have to be very subtle. Therefore, the sergeant "indirectly" accused the Anglo by implying to several of his close friends that he had "something big" on him. In this indirect way, the prisoner was led to believe that he would serve time for the killing, under the spiteful control of San Quentin officials who felt that he was guilty but did not have a case that would hold up in a court of law. After almost a year passed, the continued pressure finally pushed the named prisoner into such a mental state that he could no longer tolerate his situation. He broke down to the sergeant and started to blurt out a confession; but the sergeant refused to take the confession himself. Only after the assistant district attorney for Marin County came to the prison was the prisoner "allowed" to confess. Technically, this was a voluntary confession of a prisoner who had never even been accused of the crime. The sergeant concluded his account by noting that the prisoner would have served the time anyway, even if he personally would have had to go before the board each time that the prisoner came up for parole consideration. Actually, a concluding scene occurred after my discussion with the sergeant. The scene was set at the Marin County Courthouse in 1967, when the prisoner was convicted of second degree murder.

There are many other, often poignant examples of a prisoner's being subjected to a silent beef. However, let me merely present a final brief example that shows how a parolee can be returned to prison and be subjected to a silent beef if his maximum time is long enough. When I was writing this chapter, a parolee whom I first met in San Quentin had been accused of murder and was being held in jail. I called his parole officer to try to find out some additional details about the nature of the evidence the authorities had against him. As had most parolees, this man had committed parole violations. Normally, many parole violations are overlooked by parole officers. However, if a parolee should be arrested for a crime, but if there is not sufficient evidence to convict him, the violations may be retroactively used to build a case against the parolee, allowing the board to revoke his parole. Setting aside most particulars of this parolee's case, and regardless of whether or not he is guilty or innocent, my conversation with his parole officer proved to be noteworthy regarding silent beefs. In this instance, he agreed that if the district attorney should fail to have enough evidence to try the case in court, the Adult Authority would still be able to revoke the man's parole and make him serve the sentence for murder. Other prisoners and parolees admit that even if a man is acquitted in court by a jury, he may be returned to prison and be subjected to a silent beef. The parolee usually has no defense against this situation because the parole violations are always used as the "official" reasons for returning the man to prison; the *real* reason is never officially stated.

## Manipulation of Prisoners

How can staff members illegally, yet intentionally manipulate large numbers of prisoners for ulterior motives? I believe the "massive racial confrontation" that took place at San Quentin in January 1967 is an excellent example of how that can be done. Unfortunately, considerations of length preclude a detailed treatment of these events, which could easily be a short chapter in itself. However, let me briefly point out some of the salient factors that led many prisoners and staff members to disbelieve the "official" version that was presented to the public by prison administrators.

There were many conflicting versions of the circumstances surrounding the so-called race riots of Wednesday, January 18, 1967. The following version is based on a wide variety of sources—the most important of which were my numerous discussions with prisoners and staff members. I have tried to eliminate the obviously false and overly biased versions. Under the circumstances, the following account is as reasonable and as objective as possible. I believe that most prisoners, as well as the majority of staff members who were willing to "privately" discuss the riotous events and surrounding circumstances with me, would generally agree with the following narrative.

A minor incident that occurred on the preceeding Thursday between a black kitchen worker and a guard was interpreted by the black prisoners who worked in the kitchen as an act of racial prejudice. The intense resentment of the blacks led the staff to "fire" 12 of the prisoners from their kitchen jobs on Friday. The following day 31 more kitchen workers went on a sympathy strike. Black prisoners called for a strike of all black workers on Monday. In order to break the strike attempt, the staff ignored the routine precautions against letting men go to jobs in the industrial area when the fog precludes surveillance of the men as they go to work; three blacks were beaten, one Anglo was stabbed, and one Anglo was killed! Tuesday, either on principle or out of fear of retaliation, the majority of the 1200 black prisoners refused to go to work.

By Wednesday morning, the strike had lost its momentum, was virtually over, and would have fizzled to nothing within a day or two. However, the staff "mishandled" the nearly 3000 prisoners who gathered as usual in the upper yard after lunch to await work call. Gradually, opposing racial groups were formed. Later a small number of rabble-rousers shouted curses from one group to another. Some of the prisoners began arming themselves with boards, pipes, and the like that they were tearing from benches, picnic tables, the small guard shack, and anything else that could be ripped apart. The guards locked all exits from the yard, trapping the majority of prisoners who were there for legitimate reasons, who merely thought of themselves as spectators to the antics of a few prisoners. Then, as the guards later claimed, they found it necessary to lay down a "wall of rifle fire" to keep the opposing groups from tearing each other apart. And by 4:00 P.M., the press was told that "the danger is over for today."

However this was not so for the nearly one thousand Anglos and Chicanos who had been herded from the upper yard to the football field in the lower yard. After dark on that winter evening, many of the prisoners, who had been in shirtsleeves when things began at noon in the upper yard, ran to the bleachers to tear off wood to make bonfires in an attempt to keep warm. With rifles and tear gas, the guards tried to stop this. Later, outsiders were to assume that the eight prisoners who were wounded by bullets or ricochet slugs came too close to the "wall of fire" in the upper yard. However, the prisoners contend that most were wounded running the guards' gauntlet in the lower yard. Late that night, in groups of nine, prisoners were singled out and ordered to march away from the other prisoners. When away from the main group, they were made to strip—as a precautionary measure to prevent weapons from being taken back into the blocks—and led by nine escort guards back to their cells. This was a time-consuming process. A convict who thought he was "almost frozen" when he was led from the lower yard at 3:05 A.M. claimed that the last two prisoners were stripped and led from the lower yard at 4:05 A.M.

Most prisoners bitterly contended and many staff members generally agreed that the abuse of prisoners during the following weeks was unnecessary and entirely out of proportion. There was much more resentment toward the guards for their acts on the day of the so-called race riots than there was racial tension. Many staff members maintained that things would have rapidly cooled to normal if the prisoners had just been kept locked in their cells for a few days—often a routine measure after a prisoner strike, protest, or disturbance. However, the guards went far beyond a mere lockup; they continued their reign of abuse. But for their sheer number, the claims of needless brutality of some guards in the following days and weeks would seem unbelievable.

The prison was closed to all but staff members for nearly six weeks. When I finally was allowed to enter San Quentin again, the major subject of discussion with prisoners and staff members frequently was the so-called race riots and the associated events. In addition to relating specific details, almost every conversation, at one time or another, turned to the many unanswered questions that arose from the events on and around January 18. Even staff members were unable to make sense out of the actions of some custody staff. For example, many staff members (including several guards who stressed the "private" nature of their discussion with me) and prisoners had some strong contentions about the lengthy buildup of opposing racial groups and hostility that preceded the "wall of fire" that the guards finally laid down to keep the two opposing groups separated. It was generally recognized that at almost any time during that long buildup, the prisoners could have been stopped in a variety of ways. For example, a guard lieutenant noted that one way to clear the yard of prisoners almost immediately is to call for a "mandatory lockup." Continuing, he stressed, "The situation in the upper yard could have been controlled earlier." The lieutenant said that officials never did adequately explain why the situation was allowed to foment to the point of violence. He indicated that there was no official censure of the associate warden, custody, or the captain (of the guards) for their handling of the situation, but that there was "a lot of unofficial criticism and gossip" among custody staff. Also, there was considerable awareness among the guards that the prisoners felt they had been manipulated, and some of the guards were inclined to agree with the prisoners.

Another peculiar thing reportedly occurred during the riots. Two particular inmates played principal roles as instigators. During the buildup of opposing groups and the beginning of the riots, these two were most active. They were right out in front of the Anglo and Chicano group, cursing and threatening the blacks while a guard was taking movies from the gun rail above the prisoners. Even if there had been no movies, prisoners are quite certain that the captain would never forget being cursed and told by the two inmates that they were in charge and, in no uncertain terms, how he should sexually abuse himself. Later, B Section was filled with hundreds of prisoners being punished for their activities during the riots, but the two leaders apparently were never disciplined. Instead, it appears that they were rewarded for their efforts. Prisoners claimed that one leader was discharged for Folsom Prison less than three months after the riots and that the other was paroled from San Quentin about two months after the incident. After more than a year of effort, I was finally able to confirm that one of these inmates was paroled from San Quentin on March 21, 1967; however, there was no further record of the other inmate who was supposedly transferred to Folsom Prison on February 3, 1967.

In addition to the other reasons to disbelieve the official account of the so-called race riots, there appeared to be two major ulterior motives that may have led the higher levels of the custody staff to precipitate the prisoners into the crisis. First, a fundamental reorganization of the institutional structure (called "unitization") was being prepared for at San Quentin, which was intended to counter the sheer size of the prison and allow each cell block to function as a separate unit in many ways. It would have effectively shifted some power and authority to the treatment staff, with a deemphasis of custody. The reorganization being brought about by "unitization" caused considerable anxiety and tension among many higher level custody staff members who felt that a major readjustment or shift in power was taking place in the custody-treatment relationship (a relationship that had always been *at least* tacitly antagonistic in nature). Custody faced a serious problem. How could it counter the changes that would be brought about by "unitization?" How could it regain the power that it was losing to treatment staff?

To the above situation was introduced an additional factor which greatly intensified staff anxiety. The newly elected Governor Ronald Reagan announced that all departments of the state government would be required to cut their budgets by 10 percent. A lieutenant later confided that the resultant apprehensions about potential cuts in staff and programs, coupled with custody's fear of losing its position of power to treatment staff, caused a state of near panic among some of the staff on the powerful high levels of custody.

However, even if we assume that these were the ulterior motives and that some among the high levels of custody staff were responsible for purposely allowing a minor incident to swell into a major "racial confrontation," we are, and probably always will be, without direct evidence to support the view—because those who actually were involved in this purposeful manipulation of the prisoners have too much to lose to ever admit to such dealings. In lieu of documentation, let us consider the net results of the race riots, because they were repeatedly cited by prisoners and staff members as additional indirect evidence for their belief that some staff members acted for ulterior motives.

Staff members were reluctant to discuss officially the final outcome of the race riots. However, many staff members were willing to convey "privately" what they had "picked up" from other staff members. Concerning the budget, cuts were made in the treatment programs. A lieutenant indicated that the strike, the rioting, the prolonged unrest after the confrontation, and the staff movies of some of those activities ultimately enabled custody to avoid cutting its budget. Instead of decreasing the number of guards, custody was able to hire additional guards and spend a large amount (reported by several sources to be about a quarter of a million dollars) for overtime pay for the guards—supposedly necessary to properly control the prisoners as things gradually calmed down after the riots. Some claimed that custody's budget actually was increased. Regardless of whether or not this was true, there was no question among staff members that, budgetwise, custody definitely had prevailed over treatment.

The apparent (though dubious) need to impose extraordinary control over the prisoners during and after the so-called race riots allowed custody to clearly reestablish its position of power over treatment. At the time of the riots, the situation appeared to be so critical that treatment staff were required to temporarily fill custody roles. The meager effectiveness that counselors and other treatment staff had before the riots was *greatly* diminished in the eyes of most prisoners when many members of the treatment staff took up rifles, billy clubs, and other weapons to help put down the prisoners. As a prisoner said, "We thought so before, but now there's no question about what side the counselors are on. They're just bulls too." From many similar comments, it was obvious that the prisoners had been duly impressed. However, it was a negative impression that merely confirmed what many of them had earlier suspected. Some members of the treatment staff later expressed their regrets about the riots. They had been extremely reluctant to do what they were ordered to do; yet, technically, maintaining custody is part of their job, when and if necessary. Had a treatment staff member refused to join the guards, he probably would have been fired. Subsequently, there was no doubt that custody was in control of the prison and that treatment was subordinate to custody. In the area of staff power, too, there was no question that custody had definitely prevailed over treatment.

I openly admit that much of the evidence presented above is indirect. However, if the conclusions that so many staff members and prisoners drew from the evidence are correct, then it is obvious that a relatively small group of staff members were able to intentionally and successfully manipulate the prisoners (and many of their fellow staff members) for ulterior motives. Consequently, it can be seen that the staff's power to control the prisoners and maintain custody is an excessive, unrestrained power that also allows for, and perhaps generates, misuse of that power.

### Misleading the Public

To conclude this discussion of the illegal type of unofficial staff social control over prisoners, I would like to make some personal observations that apply not only to the so-called race riots treated above, but to other cases as well. (It should be noted that both prisoners and staff members have agreed with these observations.) A wide variety of factors have led me to conclude that prison administrators, on occasion, have grossly abused prisoners and intentionally misled the public —including the news media and state legislators. I personally believe that some prison administrators have quite deliberately capitalized on two things: the long-lived racial problems and tensions that exist inside and out of prison, and the negative attitude the public generally has toward the youthful "revolutionaries" or "militants" who, in recent years, have tried to bring about changes in our culture through radical means. Prison administrators have purposely done this to distort or hide the real issues that often are involved when violent incidents or disturbances occur among the prisoners, or when there is an organized demonstration by prisoners—such as a strike against abusive aspects of the prison system.

To illustrate how racial problems and tensions may be used advantageously by the staff, let us assume that there has been a series of violent incidents or a major disturbance inside a prison. The public generally is ignorant of the complexity and depths of the prisoner culture. The vast amount of covert activity (economic, sexual, and other) that takes place in spite of staff efforts often gives rise to violence. Granted, racial problems and tensions do exist and are very intense; but, as in the so-called race riots, race seldom is an issue behind eruption. The prisoners rarely would allow race to become an issue of general violence, because they know a *real* racial conflict on a prisonwide basis would result in tumultuous chaos. However, when either a series of violent incidents or a major disturbance does occur, the public's interest is temporarily aroused. Members of the news media will question prison administrators about the situation. Not wanting to publicly admit their inability to maintain control over the prisoners in so many ways, administrators have found an extremely effective way to stop the flow of frequently embarrassing questions and to hide the real causes. If they claim that the incidents are based on racial conflict, the public feels that it understands the situation and seems satisfied. Consequently, the real causes remain hidden, and the staff avoids public criticism.

Since the 1950s, California prisoners have repeatedly organized demonstrations to protest what they feel are abuses of the prison system. These protests have principally been against the Adult Authority and the indeterminate sentence system. Prisoners have gone through great personal sacrifice in hopes of bringing about significant, legitimate changes in the prison system. Unfortunately, the striking prisoners usually include other issues as reasons for their protest. This allows the administrators (who control the flow of information from behind the walls to the news media) to emphasize some issues and obscure others. If other issues are not involved in a protest, administrators can easily fabricate their own causes for release to the public. By using false or minor issues, the legitimacy of the protest can be brought into question and the leaders can be discredited.

For example, early in my research I discovered that administrators had been able to minimize and almost completely avoid the major issues behind an October 1963 work strike by prisoners at Folsom prison. I read original memos from prison administrators in the record jacket of a Chicano prisoner who had been one of the leaders of the strike. The main and *real* issues involved policies and actions of the Adult Authority that prisoners felt were abusive. However, a review of the *San Francisco Chronicle* and *Sacramento Bee* for that period of time revealed a very different "public" version: Prison administrators repeatedly indicated that the prisoners were striking for better food, more pay for their prison jobs, and shorter prison terms. The press and the public was never allowed to know the *real* issues.

Unfortunately, this pattern has not changed in any significant way. As late as January 1973, prisoners went on strike at San Quentin. The prisoners' list of 17 demands included some very old, yet extremely important issues: abolition of the Adult Authority, abolition of the indeterminate sentence system, and legal representation at parole hearings. These particular demands are rather complex in nature, though, and they were minimized and/or ignored in subsequent news reports. Instead, some of the less important, yet more colorful demands were stressed, including the resignation of the warden and the associate warden custody, the right to wear long hair and beards, conjugal visits, and public telephones inside the walls. In recent years, administrators have discovered new, more effective terms to call the leaders of a protest. It is easier to deprecate and discredit the previously-called "tough felons" or "ringleaders" by naming them "revolutionaries" or "militants." In this particular case, administrators claimed that a small group of "militants" was behind the strike, that this small group of "dissident inmates" intimidated the others into striking. Those who know the prisoner culture also know that a small group could not pressure or intimidate two-thirds of the prisoners at San Quentin into striking if some of the demands were not extremely important. Yet again, the public was intentionally and successfully misled by the administrators.

Prison administrators apparently realize that the simplest way to minimize the effect of protest against the prison system is to publicly discredit the prisoners. This tactic is used against outside critics, too. Occasionally a few of the outsiders who are knowledgeable of the prison system and understand the reasons behind these demonstrations openly support the prisoners during one of these demonstrations. By calling these outsiders "revolutionaries" or "militants," prison administrators attempt to degrade the outsiders, too. It should be noted that the prisoners who have been protesting against the abuses of the prison system for many years now are not what the general public expects when the term "revolutionary" or "militant" is used. Most of these prisoners are reasonable men who have long endured the abuses of the prison system, and who usually strike peacefully in protest against what they believe to be a misapplication of the ideals of the prison system. These prisoners have *not* been demanding that the walls be torn down, or that they be allowed to escape. Instead, they are trying to initiate some legitimate changes which might bring the real prison system back into accord with the ideal prison system. Prison administrators, from their position of power, have been able to keep the public ignorant of much that actually occurs inside prison by discrediting and obscuring this type of criticism. The intense bitterness and extreme frustration that lead to such demonstrations are beyond the comprehension of most outsiders. These strikes have been protests of desperation for prisoners who feel that all the legal means have generally failed them. These men have been willing to serve additional time in prison if necessary to bring these abuses to the public's attention, hopefully to bring about significant changes.

I contend that the public should be allowed to know. The prisoners should be taken seriously, because many of the reasons for their protest are legitimate. Many of the abuses of the prison system have been the subject of earnest efforts by attorneys and state legislators. Those efforts have resulted in some recent changes, but the changes fall short of what is needed. However, without some sort of safety valve for the legitimate complaints of prisoners and without significant changes to curb or eliminate abusive practices, I can only hope that an Attica-type massacre will not occur in other prisons. The root causes of protest lie well beyond the details of any incident. Unfortunately, the *real* causes probably will remain hidden from the public.

## UNOFFICIAL:   PRISONERS OVER PRISONERS

The manner in which social control is unofficially exercised by prisoners usually is either obscured from, unknown to, or distorted by outsiders. Even among the prisoners, there are many who never really understand how social order is maintained. An outsider, when considering the prisoner culture as a closed system, might expect to find a simple, lucid pattern of social control. However, if he is reminded of the official power and authority of the staff and of the absence of continuing sociopolitical leadership among the prisoners, the outsider might reconsider; he might imagine a state of anarchy existing in those areas of activity that are beyond the control of the staff. The prisoner culture is far from a state of anarchy. The outsider would be mistaken in either assumption.

Several complex things combine to complicate analysis of how prisoners unofficially exercise social control in areas of their activity that are beyond the control of the staff. For example, since prisoners must keep much of what they do hidden from the staff, things seldom, if ever, are formalized in written form; they merely are understood in a general way by those involved. As on the streets, most of the acceptable norms of social behavior need not be written down. However, unlike the outside world, in prison there are no rules or laws in written form that define the limits of acceptable social behavior. There is no listing of what penalties will be imposed for what violations. There are no written guidelines outlining how social order will be maintained. No prisoner is able to assume a *real* position of leadership or authority on an overt basis. No prisoner has the power to actively command other prisoners. No prisoner has the authority to openly establish a court, act as a judge, or execute ordered penalties for violations of the prescribed social norms that govern prisoner-controlled activities. Seriously considering these consequences that arise from the need to keep certain activities covert, one might have reason to wonder how the prisoners are actually able to exercise unofficial social control. It certainly cannot be done in an open manner.

### Three Sets of Social Norms

When engaging in the many activities that generally lie beyond staff control, the prisoners themselves exercise a considerable amount of unofficial, yet patterned control according to certain social norms. This enables most prisoners to manage this part of their lives with a relatively high degree of certainty—to evoke anticipated responses to their own activities and to predict the actions of others. However, this is a complex situation for the prisoners, because their behavior is subject to three different sets of social norms. Each set has corresponding patterns of acceptable behavior and sanctions for deviation from that behavior, but two of these sets are drawn from cultures that are in conflict with each other. The third set pertains to the manner in which prisoners ideally should handle the dilemma that arises from being subject to the social norms of two conflicting cultures.

First there is the official staff set of social norms. The staff expects the prisoners to behave in accord with these norms, which are primarily drawn from the larger culture of the streets and tailored to meet the staff's need to assure a reasonable degree of peace and security in prison. Most of these prescribed social norms are not detailed in written form; but they are generally understood by both prisoners and staff and would not be unfamiliar to most readers. In addition, there are written rules and laws, in accord with this official staff set of social norms, that define the limits of acceptable behavior for prisoners. These rules and laws are official, and the staff attempts to enforce them. However, many of the prisoners' unofficial activities are illegal or rule-breaking. Consequently, it can be seen that the official staff set of social norms does have a considerable impact on the daily lives of prisoners, because the prisoners must keep many of their activities on a covert level to avoid being subject to control by the staff.

A second set of social norms is the unofficial prisoners' set, generally governing the behavior of prisoners as they interact with each other while engaging in their unofficial and often secret activities—most of which are in violation of the official staff rules or laws. Since these unofficial activities normally lie beyond the control of, and often are completely hidden from the staff, the prisoners have established their own set of social norms that are strikingly similar to many that are found in the larger culture outside prison. Unlike the outside culture, this set of norms has no written laws to define the limits of acceptable behavior; however, these unofficial prisoner norms are generally understood by the prisoners. When a prisoner is caught violating one of these unwritten laws, the staff usually knows nothing about it. The prisoners normally are the ones who apprehend the violation, and the prisoners (*not* staff members) apply the sanctions for the offense.

It should be noted that a considerable amount of the prisoners' unofficial activity actually takes place within the view of staff members. Because of the similarity of these first two sets of social norms, much of the interaction of prisoners generally appears to be the same for both official and unofficial activities. Therefore, it is not necessary for them to keep certain aspects of their unofficial activity hidden from view. It often does not matter if staff members can see them or not. Only when a staff member comes within hearing range may the topic of conversation have to change abruptly, but without noticeable changes in the observable behavior of the prisoners.

The third set of social norms to which the prisoners are subject is the set that influences how prisoners interact with the staff when the prisoners' unofficial activity comes in conflict with the official staff set of social norms. The rules that arise from this third set of norms can be seen as a type of military code. Most prisoners know them as the convict code or "the code." As noted in Chapter 4, this code is the convicts' unwritten law that sets the limits of acceptable behavior under certain circumstances. It generally forbids a convict from snitching or doing anything that would be detrimental to the group or another member of the group. There are no specific details to the convict code, but the prisoners generally understand how the code applies to a wide range of circumstances.

Even though relatively few prisoners actually are convicts, most prisoners do observe "the code" to *some* degree. The adherence of inmates is *very* weak compared to the strong fidelity of convicts. Convicts claim that inmates do not live up to the convict code, but inmates claim that they do. Actually, "the code" to which the inmates do adhere is an *extremely* weak, distorted, partial interpretation of the convict code. This version of the code probably should be called the "inmate code"; it has some influence on inmates as they engage in unofficial prisoner activities. It should be remembered, though, that inmates normally are not privy to convict and Family activities. Therefore, unless the unofficial prisoner activities in which an inmate engages become too serious (an inmate can exchange details about those activities for personal gain or favors from the staff), or unless an inmate is personally put on the spot by another prisoner or staff member, an inmate generally will make some effort to keep covert the unofficial prisoner activities of which he is knowledgeable. A weak sense of unity in opposition to the staff does exist among inmates, but it seldom begins to even approach the strong unity felt among convicts. Consequently, if it is in the inmate's best personal interest to set that unity aside for personal gain, he will do so. When an inmate does violate this weak inmate version of the convict code for personal gain or to avoid punishment, usually there is less at stake than when convict or Family activities are involved. For this reason, relatively few sanctions are used against an inmate compared to what happens to a convict who breaks the convict code.

Two Unwritten Prisoner Codes

In other words, from the three sets of social norms to which the prisoners' behavior is subject, three different codes arise which direct and limit certain aspects of the prisoners' behavior. I will designate the first code as the *official staff civil-criminal code*; it pertains to what is right, fair, and lawful within the official staff controlled activities. I will refer to the second code as the *unofficial prisoner civil-criminal code*; it deals with what the prisoners consider to be right, fair, and lawful within the unofficial prisoner controlled activities. The third code, the *convict code*, has already been distinguished as such; it guides and controls the behavior of prisoners when their activities conflict with the official staff civil-criminal code. Even though the two prisoner codes are in unwritten form, they are generally understood by the prisoners. And, without any form of open leadership or authority, the prisoners are able to enforce these two unwritten codes to a reasonable degree—ensuring social order in the areas of their activity that are beyond the control of the staff.

It should be stressed, however, that this is a complex situation for the prisoners. They face a dilemma in which they ideally are expected to live up to the norms of two conflicting cultures and to abide by all three of these codes; yet it is impossible to do so. The staff expects a prisoner to obey the official staff civil-criminal code, yet it is virtually impossible for a prisoner to avoid involvement in the unofficial prisoner activities that are subject to the unofficial prisoner civil-criminal code. From the staff perspective, the perfect prisoner is one who abides by the official staff civil-criminal code, ignores the convict code, and reports all violations of the official staff civil-criminal code. In contrast, the prisoners ideally expect a prisoner to obey the two prisoner codes, disregarding or circumventing the official staff civil-criminal code whenever necessary; and, if violations of the unofficial prisoner civil-criminal code do occur, prisoners are expected to deal with the violators themselves, without involving the staff and the official staff civil-criminal code. In reality, there are *no* prisoners who actually fit the staff ideal, because even the *best* of the inmates engage in unofficial prisoner activities. It is impossible for any prisoner to be an exemplar prisoner from both the staff and the prisoner perspectives.

Inmates never satisfactorily solve the dilemma arising from being subject to the norms of two conflicting cultures. When engaging in unofficial prisoner activities, inmates may rely on the unofficial prisoner civil-criminal code to control their behavior with other prisoners; or inmates may resort to the official staff civil-criminal code, in violation of the convict code. As viewed from inside, inmates fail to take a moral stand to uphold the ideals of the prisoner culture; yet they do not live up to the ideals of the conflicting culture of the streets either. In contrast, convicts do solve this dilemma. They make a definite choice. Convicts may be adept at superficially appearing to go along with the official staff civil-criminal code; but they disregard it whenever necessary, remaining loyal to the two prisoner codes at all times. Only convicts take a moral stand to be true to the ideals of only one of these two conflicting cultures.

Another factor pertinent to our analysis of how prisoners unofficially exercise social control is the fluidity that exists among the prisoner population. Prisoners are continually moving in and out of the prison system, often being transferred from one prison to another. Since these moves are frequently imposed on them by the staff, the prisoners must allow each other to move in and out of relationships with comparative ease. For most prisoners, interpersonal bonds appear to be temporary and expedient, with little commitment or loyalty to one another. Also, in a single prison, the population is large, and potential individual and clique relationships are numerous. Therefore, if a prisoner wants to move in or out of one or more of these relationships for his own personal reasons, he normally will be able to do so with relative freedom. This frequent movement of prisoners normally prevents stability of membership in prison—either among the entire population or among small groups such as cliques. However, in spite of this fluidity, the configuration of the prisoner population normally remains somewhat the same, with only the individuals changing as prisoners move from one relationship to another, from one prison to another, or in and out of CDC. Nevertheless, this inconstancy is one of the many factors that detract from any strong sense of unity that the prisoners might feel in opposition to the staff; it is one of the numerous reasons why most prisoners have little commitment or loyalty to one another. Even if the staff were to allow prisoners to develop leaders with significant power and authority over others, this fluidity would make it difficult for those leaders to succeed. There would be no sense of unity on a larger, prisonwide basis; and, on the clique level, it would be too easy for a prisoner to leave one group and join another to avoid an undesirable leader. Consequently, this ease of movement is another factor which—in conjunction with the power and authority of the staff—tends to prevent prisoners from establishing meaningful overt authority above the individual or clique level. (Although it deals with a relatively simple type of culture with different determinants, the reader may wish to refer to Lee and DeVore 1968:132–137, 153–156 for a treatment by Turnbull and others of a comparable fluidity and absence of centralized authority among hunters and gatherers.)

### Private Law and Prisoner Legal Sanctions

As noted earlier, the two unwritten prisoner codes generally lie beyond staff control and usually involve only the prisoners. Unlike the public law implied in the official staff civil-criminal code, no staff member or public officer has the authority to enforce the two prisoner codes. If these codes are to be implemented, the prisoners themselves must do it. Without recourse to any organized authority, for the prisoners, these two codes fall into the realm of private law; and the prisoners resort to the means of private law to enforce these codes when the violator is discovered.

The private law of the prisoners is not unlike that which is found among primitive cultures. In the absence of a strong sense of community of interests among all the prisoners, a violation of either of the two prisoner codes (or sets of private laws) is seen as a private wrong. Even though most prisoners as a whole would recognize a breach of these codes, the largest significantly effective group in prison generally is the clique. Consequently, violations of the two prisoner codes are seen and treated as injuries to individuals and cliques, rather than against the prisoner population as a single group or entity. If these codes are to be enforced by the prisoners (who as a group are lacking in centralized authority), the wronged prisoner or clique must punish the violator—assuming he is discovered.

Although the means by which the prisoners privately enforce their two codes are judged as illegal or rule-breaking by the staff, the prisoners generally regard the sanctions that they use as reasonable. From within the prisoner culture, when the prisoners' illegal or rule-breaking activities are involved, the disciplines that make most sense to the prisoners are their own, not those of the staff. To the prisoners, their own actions are like legal sanctions, and they directly apply to the prisoners' illegal and rule-breaking activities. In order to keep these sanctions distinct from the official and unofficial type used by the staff for violations of the staff civil-criminal code, I shall refer to the prisoners' own actions as *prisoner legal sanctions*. The prisoners are aware that individuals and cliques *may* impose these prisoner legal sanctions, and such private use is generally understood and viewed as legitimate by most prisoners. However, prisoners realize that the punishment of a violator also depends on the desire and ability of the wronged party to impose sanctions. Even when the wronged party desires to punish the violator, the size and complexity of the prison and prison system, or the power and connections of the violator, may often preclude success. Inmates are the least inclined to take action and the least successful when attempting to enforce the prisoner codes. Since convicts have a greater inclination to engage in serious illegal and rule-breaking activities and have a better knowledge of the depths of the prisoner culture, they usually are more successful in their attempts to impose prisoner legal sanctions against violators of the two prisoner codes. Also, it must be noted that it is more difficult for an individual to do this than it is for a clique; yet even cliques of convicts fail to implement action against a violator at times. Family, in contrast, with its unity and power throughout CDC and on the streets, is able unfailingly to impose prisoner legal sanctions whenever it decides they are called for.

The prisoner legal sanctions involve the covert use or threat of physical force. Although they may be reluctant to do so, unless they are the object of the sanctions, most prisoners either tacitly approve of, or at least ignore the use of these measures by other prisoners. When a prisoner actually resorts to physical force, it is likely to result in the beating or stabbing of another prisoner; and it is not uncommon for death to be the final outcome. As an extreme example, when Family decides that physical force is necessary, it would be an exceptional situation that would not end in the death of the violator. It should be stressed that these sanctions normally are imposed in an undercover manner; to do so openly would be foolish. The consequence could be apprehension by the staff and subjection to the official staff civil-criminal code.

### Prisoner Social Sanctions

When prisoner code violators are determined and yet are not punished by the wronged parties, a different kind of sanction may be exercised by other prisoners to try to keep the behavior of the violators in accord with the prisoner social norms. I shall refer to these sanctions as *prisoner social sanctions*. They also may be used against those who deviate from the prisoner social norms in ways that are not serious enough to be judged actual violations of the prisoner codes, yet are serious enough to warrant imposition of some restraints by other prisoners.

The prisoner social sanctions do not involve physical force. Instead, they normally entail the use or threat of ridicule, shaming, exclusion from certain activities, social isolation, or virtual ostracism. No single individual imposes these prisoner social sanctions; it is done by groups of prisoners and occasionally by all the prisoners in cases where a prisoner is a blatantly obvious repeated violator of the prisoner social norms. These reprimands are conveyed in an apparently casual, yet quite deliberate manner by the prisoners. The fear of these sanctions usually prevents most prisoners from deviating too far or too often from the prisoner social norms. If a norm deviation or code violation should occur, the threat of, or temporary use of, any of these sanctions ordinarily will bring the prisoner back into line. If the measure should fail, stronger social sanctions may be imposed. Ultimately, if all else fails, social isolation or strict ostracism will succeed at least in protecting other prisoners—by making the deviate so alien to the prisoners and most of their activities that he is a relatively harmless oddity to be avoided under most circumstances.

However, the manner in which prisoners are able to assure a reasonable compliance to the prisoner social norms and codes is more complex than indicated above. It should be stressed that various types or groups of prisoners have different understandings of and adherence to the prisoner norms and codes. This leads to divergent behavioral expectations for each type. Consequently, there is a differential involvement of prisoners in various levels of prisoner activities. In turn, the treatment of prisoners who deviate from prisoner norms or violate prisoner codes varies according to the type of prisoner they are, the type of prisoner the wronged party is, the type or level of prisoner activity involved, and the degree of seriousness of the deviation or violation. The wronged party or group can be any of the following: inmates, convicts, Family, blacks, Anglos, or Chicanos. In addition, the deviant or violator can belong to any of the same above-named groups. This may be complex and confusing to outsiders, and even to many prisoners. However, it actually is patterned, reasonable, and generally predictable to those prisoners who truly understand the prisoner culture. They may not be able to articulate it, but they do act in accordance with what they know as acceptable prisoner behavior.

Since a single act may not be vitally important to the prisoners as a group, an isolated norm deviation or code violation by a prisoner may seem to be ignored and tolerated by the wronged party and other prisoners as well. Several, or even many, norm deviations or code violations may occur before a prisoner gets a bad reputation among other prisoners; but convicts only need to see certain things once to know a prisoner is an inmate. Convicts carefully note such acts and use this information to classify a prisoner as an inmate or to reclassify a convict into an inmate. Therefore, usually without the prisoner knowing it, if his single act becomes known by a convict, it probably will result in his being branded as an inmate by all convicts. Unbeknownst to him, the inmate purposely will be excluded from all second-level activities; and regardless of how long he stays in prison, he probably will never become knowledgeable of the convict or Family levels. Also, a convict usually would have to be found guilty of only one such norm deviation or code violation to lose his status as a convict and cease to be privy to convict-level activities.

## Snitching

For a more detailed indication of the variety and complexity of situations that could give rise to the use of prisoner social and/or legal sanctions, let us consider some aspects of snitching—a violation of the convict code. For example, since inmates potentially will snitch to the staff about prisoner illegal and rule-breaking activities, convicts consider inmates as enemies when convict-level activities are involved. Consequently, convicts use a prisoner social sanction against inmates and generally exclude them from direct involvement in second-level activities; they assume the responsibility for keeping details about convict-level activities hidden from inmates. Convicts do not expect inmates to follow the convict code in the same way that convicts are expected to. Therefore, convicts often allow gunsels to serve as both a connection and a buffer between second-level economic activities and inmates—especially between themselves and inmates who have a known reputation for snitching. The gunsels' reputation for unpredictable behavior and violence seems to effectively counter the inmates' inclination to snitch much of the time. When an inmate does snitch, only the identity of the gunsel is revealed to the staff, because the gunsel will "ride the beef" (take the punishment from the staff —usually time in "the hole") and proudly refuse to implicate the convict or convicts involved. The inmate may have legitimate reasons to fear the gunsel upon his release, for he may attempt to impose prisoner legal sanctions if he knows who snitched.

A convict may also deal directly with an inmate whom he judges to be trustworthy *to a degree*—as far as the inmate's self interest is concerned. The inmate's desire for drugs, to gamble, to borrow money, to run a store, or similar things often assures a reasonable adherence to the convict code. Nevertheless, the inmate cannot be trusted with details beyond knowing the convict connection to those activities. If an inmate accidentally learns some details about second-level activities and snitches to the staff about those details, convicts usually see the fault as lying in the circumstances; and no convict is blamed for the accident. Sanctions seldom are taken against the inmate snitch unless the wrong is keenly felt by an individual convict. However, if a convict *knowingly* reveals details about second-level activities to an inmate, and if the inmate snitches on other convicts, that convict is guilty of violating the convict code. The convict, *not the inmate*, is subject to prisoner legal sanctions from other convicts. Also, if the inmate does snitch, only the individual convict is punished by the staff. The convict rides the beef and serves as an effective buffer between the inmate snitch and other convicts. In many cases, convicts judge this as one of the risks of doing business with inmates. The inmate snitch acquires a wider reputation; and, in turn, it becomes more difficult and expensive for him to satisfy his illegal or rule-breaking desires. However, the inmate may have profited enough from this connection; or the convict personally may feel so strongly about a particular wrong that he will privately impose violent prisoner legal sanctions against the inmate who (as a prisoner) has actually violated the convict code against another prisoner. This potential for violence often effectively lessens the inmate's inclination to snitch and, by intimidation, frequently creates some degree of dependability in many inmates.

Since inmate snitches seldom know much about second-level activities, they usually snitch to the staff about inmate-level activities. Even though many first-level activities are illegal or rule-breaking, most prisoners and staff members recognize that all prisoners engage in these activities and that they are rather superficial or trivial compared to second- and third-level activities. Many of these activities are frequently seen and tolerated by staff members themselves. In the majority of cases, staff members choose to conveniently overlook this type of activity, because there is too much of it taking place to even begin to stop and there are more serious prisoner activities to try to thwart. Consequently, the impact of snitching about first-level activities is minimal. When an inmate snitches on this type of activity, he is not likely to receive much recognition or reward from the staff. When the staff does punish a prisoner for first-level activity on the word of a snitch, the wronged prisoner seldom sees the action of the snitch as being serious enough to warrant the imposition of prisoner legal sanctions—but sees it merely as an annoyance and tolerates the minimal punishment from the staff.

However, the snitch does gain a wider reputation among the prisoners and may be subjected to prisoner social sanctions. As the frequency and importance of the details passed to the staff increases, the more stringent the prisoner social sanctions become. If the snitch becomes too obvious, then he may be virtually excluded from all prisoner illegal and rule-breaking activities. Therefore, most inmates normally do not find it profitable to snitch on first-level activities—at least not too often or too openly.

In contrast to inmates, convicts are expected to be faithful to the convict code without exception. Therefore, real convicts can be trusted and frequently are privy to details of second-level activities of other convicts. But, as a convict said, "There may be a rotten apple in any barrel." In rare instances a convict does snitch, but the information has to be so very significant—on the convict or Family level— that it results in a large reward for the snitch from the staff. The convict does this only if he thinks he can do so without being discovered by other convicts. If the identity of the snitch is discovered and if second-level activities are involved, the wronged convict usually attempts to impose prisoner legal sanctions against the convict snitch. Even if the wronged party does not choose, or is unable to exercise prisoner legal sanctions, other convicts immediately use prisoner social sanctions to reclassify the snitch as an inmate and exclude him from *all* second-level activities. If the snitch is discovered and third-level activities are involved, prisoner legal sanctions *are* imposed by Family. If the snitch did not know that Family was implicated but merely thought that convict-level activities were involved, he may not be executed. However the prisoner legal sanctions used are serious ones, and the snitch is immediately reclassified as an inmate. But, if the snitch has been privy to some Family activities and knowingly snitches on Family, he usually is executed by Family.

Because the majority of Chicano prisoners are either convicts or convictlike and since all inmates are possible snitches, Chicano prisoners generally exclude inmates from their truly important activities. In addition, since Chicano prisoners see most Anglos and almost all blacks as either inmates or inmatelike, they find that it is easier to limit their interaction with the majority of these prisoners and deal only with the relatively few Anglos and blacks who have been tested and classified as convicts. Consequently, it is understandable that many Anglos and blacks express feelings about never getting to know Chicanos, because their dealings with Chicanos never are more than superficial. Family members take those Chicano convict feelings one step further. For example, since Family members have such strong feelings about snitches and since blacks have such a reputation for snitching, it is difficult to get a Family member even to admit that black convicts exist. The few black convicts in San Quentin are excluded from any direct knowledge of third-level activities. Even though a black convict can be trusted as an individual, he must deal with other black prisoners, who may be snitches. Family members see no reason to take the risk of using such a potentially weak buffer between third-level activities and inmates. Also, the Family member who would vouch for the trustworthiness of a black convict might be held responsible if someone snitched on a third-level deal in which the black convict was involved. In addition, just to be seen dealing with a black might cast doubt about the reliability of the Family member in the minds of others who are not aware that the black is a convict. Therefore, Family members almost never deal directly with black convicts.

### Failure to Live up to an Economic Agreement

As further evidence of the use of prisoner social and/or legal sanctions, let us now consider some aspects of failure to live up to an unwritten economic agreement—a violation of the unofficial prisoner civil-criminal code. Written agreements could be used by the staff as proof of illegal or rule-breaking activity of prisoners. Consequently, prisoner economic agreements are unwritten, and prisoners generally understand that they are expected to abide by the terms of a verbal economic agreement. However, the situation is complicated by the various types of prisoners, different levels of economic activities, degrees of involvement in those activities, and varying ability to impose sanctions. Therefore, disparate compliance to the terms of an unwritten agreement may be expected by prisoners, according to the level of activity involved and the types of prisoners concerned; and hence, diverse retributions may be taken by the wronged parties.

When a prisoner is unable to live up to an unwritten economic agreement (such as paying back a loan), he may do nothing and hope that the lender will not impose prisoner sanctions against him. Alternatively, he may try to work out other arrangements for repayment; and if that fails, he still may choose to do nothing. Or, if he is fearful of his physical well-being, he may choose to break the convict code as well. He does this by going to the staff and requesting to be locked up for protective custody, hopefully to be subject only to the official staff civil-criminal code, avoiding the punition of the prisoner codes. If the staff is obliging, the guilty party usually is safe from the lender for a period of time, since the lender normally is unable to exercise prisoner legal sanctions against the guilty party while the latter is in "the hole" or the Adjustment Center. The violator hopes that by the time he is released from protective custody that at least one of several things will have happened: the lender will have cooled off enough to not inflict prisoner legal sanctions on him; the lender will have resigned himself to the situation and written the loan off as a bad debt; or the lender will have been transferred to another prison. Often, in the process of convincing the staff of the necessity to be locked up in protective custody, the guilty prisoner further violates the convict code by telling the staff details about prisoner illegal or rule-breaking activities—at least those involved in the loan in question. This may lead to the lender being punished by the staff for violation of the official staff civil-criminal code. When this occurs, the lender obviously has additional reason for imposing prisoner legal sanctions against the prisoner who has broken the prisoner codes in three ways.

Most prisoners are reluctant to be locked up for protective custody, and there are several valid reasons for their attitude. For example, if the prisoner snitches to the staff about prisoner illegal or rule-breaking activities in seeking protective custody, as noted above, the prisoner may give the wronged party additional reason to use prisoner legal sanctions against him. Also, there is no guarantee that the prisoner will avoid prisoner legal sanctions while in protective custody or after release. In addition, being in protective custody is not a pleasant experience; going through the three grades of segregation in either "the hole" or the Adjustment Center generally is viewed as something to be avoided if possible. Furthermore, if the broken agreement is important enough to warrant protective custody, it usually necessitates the imposition of prisoner social sanctions, too; and being locked up will not prevent retribution when the guilty prisoner returns to the general prisoner population, or possibly sooner. Through those sanctions the prisoner could acquire such a poor reputation and credit rating that he would be unable to purchase prisoner goods and services on credit; and, since a major portion of prisoner economic activities are on a credit basis, the guilty prisoner could be excluded from normal participation in a major part of the prisoner culture.

The innumerable unwritten economic agreements usually involve the use of credit or three-for-two loans among prisoners. These agreements range in amounts from a single package of cigarettes owed for the purchase of candy on credit from an inmate store all the way to the loan of $30,000 to a group of convicts by Family (as noted in Chapter 6). The limit of the credit or the loan is dependent on the prisoner's income. For example, an inmate's income generally is limited to the amount he legally draws each month. Only by converting part or all of their ducats into cigarette money are most inmates able to either purchase prisoner goods and services or pay their prisoner economic debts; and, like many people on the streets, many inmates depend on credit purchases and small loans to make it from payday to payday. But, because inmates seldom are able to hustle for significant amounts above their draw on a dependable, routine basis, economic agreements involving an inmate as one of the parties tend to be relatively small. Prisoners usually take care to limit the amount of credit they extend or the size of loan they make to an inmate. The limit seldom exceeds a sum that can reasonably be paid back from the inmate's draw.

In contrast, convicts usually have a keen ability to hustle effectively—often for considerable amounts. Also, most convicts are able to succeed in their various economic enterprises. Consequently, even though many convicts do not have a legal monthly draw, they are able to generate income that makes even a full $45 monthly draw rather insignificant in comparison. Economic success and proven adherence to the prisoner codes gradually earn a reputation for a convict. Therefore, most convicts would be able to borrow a thousand dollars, or obtain that amount of wholesale goods on credit without much difficulty. Unlike dealing with inmates, the existence or absence of a fixed monthly income is not the key consideration when granting credit or a loan to a convict.

Prisoners know that inmates frequently overextend themselves beyond their limited income. When this happens, they normally are unable to meet all of their financial obligations, so something has to go unpaid. For example, assume an inmate routinely purchases goodies from an inmate store on credit each month and pays his bill when he receives his monthly draw. With the amount in excess of his monthly canteen and inmate store purchases, he buys drugs for occasional use and gambles. To cover gambling losses, the inmate frequently borrows at three for two. If the inmate loses an excessive amount gambling, he finds himself unable to pay all of his debts. At this point, the inmate must consider several factors. Gambling, drugs, and three for two are handled by convicts and these goods and services are quite important to him compared to store goodies which are sold by inmates. So, it is of primary importance to maintain his ability to get those convict-level goods and services on credit. In addition, convicts have a greater ability and inclination to impose prisoner legal sanctions than inmates do; and prisoner social sanctions imposed by convicts (such as spreading the word among other convicts regarding the inmate's poor credit, with a resulting loss of credit) are much more restrictive than those imposed by an inmate, because inmate stores are so numerous that a poor credit rating with one inmate usually will not prevent credit from another. Also, if the inmate chooses protective custody (a very poor way to declare bankruptcy in prison), he loses his credit standing and potentially faces prisoner legal sanctions from the convicts *and* the inmate store owner. Therefore, considering all these factors, the inmate tries to preserve his good credit standing with the convicts by paying them or, if necessary and possible, by making new arrangements to pay them over an extended period of time. He also hopes that the store owner will not impose prisoner legal sanctions against him. An inmate usually is able to successfully extricate himself from his economic bind in this manner, with only the inmate store owner losing a relatively small sum.

The amount one inmate might fail to pay another would be relatively small compared to the quantities involved in second- and third-level economic transactions. However, to an inmate who has his own financial obligations to meet and his own credit standing to protect, the amount may be quite large and important. Consequently, the failure of one inmate to pay even a small debt to another can lead to the use of prisoner legal sanctions and even to the loss of lives among inmates. In contrast, the debt limit a convict would normally allow an inmate might be larger, but still it probably would be relatively low, too. Even though the convict normally could write off the amount as a bad debt and still meet his financial obligations, he usually is reluctant to do so—for, if he frequently let things pass, he would soon gain a reputation that convicts purposely avoid. Lesser prisoner legal sanctions in the form of threats usually are sufficient to bring the inmate into compliance with his economic agreement or force him to seek protective custody, because inmates are fully aware that convict threats are not empty ones.

Convicts are inveterately astute in their economic dealings; however, once an agreement has been reached, a convict usually can be trusted to carry it out. Granted, convicts often may be somewhat abusive of inmates in particular, such as knowingly overcharging for prisoner goods or services. Whether one judges the treatment of inmates by convicts as corrupt or not depends on one's perspective. Convicts shrewdly taking advantage of naive inmates may be balanced against inmates frequently snitching on convicts. Although inmates are the enemy in many respects when second- and third-level activities are involved, convicts do not snitch on inmates. Also, as noted in Chapter 6, inmates have a better and more reasonably priced supply of prisoner goods and services because of the second- and third-level activities of convicts. If an inmate wants those goods and services, it is only reasonable to make him pay. Ordinarily the inmate ends up owing money to a convict. But, there are situations where a convict will be obliged to an inmate. For example, the relatively few inmates who are able to illegally bring cash in from outside resources normally use that money for cash purchases which are delivered either immediately or steadily over an extended period after the actual purchase. As illustration, an inmate may pay cash to a convict for a regular supply of drugs for a specified period of time into the future. The inmate has no actual guarantee that the convict will honor the agreement, and he probably would be unable or unwilling to impose prisoner legal sanctions against the convict if the latter should refuse to honor the agreement; but the inmate does have reason to expect the convict to meet the contract, because the behavior of convicts normally falls within the limits of the prisoner codes.

Many times prisoners—even convicts—successfully avoid unwritten economic obligations when they are transferred to another prison. The prisoner can later claim the difficulty he encountered in trying to make connections for the payment of the debt, knowing that he really did nothing because a lender usually is unable to impose prisoner legal sanctions from another prison. However, some convicts may have the right connections with convict friends in the other prison and be able either to indirectly collect the debt or to have prisoner legal sanctions imposed on his behalf. Though frequently nothing is done, and the obligation is forgotten—unless the two parties should meet by chance in the future. When dealing with Family, the situation is different. Family almost always does business only with convicts, seldom directly with inmates. However, if Family has an agreement with a prisoner—it does not matter where the prisoner is transferred, because Family is active in all California prisons and on the streets—the obligation will be met. If a prisoner should find himself unable to meet the terms of an economic contract with Family, realistic alternative repayment plans are willingly arranged by Family (much like an employees' credit union is willing to work out some arrangement for a member who has encountered unforeseen financial problems). Most prisoners realize the seriousness of trying to cheat or walk out on Family; it is almost impossible to avoid paying a debt to Family. If a prisoner should continue to be recalcitrant, he would be subjected to the ultimate prisoner legal sanction and pay the debt with his life.

In order to stress the patterned nature of the prisoners' behavior and the behavioral expectations which result, let me present a comment that prisoners made repeatedly. They contend that "Folsom is an easier joint to do time in than San Quentin." When explaining what they mean by that statement, the prisoners note that the men serving time in Folsom prison tend to be older prisoners who have spent more time in CDC prisons than the majority of prisoners have. And, by having served more time, those prisoners have come to know certain aspects of the prisoner culture well. Even inmates learn what type of behavior to expect from the different types of prisoners with whom they interact. The behavior of most Folsom prisoners generally is quite predictable. Unlike San Quentin, in Folsom a prisoner is much less likely to be killed unexpectedly over something trivial. When that type of violence occurs in San Quentin, it usually is done by a younger, relatively new prisoner who acts out of fear and out of ignorance of the normal behavioral expectations.

It should be stressed that the enforcement of the prisoner codes through the means of private law by the wronged party does not result in a feud between opposing groups of prisoners. The prisoners generally understand the prisoner codes; and when a violation occurs, the facts surrounding it soon become known to the interested prisoners. Consequently, when prisoner sanctions are imposed by the wronged party, other prisoners usually recognize the legitimacy of their use. The prisoners realize that unresolved, continuing conflict or feuds would border on anarchy. Most prisoners appreciate the dangers of such anarchical conditions, knowing that the behavior of others would no longer be predictable and that social order would seriously deteriorate or cease to exist. Since prisoners usually can predict the behavior of others and avoid disputes if they want to, they appreciate the orderliness of their culture. They realize that cooperation in avoiding unresolved, continuing conflict or feuds is beneficial to them. For example, the basic ethnic differences and causes of racial antipathy between ethnic groups on the streets are intensified by the forced, continual interaction between ethnic groups in prison. In particular, the resulting antagonism between the Chicano and black prisoners is but thinly veiled. The prisoners actually have no mechanism for avoiding periodic or even continual racial conflict between these ethnic groups. However, most Chicano and black prisoners recognize the dangers of such anarchical conditions; so actual manifestations of racial conflict seldom become a reality—even though the potential causes continue to exist. For example, when there is a violent incident between a Chicano and a black, the knowledgeable black and Chicano prisoners quickly spread the word among their respective groups, stressing that it is *not* a racial incident and carefully note the actual legitimate reason behind the violence—such as an unpaid debt. When this type of situation occurs, the serious and usually successful efforts of many prisoners to avoid a racial confrontation seems to emphasize just how far from anarchy the prisoner culture actually is.

## UNOFFICIAL:   PRISONERS OVER STAFF AND CDC

When a staff member or the prison system becomes too abusive and goes beyond the rather high limits of maltreatment that prisoners normally tolerate, the prisoners attempt to exercise social control over the staff member or the prison system. The prisoners experience more success in controlling excessive abuse from an individual staff member than they do when trying to control the maltreatment in the prison system. For example, if a guard should become inordinately abusive, the prisoners can complain to other staff members; and the word will soon reach the bull's superiors. In turn, the staff may impose sanctions against the guard (in some respects, on behalf of the prisoners) such as changing his assignment to an undesirable one at an isolated post on the gun rail at the far end of the lower yard. The bull usually gets the message. However, if the guard should persist in his excessive abuse of prisoners after returning to a more favorable assignment, a few covert threats of potential violence from prisoners may be effective. After all, occasionally staff members *are* the object of prisoner violence. For example, a garbage can dropped on an unrelenting bull from the fifth tier railing quite effectively eliminates the prisoners' immediate problem.

It should be noted that staff members also can become subject to the prisoner codes. For instance, if a bull starts running drugs, it may be possible that he is doing so as a representative of the staff, to try to catch prisoners in the commission of a felony. However, if the bull repreatedly runs drugs and it becomes obvious that he is personally partaking of the considerable profit, he too will become subject to the prisoner codes. This bull understands that he should not do anything foolish, like skipping out with the money for some transaction or snitching to other staff members. The threat of death usually is sufficient to ensure compliance with the prisoner codes. However, if a violation should occur, it is quite likely that the ultimate prisoner sanction will be imposed. For example, not all of the 73 individuals executed by Family for serious violations of the prisoner codes have been prisoners.

The prison administrators' minimization and distortion of the prisoner efforts to bring the extreme maltreatment in the prison system to the attention of the public and legislators was discussed earlier in this chapter. Even though these efforts by prisoners have fallen far short of what the prisoners would like to accomplish, their demonstrations may have tempered the excessive abuses and prevented them from becoming worse. Therefore, through their protests, the prisoners may have exerted a small degree of social control over the prison system. Although outsiders have been led to believe otherwise, the majority of demonstrations by California prisoners in recent years have primarily been against abusive aspects of the prison system—principally against the Adult Authority and the indeterminate sentence system.

### Convict Unity Holiday and *The Outlaw*

One major demonstration at San Quentin is an outstanding exception to the pattern of prison administrators deluding the public. It should be considered in some detail. The prisoners' Convict Unity Holiday, which was held on February 15, 1968, revealed some of the stark reality behind the ideal prison system to the public. It made certain state legislators more aware of many of the major abuses of the prison system, and ultimately led legislators, attorneys, and other outsiders to try to bring about legitimate changes. Unfortunately, it has taken great effort by outsiders to bring about even minimal changes so far; however, there is a growing recognition among the general public that the prison system is not quite as ideal as prison administrators would have outsiders believe.

In order to understand the background that led up to Convict Unity Holiday, let us first consider some facts about *The Outlaw*, because it initiated Convict Unity Holiday. As noted earlier, *The Outlaw* was the underground newspaper that convicts illegally published inside San Quentin for 14 months, despite all staff attempts to suppress it. *The Outlaw* began serious publication in June 1967. Its major articles dealt with important issues and rumors within the prison. As a service to the prisoners, through its investigative reporting, *The Outlaw* tried to get to the source of rumors—to either confirm or dispel them.

The staff went to great efforts to stop *The Outlaw*. Soon after the convict paper began publication, every duplicating machine in the prison was under lock and key; but it continued to be published, and a copy of each issue appeared on the warden's desk! Later, any prisoner who was caught with a copy of *The Outlaw* in his possession was "thrown in the hole" for 29 days. Prisoners who were believed to be directly involved in its publication were transferred to other prisons and put in "the hole" there. (A convict who was *accused* by the staff of being "the editor" spent nearly two years in the adjustment center at Folsom because of that allegation which never was proved.) The prisoner cost of stencils, paper, and ink became greatly inflated. Even after 50 or more convicts had been transferred to other prisons, *The Outlaw* continued. Only when it had succeeded in enlightening some outsiders (particularly some state legislators) did *The Outlaw* voluntarily decide to publish its final issue in August 1968.

Although the convicts who published *The Outlaw* hoped that some editions would reach the streets and be brought to the attention of the public, they realized that the only way they could exert more pressure on the prison administrators would be to successfully publicize some of the major problems facing the prisoners. A January 1968 issue of *The Outlaw* set forth the details about Convict Unity Holiday as shown on pages 186–187.

Unlike most San Francisco Bay Area newspapers, the underground press was not reluctant to report about the forthcoming Convict Unity Holiday. Beginning in January, the *Berkeley Barb* ran a series of front-page articles that presented the *prisoners'* story about the strike—in detail, *before* it happened. On February 15, in spite of staff efforts to thwart the strike, about 20 percent of the almost 4000 prisoners went on strike (as noted in Chapter 1). Since their day had started early, all the prisoners had been returned to their cells an hour early, in time for many of them to see and/or hear the combined rock bands—The Grateful Dead and The Phoenix—that were playing at full amplification for the prisoners and the roughly 400 to 500 outsiders who had gathered at the main gate to show their support for the prisoners. Realizing that they actually did have support on the streets, about 75 percent of the prisoners struck the following day. The strike lasted for over a week, with a sympathy strike taking place at Folsom for nearly a week.

Convict Unity Holiday and the ensuing strike led to a series of communications between the prisoners and the chairman of the Criminal Procedure Committee of the California Assembly, with that committee finally holding hearings about abusive practices of the Adult Authority at San Quentin a year later. At those hearings, in spite of the warden's forbidding, a prisoner-prepared report *was* presented to the members of the committee. The entire report, "A Convict Report on the Major Grievances of the Prison Population with Suggested Solutions" is printed in Robert Minton's book, *Inside Prison American Style* (1971:209–325). Indicative of the importance of that report is the "Bill of Particulars" which is outlined on page 3 of the original report:

I.    Objection to Adult Authority Resolution #171, primarily the refixing of the term of imprisonment at a length greater than originally fixed;

ON FEBRUARY 15, 1968, THOSE AREA'S WHICH WILL BE EXEMPT FROM
THE MOVEMENT WILL BE AS FOLLOWS: THESE AREA'S ARE ESSENTIAL
AND SHOULD CONTINUE TO OPERATE.

1. HOSPITAL  2. MESS-HALL  3. BOILER ROOM  4. BLOCK WORKERS

LET US TAKE THE OPPORTUNITY TO ASSURE EACH AND EVERYONE OF
YOU THAT WE CAN BE SUCCESSFUL IF, AND ONLY IF, WE REMAIN
UNITED.  THE EFFORTS OF EACH MAN WILL BE VITAL TO THE ULTI-
MATE OUTCOME.  ON FEBRUARY 15, 1968, THE EYES OF MANY PEOPLE
WILL FOCUS UPON YOU, CONVICTS AND FREE PEOPLE ALIKE, ANXIOUS
AWAITING TO SEE IF WE HAVE THE ABILITY AND COURAGE TO STAND
UP FOR SOMETHING WORTHWHILE.  LET'S NOT DISAPPOINT THEM.
ABOVE ALL, LET US NOT DISAPPOINT OURSELVES.  UNITY, THAT'S
WHAT WE NEED.

...WE MUST NOT RESORT TO ANY TYPE OF VIOLENCE, OTHERWISE WE
WILL DESTROY WHAT WE HAVE WORKED SO HARD TO GAIN.  WE, OF THE
OUTLAW, HAVE TAKEN MANY CHANCES IN KEEPING YOU POSTED ON THE
EVILS WHICH EXIST WITHIN THE ADMINISTRATION.  NOW, WE OFFER
YOU A FEW OF THE THINGS WE EXPECT TO GAIN, IF WE STAND TO-
GETHER.  REMEMBER, ON FEBRUARY 15, 1968, ON CALL FOR LOCKUP,
GO TO YOUR CELL.  DO NOT BECOME INVOLVED IN ANYTHING.  THIS
IS IMPORTANT.  THE FIRST SIGN OF A DISTURBANCE, THIS ADMIN-
ISTRATION WILL FIRE TEAR GAS AND BULLETS.  SOME WILL BE IN-
JURED, AS WE PANIC IN AN ATTEMPT TO SCATTER.  WE MUST NOT
PERMIT THIS.  IF NO LOCKUP IS CALLED ON THIS DAY, THE SAME
MOVEMENT WILL REMAIN IN EFFECT FOR THE FOLLOWING DAY, AND
WILL REMAIN IN EFFECT UNTIL THE ADMINISTRATION CALLS A
LOCKUP.  DO NOT REPORT TO WORK...

HERE ARE A FEW CHANGES WE EXPECT TO BE BROUGHT ABOUT.

1.  AN OPPORTUNITY FOR ALL PAROLE VIOLATORS TO BE AFFORDED
    A HEARING IN A COURT OF LAW: TO CALL WITNESS'ES IN
    THEIR BEHALF: TO CROSS EXAMINE THOSE WITNESS'ES WHO AP-
    PEAR AGAINST THEM: TO BE REPRESENTED BY COUNSEL.

2.  COMPLETE ABOLISHMENT OF THE INCREASED PENALTIES FOR
    NARCOTICS OFFENDERS WITH PRIOR FELONY CONVICTIONS.
    SEVERAL MEN HERE ARE NOW SERVING ANYWHERE FROM 10 TO
    15 YEARS TO LIFE AS A RESULT OF THIS STUPID LAW.  ISN'T
    5 YEARS TO LIFE SUFFICIENT?  THE PENALTY IS NO DETERRENT
    TO CRIME.  THIS HAS BEEN PROVEN TIME AND AGAIN.

3.  THAT MORE FAVORABLE CONSIDERATION BE GIVEN TO FIRST OF-
    FENDERS WHEN THEIR MINIMUM TIME IS COMPLETED.  TO COMPEL
    A PERSON TO LINGER IN PRISON CAN ONLY LEAD TO FORMING A
    HARDENED CRIMINAL.  TO MUCH TIME DESTROYS ANY CONSTRUC-
    TIVE THINGS THE PRISONER HAS ACCOMPLISHED.

4. A DEMAND FOR THE REMOVAL OF ALL EX LAW ENFORCEMENT
   OFFICERS FROM THE ADULT AUTHORITY, AND THAT THEY BE RE-
   PLACED WITH PROFESSORS, PSYCHOLOGISTS, ETC., WHO ARE
   MORE FAMILIAR WITH THE CRIMINAL.

5. THE IMMEDIATE REMOVAL OF ALL CHILD SEX OFFENDERS TO
   MENTAL HOSPITALS WHERE THEY CAN RECEIVE THE HELP NECES-
   SARY TO OVERCOME THEIR ILLNESS.

6. TO COMPEL THE ADULT AUTHORITY TO RECONSIDER ALL CASES
   WHO APPEARED BEFORE THEM SINCE OCTOBER, 1967, AT THE
   TIME WHICH THE NEW TIME SCALE WENT INTO EFFECT. ALMOST
   ALL PRISONERS WHO APPEARED BEFORE THE BOARD SINCE
   OCTOBER HAVE BEEN DENIED. A GOOD INDICATION THAT YOU
   WILL DO MORE TIME.

7. DEMANDS FOR BETTER FOOD AND LIVING CONDITIONS WITHIN THE
   PRISON. APPROXIMATELY $2,600.00 IS APPROPRIATED ANNUALLY
   FOR YOUR SUPPORT. DID YOU KNOW THAT $14.00 IS APPROPRI-
   ATED EACH YEAR JUST SO YOU CAN HAVE A NEW MATTRESS? HOW
   LONG HAS IT BEEN SINCE YOU'VE HAD ONE? THIS IS JUST ONE
   ITEM. WE COULDN'T BEGAN TO LIST THEM ALL.

8. COMPLETE REVISION OF THE PRESENT PAY SCALE. PRICES IN
   THE CANTEEN CONTINUE TO SHOOT SKYWARD. THE DRAW HAS BEEN
   RAISED TO $30.00 A MONTH. CAN YOU DRAW $30.00 ON YOUR
   PRESENT PAY?

9. DEMAND THAT A DOCTOR BE AVAILABLE WITHIN THE PRISON
   AROUND THE CLOCK IN ORDER TO PREVENT UNLAWFUL DEATHS
   SUCH AS THAT OF WALTER ATKINSON, A-82632, ON NOVEMBER
   5, 1964. DIDN'T THINK WE KNEW ABOUT THAT. DID YOU,
   DOCTOR McNAMARA? WANT US TO GIVE YOU A FULL REPORT?
   HE DIED AS A RESULT OF RESPIRATORY DIFFICULTY, THIS IS
   TRUE. BUT, ONLY BECAUSE HIS JAWS WERE WIRED TOGETHER
   FOLLOWING SURGERY, AND HE STRANGLED ON HIS OWN VOMIT.
   YOU WERE DRUNK WHEN YOU FINALLY DID SHOW UP, WERN'T YOU
   DOCTOR? WE KNOW. WE ALSO HAVE PHOTOSTAT COPIES OF THE
   COMPLETE RECORDS. WONDER IF JOHN CONLEY, D.D.S., WOULD
   SUPPORT YOUR CLAIMS? WE WILL SEE SOON ENOUGH.

10. THAT YOUR PAROLE OFFICER BE COMPELLED TO PUT THE AP-
    PROVAL OF ANY REQUEST YOU MAKE IN WRITING IN ORDER THAT
    HE MAY NOT BE PERMITTED TO USE THESE THINGS TO JUSTIFY
    VIOLATING THE CONDITIONS OF YOUR PAROLE AT HIS OWN WHIM
    OR CAPRICE.

THESE ARE THE MORE IMPORTANT THINGS WE EXPECT TO ACCOMPLISH
AS A RESULT OF OUR MOVEMENT. THERE ARE OTHER ISSUES, SOME
MORE IMPORTANT, OTHERS LESS, WHICH WE WILL BRING TO YOU AS
SOON AS THE COMPLETE FORMAT HAS BEEN DRAWN...

II.    Objection to the method of effecting parole violations;

III.   Objection to the long terms served by parole violators;

IV.    Objection to the Adult Authority speculating about the degree of criminal involvement greater than the facts warrant;

V.     Objection to the inordinate amount of time being served by first termers in certain offense categories;

VI.    Objection to apparent lack of consideration given to time served in the deliberations that pertain to the determination of the term of imprisonment;

VII.   Objection to allowing criminal acts of recent offenders to aggravate the standards used in fixing the term of imprisonment of inmates who have already served x-number of years for similar offenses;

VIII.  Objection to basing denial upon the so-called "voice of the public" or the "public mood," when in fact the public hasn't said a word or otherwise manifested its mood;

IX.    Objection to the constantly changing structure and policies of the Adult Authority and the failure to give the inmate population any indication of the reasons for, or the ramifications of, the changes;

X.     Objection to the inadequate record kept of the Adult Authority hearings, and the lack of meaningful comment therein;

XI.    Objection to the lack of continuity in Adult Authority expectations, demands, and policies from hearing to hearing and from member to member;

XII.   Objection to the fact that the inmate body has no organized voice or other means calling for mitigation, while forces demanding aggravation have full and free access to the communications media.

The events which were initiated by *The Outlaw* and Convict Unity Holiday show that in exceptional cases, when the prisoners' story is detailed to the public in advance, the prisoners are able to exercise some degree of social control over the staff and the prison system. Since the prisoners are not allowed to have meaningful sociopolitical leadership, *The Outlaw* served as the voice of the prisoners and functioned as the centralized form of leadership for the prisoners at that time. The prisoners were able to act as a body. It was not necessary for individual prisoners to step forward as spokesmen and consequently be transferred and silenced in "the hole" of another prison.

Unfortunately, the great efforts of prisoners to exert social control over the prison system produced very limited, temporary results. The root causes that led to the publication of *The Outlaw* and Convict Unity Holiday at San Quentin still remain. Perhaps the prisoners are correct when they urge that the legislature must make significantly legitimate changes to eliminate the prime sources of many of the major abuses of the prison system.

# 9 / Conclusion

The purpose of this book has been to present the prisoner culture as a complete world as the prisoners perceive, experience, and know it. Within space limitations, I have attempted to capture and communicate the essence of the prisoner culture, allowing you to see it at a depth that many *inmates* never know —even though they may live in the prisoner culture for years. I want to stress that this work is not written to embarrass any group or type of prisoners, staff members, or prison administrators. Nor is this book intended to be a polemic against CDC. Instead, I have attempted to present the reality found hidden behind prison walls in the California system. Even though that reality may be stark or harsh at times, and particularly so to certain individuals or groups, I believe it should be confronted by outsiders. As an anthropologist, my methods of study were different from those used by most others who have studied prisons; and many prisoners agree with my personal belief that the results, too, have been different. For those who would aspire to change either the prisoners, the prisoner culture, or the prison system, I personally hope that the results presented in this book will enable them to do so from a better informed, more realistic position.

Because of my understanding of the prisoner culture and my position as an anthropologist, concerned citizen, and taxpayer, I feel that I have a duty to make some observations and recommendations. Although some of these remarks may technically lie beyond the scope of this book, I feel that I would be remiss if I failed to make them. First, I will comment on the general failure of rehabilitation efforts inside prison; and then I will recommend some changes that I believe would lead to a more realistic treatment of convicted felons and would substantially reduce the disparity between the ideal prison system that administrators present to outsiders and the real prison system that the prisoners know and experience.

## REHABILITATION?

Even though there are a few exceptions in the area of educational or vocational training, most prisoners contend that rehabilitation programs generally fail to accomplish their goals and are nothing more than hypocritical farces. Rehabilitation is a cruel myth, and the use of euphemistic terms such as "treatment" and "correction" deceive outsiders. For many years, California prisoners have strongly contended that the "corrections" system not only fails to accomplish its rehabilitation goals, but that it adds emotional brutality and the torture of uncertainty to the lengthy sentences they serve. The Criminal Procedure Committee concluded that "There is no evidence that prisons rehabilitate most offenders" (California Legislature 1968:25); yet under the indeterminate sentence a prisoner's release theoretically is contingent on his becoming rehabilitated. The associate warden, care and treatment, commented to another staff member about rehabilitation activities: "It doesn't really matter what they do or what they accomplish, as long as they look good on paper" (Hastings 1967). Rehabilitation is doomed to failure in the prisoner culture—where to identify too closely with the social norms of the outside culture is to be a deviant, most commonly a snitch. Life in the prisoner culture reinforces cheating and other rule-breaking and illegal activities (so-called criminal behavior). Those who believe that prisoners should abide by the norms of the outside culture would profit by viewing the prisoner culture as a vast morass and rehabilitation activities as pure water. However, this vision would portray that weekly hour or so of largely extraneous rehabilitation activity as a single drop of pure water; when it is dropped into that morass, it is lost!

Prisoners have discussed their feelings about the condescending manner that some care and treatment staff exhibit when dealing with them. Some of the rehabilitation activities seem to be based on what has been called a "sickness image" of the prisoners, which assumes that crime is analogous to disease, that prisoners are sick, and that prisoners need to be treated and cured if possible. Prisoners contend that this sickness image is based on questionable suppositions. Is the individual sick? Or does his subculture conflict with the larger United States culture? Most prisoners are normal human beings who have acted in accord with the social norms of their subculture—in a manner that is seen as right, normal, and moral from within that subculture. A Chicano prisoner commented,

> They treat us as if we're sick. We're not sick; we just live in a different world than they do. We know the right things to do in our world, even though we can't make it very well in their world. It's easier for them to try to *treat* us than to get at the root causes of our so-called crime, because that would involve making basic changes in the existing system—inside and on the streets.

## CHANGES FOR THE MAJORITY

My suggestions are based on a combination of my understanding of the prisoner culture, changes that have been suggested by others, and the prisoners' own views of the prison system. I strongly contend that the prisoners' perception of the pertinent problems and possible solutions should *not* be deemphasized. Prisoners generally are reasonable human beings who know and understand the prisoner culture and the prison system *as few outsiders do*; to ignore the prisoners' views and ideas (as prison administrators, staff members, and outsiders have traditionally done) is a tragic mistake. Major changes are needed *now*—to save taxpayers' money, to avoid abuse and neglect of human beings, and possibly to avoid an Attica-type massacre in California. These needed innovations must be initiated by the legislature.

By now, it should be obvious to most readers that rehabilitation efforts *in* prisons (as they now exist) generally are unrealistic and usually are lost in the prison*er* culture. Instead of serving to discourage repetition of crime, prison terms often foster a negative attitude toward laws and rules, impairing rehabilitation efforts—the longer the sentence, the more negative the attitude. Studies conducted by the California Legislature (1968 and 1970) have confirmed the general failure of rehabilitation efforts in California prisons and have indicated that severe penalties (lengthy sentences) do not deter crime or reduce recidivism. Furthermore, in a May 7, 1973, press release, California Assemblyman Alan Sieroty indicated that "Under its indeterminate sentence law, California now leads the nation with a 36-month median time being served by inmates." It also should be noted that many prisoners quite seriously contend that few prisoners in CDC have a real commitment to crime; that some may have made serious mistakes in the past; but that many have never been in a position to establish what might be called "normal" patterns of social behavior. Repeatedly prisoners stressed the absence of job and/or educational training as the underlying causes of much crime. Without basic reading and writing skills, one may even be refused a job as a laborer at times. Without the skills or training to overcome these deficiencies, the prospects for a happy life are somewhat dim for many prisoners. These are economic factors, not moral ones. Yet, many prison administrators and penologists have indicated that the majority of the men in prison could be released to the streets without any additional threat to the community. For example, the director of CDC personally indicated to me that a reasonable figure for California prisons would be about 75 percent. If all of the above factors are considered, it can be seen that it is unrealistic, under the present system, to try to rehabilitate the majority of men in prison. I believe most of these men should be kept out of prison in the first place; they should remain on the streets, in the culture in which they eventually are expected to live. If at all possible, probation should be used in order to avoid sending a man to prison. However, some fundamental changes also must be made in the probation system if it is to effectively reach the bases of much criminal activity.

In 1965, it cost approximately $2,000 more annually to keep a man in prison than it did to have a man on probation. Many people who recognized the shortcomings of rehabilitation efforts in prisons argued that some of that money could be spent more wisely in the community, where probation supervision was a sham, but where meaningful rehabilitation could take place if significant programs were implemented. Consequently, in 1965 the legislature adopted a "probation subsidy" program which was implemented the following year. Under the probation subsidy program, participating counties were paid up to $4,000 per felon for keeping them under locally supervised probation rather than committing them to state prison. Although this was seen as a step in the right direction, the program has been severely criticized. Critics agree that probation subsidy *is* being used to bring more money to the local level. However, the critics contend that significant programs still are nonexistent; that county governments still are ill-equipped to deal with rehabilitation; that the funds are primarily used for administrative costs and salaries of the probation department; and that there has been little significant change in probation supervision throughout the state. Even though the probation subsidy program has generally failed, I contend that the additional funds can and should be used on the streets for educational and job training. Men should be trained in *real* jobs, in the *real* world in which they ultimately are expected to live —*not* in the atypical world of the prisoner culture. Help should be given to these men so that they can broaden their opportunities, but the help should be given in such a manner that the men are allowed to maintain their human dignity and self-respect.

Concerning probation and parole, I feel some fundamental changes must be made in the existing system. An entirely new, statewide probation-parole department should be established. The new department should limit its activities to providing a few vital, supportive programs or services for convicted felons. Probation and parole officers should not be expected to play the police-type role that has been so unsuccessful and unrealistic, that has alienated them from those they are supposed to help. Since most crimes committed by probationers and parolees are discovered through citizen complaint and police apprehension, this regulatory role should be left to the police. This would free probation and parole officers from the dilemma of having to play conflicting roles and allow them to fill the supportive role with a much greater degree of success.

Since the major problem facing most convicted felons is economic in nature, the few vital programs offered by the new probation-parole department should focus principally on job training and placement. Secondary emphasis should be placed on basic educational training if necessary and on financial and social services. Using some of the savings (about $2,000 per man annually) derived from having men on probation or parole rather than in prison, the new probation-parole department should establish a statewide job placement service to help overcome the obstacle most convicted felons encounter when trying to find employment. Some of the yearly savings also could be used as incentives for employers to hire felons in real jobs, to train them if necessary, to pay them real wages, and to keep them as permanent employees after they have been trained. In addition, some of the savings could be used to set up bonding procedures to protect the employers from potential employee dishonesty. Some of the savings also could be used to set up a fund whereby a convicted felon initially is given adequate, realistic financial support until he is paid by his new employer, or during brief periods of unemployment. Such programs and services would provide probationers and parolees meaningful contracts with the real culture of the streets—where they must ultimately succeed if they are to avoid spending their entire lives involved in either criminal or prisoner activities. Under the proposed program, many felons would find themselves in an entirely new situation for at least forty hours a week; it would enable many of them to establish "normal," responsible patterns of behavior.

I readily admit that a statewide probation-parole system such as that briefly outlined above would never be completely effective, because some convicted felons *do* have a commitment to crime. There are some who will abuse and/or circumvent any type of system. However, for the large number of convicted felons who are not dedicated to crime, yet who are not adequately trained to succeed economically on the streets, the above probation-parole system would allow better opportunities to avoid the necessity of engaging in criminal activities. I contend that using tax dollars in this manner would be more fruitful than using similar amounts for crime prevention programs, which merely deal with the ultimate manifestation of criminal activity. The changes I have suggested would reach the root causes of the criminal activity of many convicted felons.

## CHANGES FOR THE MINORITY

I personally believe that the minority of the prisoner population that does actually pose an additional threat to society (roughly 25 percent of the prisoner population or less) should not be allowed to live unrestrained among society. For these men, I have no answer other than to abolish prisons as we now know them. Society probably will always need some kind of system of protecting itself against violently antisocial individuals; but only when necessary should men be put in prison.

When the imprisonment of an individual is necessary for society's protection, the punishment should be much shorter than the average length of sentences under the present system. Even then, imprisonment should still allow the prisoners to maintain their human dignity and self-respect. In order to accomplish this, I agree with the prisoners' contention that the indeterminate sentence system—including the Adult Authority—should be abolished. This would eliminate much of the hypocrisy and abuse that the prisoners presently perceive and experience. A fixed sentencing system with time off for good behavior should be instituted. Although a fixed sentencing system is not perfect, it would avoid much of the usurpation of the present system, such as the absence of due process of law and double jeopardy that result from disciplinary court actions, and the mental cruelty of uncertain, lengthy sentences.

In addition, the state's huge, isolated prisons should be replaced with *very* small ones. These small prisons should be located in cities—in the real world of the streets. If supportive efforts of the community and of the prisoners' families are ever to succeed, the isolation (and even sexual deprivation) of prisoners must be avoided wherever possible. And, if these new community prisons are small enough, the type of prisoner culture described in this book may never develop. Also, even though I have some deep personal reservations about the possibility for their success, efforts should still be made to *try* to rehabilitate the minority of men that would be sent to prison. These small community prisons should concentrate their rehabilitation efforts primarily on job training and basic education when necessary. This way, when and if a man does finally decide to try to make it legally, he will have at least some minimal qualifications which may enable him to do so. By virtue of their size and location, these prisons might be more successful than prisons have been in the past.

It should be obvious to readers by now that prisons are protected from outside scrutiny. Frequently, there is a discrepancy between the image presented to the public and the facts known to insiders. The prison system should be opened up to the view of outsiders. One way to achieve this—at least partially—is to establish a prison ombudsman. The ombudsman would be an independent officer, appointed by the legislature to investigate prisoner and staff complaints; correction of abuses of the system would come through his freedom to publicize his knowledge and his close relationship with the legislature. The establishment of a prison ombudsman also would lessen the chances of the existing ills finally manifesting themselves in the form of prison riots, by giving the prisoners an outlet for calling injustices to the attention of outsiders. Since the early 1950s, the majority of prison riots, strikes, and demonstrations have *not* involved attempts to escape; instead, they have been attempts of prisoners to bring the *reality* of prison life to the notice of the public. Unfortunately, Governor Reagan has vetoed bills to establish an office of prison ombudsman in 1971 and 1972. I hope that he and others who oppose a prison ombudsman soon come to realize that such an officer would help increase the visibility of a prison system that has generally been too isolated, that his mere presence would serve to discourage illegal, unfair, or inhumane practices. I contend that we must help the prisoners to effectively and nonviolently redress legitimate grievances.

An impetus for change has gradually arisen from a slowly growing public awareness of how prisoners are mistreated under our present prison system. The public must know the reality behind those prison walls if valid criticism and suggestions for change are to be made. I hope this book will serve as an enlightenment for that purpose.

## POSTSCRIPT

The unity of Family, as a single organization, no longer exists. During the latter part of 1972, some significant changes began taking place. For some members, the loyalty to Family came to be too much in conflict with the allegiance they felt toward their own sub-Family or toward a Third Family member. These complex, opposing loyalties have resulted in a major split in Family. In 1973, an extremely brutal power struggle continued between two major factions of Family, with much bloodshed and many deaths on the third level of the prisoner culture throughout CDC, and on the streets. Authorities could do little more than treat the wounded and occasionally try to prosecute some of the very few who are caught in their acts of violence. CDC statistics *will* certainly show that Chicanos were more violent than other ethnic groups in 1973. And, there *will* be subcultural factors behind this excessive violence. Actually, it was quite amazing that Family was ever able to establish and maintain the type of leadership and unity it did among such a large group of Chicanos, because such unity and leadership normally are effective only on a small-group or clique basis, such as within a sub-Family. At the present time, what was formerly called Family has broken up into two warring factions. One faction is comprised of *Familia* (the Spanish pronunciation for what I have referred to as Family), *Familia Cinco*, and *Familia Nuevo*. The other faction is a combination of "Mafia" (from the earlier name of Family when it was called the "Baby Mafia") and "EME" (which merely is the Spanish pronunciation of the letter "M," referring to the "M" in "Mafia"). Presently the *Familia* faction has about 1500 members and maintains control over all California prisons except Folsom and Tehachapi. The Mafia-EME faction now has roughly 300 members who are able to control Folsom and Tehachapi prisons. It is very unhealthy for a member of either faction to be transferred to one of the prisons under control of the opposing faction. The Mafia-EME faction appointed two "generals" to expedite matters; one of those generals was killed, being stabbed 58 times by members of the opposing faction. The *Familia* faction still functions under the type of leadership described in Chapter 4. Unfortunately, it appears that this warfare will continue below the surface and generally beyond the control of authorities for a long time into the future, with neither side being able to eliminate the other, because new members are being brought into both factions faster than they are being killed.

# References

Bock, Philip K., 1970, *Culture Shock*. New York: Alfred A. Knopf, Inc.

California Legislature, 1968, *Deterrent Effects of Criminal Sanctions*, Progress Report of the Assembly Criminal Procedure Committee.

————, 1970, *Parole Board Reform in California*, Report of the Assembly Select Committee on the Administration of Justice.

Campbell, A. J., 1967, "A Statistical Study of Incident and Infraction Reports: 1966, 1965, 1964, 1963, 1962, California State Prison at San Quentin," a mimeographed report prepared by Correctional Lieutenant Campbell.

Goffman, Erving, 1961, *Asylums: Essays on the Social Situation of Medical Patients and Other Inmates*. Garden City, N.Y.: Doubleday and Company, Inc.

Hastings, Homer, 1967, Comments made by Dr. Hastings, Associate Warden, Care and Treatment, to another staff member during lunch, San Quentin, June 1, 1967.

Irwin, John, 1970, *The Felon*, Englewood Cliffs, N.J.: Prentice-Hall, Inc.

Lee, R. B., and I. DeVore (eds.), 1968, *Man the Hunter*. Chicago: Aldine Publishing Company.

Lowry, John, 1966, "Statistical Summary, Mexican-American Educational Participation, San Quentin, Summer 1966," unpublished paper.

Minton, Robert J. Jr. (ed.), 1971, *Inside Prison American Style*. New York: Random House.

Sykes, Gresham M., 1958, *The Society of Captives: A Study of a Maximum Security Prison*. Princeton: Princeton University Press.

Wham, Raymond, 1966, Comments made by Mr. Wham, Associate Warden Custody, at a disciplinary committee hearing, San Quentin, June 28, 1966.